THE CHANGING POSTWAR INTERNATIONAL LEGAL REGIME

The Role Played by Japan

International Law in Japanese Perspective

VOLUME 8

Series Editors

Shigeru Oda
Yuji Iwasawa

The titles published in this series are listed at the end of this volume

The Changing Postwar International Legal Regime

The Role Played by Japan

WAKAMIZU TSUTSUI

Emeritus Professor,
University of Tokyo

KLUWER LAW INTERNATIONAL
THE HAGUE / LONDON / NEW YORK

Published by:
Kluwer Law International
P.O. Box 85889, 2508 CN The Hague, The Netherlands
sales@kli.wkap.nl
http://www.kluwerlaw.com

Sold and Distributed in North, Central and South America by:
Kluwer Law International
101 Philip Drive, Norwell, MA 02061, USA
kluwerlaw@wkap.com

In all other countries, sold and distributed by:
Kluwer Law International
Distribution Centre, P.O. Box 322, 3300 AH Dordrecht, The Netherlands

A C.I.P. Catalogue record for this book is available from the Library of Congress.

Printed on acid-free paper.

ISBN 90-411-1847-0

Kluwer Law International incorporates the imprint Martinus Nijhoff Publishers.

Printed and bound in Great Britain by MPG Books Limited, Bodmin, Cornwall.

CONTENTS

FOREWORD

The Second World War was the first war fought to destroy the enemy by use of the most advanced technological means developed by states at that time. However, it may also have been the last "world war" in the sense that great wars will no longer be fought between governments. In fact, immense destruction and inhumanity have occurred since the end of the Second World War in the form of irregular warfare known as class struggles, anti-colonial or national liberation movements, and terrorism in the name of various causes.

This is a reflection of the weakening of the sovereign state system on which traditional international law developed. The Allied Nations of the Second World War may have intended to rehabilitate the system after the War, but it was precisely the practices of the Allied Nations taken against the Axis states before and during the War that brought international law to invalidation.

We were told that the activities of the United Nations would bring international society closer to being a municipal one. The fact is that international society remains decentralized, with a considerably larger number of sovereign states all accepted as members of the United Nations.

Internationalization has brought people in closer contact across national borders, decreasing the control of states over them. The United Nations has been more successful in attaining its secondary purpose of "international cooperation in solving international problems of an economic, social, cultural, or humanitarian character" than in fulfilling its principal purpose of the "maintenance of international peace and security."

Since her surrender, Japan has enjoyed remarkable success in resurrecting her war-devastated economy, but has yet to free herself from the situation where she has no discretion to choose her own means of security. Under these circumstances, Japanese students have good reason to be interested in subjects other than the law of international peace and security, just as I did in my student days. It also accounts for their tendency to take an idealistic, rather than a realistic, approach in discussing that law.

This does not mean, however, that they are indifferent to overseas affairs involving the use of armed force. In the 1960s and 1970s, students engaged in insurrections against society and universities under the influence of the Chinese Cultural Revolution and demonstrated against American intervention in the conflict between the two regimes in Vietnam.

Amid this climate of unrest, I wrote a number of books and theses on "war and law" in Japanese. Some students agreed with my arguments, while others – especially those who eagerly supported anti-war demonstrations – resisted on the ground that discussions on war were at odds with the peace movement.

The tragedy caused by the terrorist attacks on New York and Washington on 11 September 2001 brought to mind our former fear of air raids. They were a daily phenomenon in cities in belligerent regions during the Second World War and have continued to be so in the armed clashes that have subsequently broken out.

While it may be natural to think ourselves not in the same situation as people in belligerent regions, we must not overlook the fact that force conditions peace. As any use of force involves some degree of inhumanity, law should elucidate such activity persuasively.

I have spent most of my academic career studying and lecturing in international law and jurisprudence at University of Tokyo. Apart from some contributions to overseas journals, the results of my research have all been published in Japanese. This is my first experience of planning and writing a book in English and this work has taken me an unexpectedly long time to complete. I have revised the draft many times as incidents have occurred during the process of writing.

Dr. Shigeru Oda, Judge of the International Court of Justice, cordially encouraged me to finish this work, and Mr. John Middleton, Associate Professor of Law at Hitotsubashi University in Tokyo, kindly polished my English.

I sincerely hope this book will enable readers in English to gain a better understanding of international law from a Japanese perspective, especially in relation to international peace and security.

Wakamizu Tsutsui

INTRODUCTION

This book consists of three chapters. Chapter 1 discusses how the international legal regime has changed in tandem with the foundations of such society over the past two centuries. There have been a number of impetuses to this change, but the most significant one has undoubtedly been the Second World War, which was fought in an unprecedented manner as far as international law and human life and property were concerned.

The Second World War was destructive, not only because of the advanced technology applied to warfare, but also because there was no normative restriction. International law originates in an agreement on the "freedom of conscience" reached among the belligerents in a religious war. As far as war is fought according to international law, the loss of human rights is kept to a minimum. In a war fought to realize an ideology inconsistent with the opponents', they would cease hostilities only after the annihilation of their enemy.

International law was originally limited in application to the "Family of European Civilized Nations" among whom it had been agreed. This meant that non-European nations did not enjoy the rights of international law on account of the differences in their civilization. The principle of sovereign equality would only be established after recognition of the multiplicity of civilization.

When the world was devastated by great war, a "world government" was conceived to realize eternal peace. Most states survived the Second World War by compromising their sovereignty to the benefit of greater powers. After this practice, it became possible for states' sovereignty to be subjugated to a "general international organization." The fact that individuals had come in ever-closer contact across state borders since the nineteenth century also justified the existence of "international government."

Any scheme, if it is intended to be positive, must be based on the practice from which it came to be realized. In this light, it may have been inevitable that the postwar international regime would not deter the recurrence of religious wars and wars of colonization. The problem is how the postwar international organization can effectively realize the principle of war renunciation or no use of force, having full regard to human rights.

The following chapters argue that the United Nations has been a positive postwar international order, recognizing the right of self-defense as inherent to every state, including "enemies." The organization has therefore weakened its collective character, but outlived the Cold War by entrusting the collective function to self-defense taken individually.

Chapter 2 discusses the way in which such an international legal order has been achieved through self-defense.

The practice of self-defense is so rare under traditional international law that it cannot be regarded as comparable to any concept in municipal law. Municipal law allows individuals to take forcible action for their legitimate defense in circumstances where the government is not prepared to discharge its public function. The postwar international legal order has been realized by self-defense as an intermediate function between the individual and collective, as provided under article 51 of the UN Charter.

The United Nations has experienced some difficulty in its organizational function since the Security Council, the primary organ for peace and security, may be paralyzed by the use of veto powers. Apart from structural difficulties, it has no force of its own, so enforcement action is impracticable without the participation of the forces of individual states, including the more powerful ones. Individual states take forcible action on the express ground of self-defense under the UN Charter.

Peacekeeping is a practical activity undertaken by the United Nations for the maintenance of peace and security. It is sometimes reinforced by an act of self-defense taken by the participating states. After the Cold War, enforcement action has come to be taken more often by the United Nations as a successor to self-defense.

The conditions of self-defense are dependent upon the practice taken in that name. The conditions are not necessarily the same as those of legitimate defense in municipal society. Self-defense should be understood as activating the social function in international society.

The postwar international legal regime is a regime of self-defense in the sense that it is characterized by the social function of self-defense. It departs from the traditional international law knowing no public or collective part under the principle of free recourse to war. On the other hand, it is not assimilated with a municipal legal regime having a government under the authority of which no illegal use of individual force is overlooked except in an emergency.

The regime of self-defense is realized on the basis of regional cooperation. In fact, self-defense was conceived in the drafting stage of the UN Charter by promoting regional realities ahead of general collective principles. The concept of collective self-defense was in fact extracted from that of self-defense in order to emphasize its social aspect.

In light of wartime practices, the postwar international organization should be organized on the basis of regional cooperation. As a matter of fact, the postwar international order came to be possible by amending the original scheme of "general international organization."

Reconstructed on the basis of self-defense, the postwar international organization removes the deficiencies in the original concept, namely the limitation on membership and the incompleteness of the humanitarian principle.

Strictness in the collective principle threatens the humanitarian treatment of belligerents and civilians in armed action, including enforcement. Adherence to ideology has brought out inhumanity in the wars of recent times, as practiced during the Second World War and the subsequent wars for national liberation. If the Cold War had developed into a "hot war," it would have been so destructive as to threaten the very survival of humankind.

The "enemy" nations were neither integrated into the Allied Nations regime nor the United Nations, nor rehabilitated through peace conferences held in accordance with traditional international law. It has been in self-defense arrangements that they have found their status in postwar international society.

It is natural that "enemy" states are situated not in the regime of the Allied Nations, but in something different from it, that is, the postwar international legal regime. The postwar international legal regime is thus characterized by the status of the "enemy" states. Chapter 3 discusses this phenomenon by reference to the process of rehabilitation of an "enemy" state, Japan.

Japan has neither been integrated into the United Nations collective security system nor the system of a peace treaty concluded according to general international law. The process followed was the adoption of the Constitution of Japan 1946 and the conclusion of a U.S.-Japan Security Treaty based on the right of self-defense inherent to every state, whether Allies or their enemies.

Japan preferred the garrison of foreign forces in her territory to the non-maintenance "of land, sea, and air forces as well as other war potential" provided by the Constitution. This indicates that Japan was not convinced that the United Nations would act as her guardian in its collective function and general character despite the provision of her Peace Constitution.

This does not mean, on the other hand, that the United States and Japan will have full regard to article 51 of the UN Charter. The U.S.-Japan Security Treaty expressly provides for "the Far East," which is not necessarily conditioned on article 51 of the UN Charter. It is also noteworthy that other states are also following suit in light of the events after the Cold War.

In order to inquire where the legal regime of international society is heading, it is necessary to trace the changes to date, the most significant impetus for which was the Second World War. We must not overlook the fact that the present international legal regime derives from the practices of the Second World War, the most distinctive feature of which was the disregard of an international law originating in an agreement on "freedom of conscience."

CHAPTER 1

THE CHANGING LAW IN POSTWAR INTERNATIONAL SOCIETY

I. International Law as the General Order in International Society

(1) International law originating in a system of freedom of conscience

The first half of the twentieth century brought two great wars in succession in 1914–1918 and 1939–1945. They are usually referred to as the First and Second World Wars, but only the second one deserves the title of World War, being unprecedented both in its scale and geographical extent and having an epoch-making effect on international society. The legal situation arising from the Second World War remained unchanged in international society during the second half of the twentieth century and may well endure throughout this one.

Wars involve destruction, but the scale of this destruction is limited by normative and technological factors. War fought on a limited scale would therefore not bring the enemy to the brink of total destruction. The Second World War was fought with the latest technologies available at the time and under the grip of the most radical ideologies, and the physical destruction wrought on enemies was without limit.

In this regard, the Second World War is comparable to the medieval religious wars in Western nations, which were also fought with no normative restrictions. Opposition between Christian factions caused a series of wars in Germany from 1618. According to Hugo Grotius (1583–1645), these were waged with "a lack of restraint in relation to war, such as even barbarous races should be ashamed of." He continued: "Men rushed to arms for slight causes, or no cause at all, and when arms have once been taken up, there is no longer respect for law, divine or human; it is as if, in accordance with a general decree, frenzy had openly been let loose for the committing of all crimes."[1]

Under the conviction that "there is a common law among nations," Grotius discussed "law, which is valid alike for war and in war." The law was extracted from the intelligent achievements of learned men, that is, the results of European civilization. In doing so, he intended to minimize the inhumanity of man to man observed in acts of war.

---

[1] H. Grotius, *De Jure Belli ac Pacis* (translation) in J.B. Scott (ed.), *The Classics of International Law*, 1925, vol. 1, esp. pp. 20–21.

He developed his argument with the aim of placing normative restrictions upon warfare. It would be attained by integration of the law into the practices of nations. Since restrictions developed on a theological basis would have little effect on wars between nations without a shared religion, "Law Among Nations" needed to be secular.

The peace thus attained would be institutionalized under the principle of the equal treatment of nations irrespective of their size and the religious beliefs of their monarchs and people. For as long as this principle was maintained, the society would remain peaceful, with different political systems and ideologies. It was later formulized as the "sovereign equality of nations" in accordance with the political theory of the absoluteness of monarchs. When war is fought within this institution, it will cease when the victor is satisfied with the position of power it has gained over the vanquished. In such a war fought among legally equal parties, no party either disappears or becomes a world empire.

Under this institution, Europe remained at peace for almost a century from the end of the Napoleonic War until the beginning of the First World War. Belgium and Switzerland became independent as a result of the peace conference in Vienna, which ended the Napoleonic War following the French Revolution. They were too small to survive without the protection of a system of sovereign equality. Permanent neutrality was a means of securing such independence.

However, it would be incorrect to conclude that society is driven to disunion by being based on the principles of freedom of conscience and the sovereign equality of states. Rather, the effect of these principles in society is to bring the members into intimate and constant relations with each other. "The separate state could never be accepted as the final and perfect form of human association, and in the modern as in the medieval world it would be necessary to recognize the existence of a world unity. The rise of international law was recognition of this truth."[2]

Under the international peace attainable under this principle, the law of peace is created through the intercourse of states. Their official intercourse is through diplomatic missions and leads to laws of diplomatic relations. The commercial intercourse of private individuals, which culminated in the laissez-faire economics of the mid-nineteenth century, motivated the conclusion of commercial treaties between governments. Laws of territory are formed through the states' practices of acquiring land and using the sea and air. Laws of state responsibility are recognized through remedies for the breach of such practices.

So long as a nation remains a member of international society, it enjoys the right of international law in relation to its activities in war and peace. International law was originally conceived as a method of mitigation of acts of war, but has developed to the stage where it is now a normative body in every field of relations between nations. Both the laws of peace and of war are integral parts of international law.

The legal situation in postwar international society in the second half of the twentieth century leads us to question whether we should focus our attention on the law

---

[2] J.L. Brierly, *The Law of Nations* (6th ed.), 1963, pp. 6–7.

of war rather than that of peace. There is, by definition, no international society under the rule of international law unless freedom of conscience prevails. If the practices in the Second World War are taken as being in accordance with the rules prevalent at the time, then traditional international law must have been rendered invalid already.

Indeed, the Second World War was too destructive for the traditional law of war to be proven valid. That may be a result of the invalidation of the traditional principle of freedom of conscience. It was possible in view of the fact that traditional international law proceeded on the premise of common values held by members of that society when there was in fact no standard of common values between them. What made the situation extreme was the fact that technology had developed to the stage where it was possible to destroy any people, race or nation regarded as different.

International law originates in the "Family of European Civilized Nations," excluding non-European civilized nations from the jurisdiction. The Europeans did indeed make annihilative warfare with non-Europeans in the process of advancing outwards. From a global perspective, international law was never established until it was believed to be beginning to decline.

Most non-European nations made the Second World War an opportunity to regain their independence from European colonial rule. The War fostered the dissolution of traditional international law on the one hand, but marked a turning point in globalization on the other.

The postwar international legal order cannot be a rehabilitation of traditional international law based on the homogeneity of civilization. It must be based on a variety of races, religions and ideologies, developed economic structures, stable political orders, and so on to be a truly international system. Science and technology make it possible to create such a system, but also to destroy any opponents on account of their heterogeneity.

In this situation, traditional international law may be somewhat obsolete, but is still important for the survival of human civilization through its fundamental doctrine. It must be remembered that international law originates as a device to prevent total destruction, conditional upon tolerance of different beliefs.

(2) International law developing into a general order

a) Civilizations regard encounters with others in various ways: friendly or antagonistic, peaceful or violent.[3] Europeans showed no tolerance of outsiders in the process of their advancement outwards, taking an antagonistic and violent attitude toward them rather than a friendly and peaceful one.

According to Immanuel Kant, who distinguished between relations with "barbarians" and those with "the civilized," the situation was as follows:

> "If we compare the barbarian instances of inhospitality referred to with the inhuman behavior of the civilized, and especially the commercial, States of our

---

[3] Arnold Toynbee discussed this subject in a study of at least twenty civilizations in every corner of the world at various stages in history: *A Study of History*, 1921–1954.

> continent, the justice practiced by them even in their first contact, the injustice practiced by them even in their first contact with foreign lands and peoples fills us with horror, the mere visiting of such peoples being regarded by them as equivalent to a conquest. America, the Negro lands, the Spice Islands, the Cape of Good Hope, etc., on being discovered, were treated as countries that belonged to nobody; for the aboriginal inhabitants were recognized as nothing."[4]

A considerable proportion of the non-Europeans – the Native Americans, Oceanians, Africans, and some Asians – were subjugated by European powers. Empires in India, Burma, Indochina, Indonesia and Africa disappeared, and China stood on the brink of total subjugation. There were conquests, annexations, enslavement and destruction on the part of non-Europeans, while the Europeans remained relatively peaceful under the system of "the Law of the Family of Nations."

If the Westphalia Rule were recognized as covering every relationship around the globe, there would be no war of annihilation, even against people and nations with different beliefs and civilizations. As long as it remained the rule of law, it would be omnipresent in every corner of human society. The Roman Empire, from which most European nations descended, remained peaceful under the rule of law, although it comprised a considerable number of different races and civilizations.

In applying the different standard to outsiders, they fell into the contradiction that certain nations were excluded from natural rule. This situation was against not only the tradition of European civilization, but also that of human civilization itself.

The dynasties in mainland China contemporaneous with the East Roman Empire in the seventh century, which handed down the text of Roman law in codified form, also conceived the idea of "peace through law." In fact, the dynasties of Sui and Tang completed the codification as a means of unifying their country. This was adopted by Japan and remained in force there until the nineteenth century, when it was replaced by a system of Western law.

Law is a synthesis of philosophy, theology and political science. The role taken by law in society as a social norm is different according to the civilization on which the society develops. Notwithstanding its similarity to the codified Roman law, a statute in Chinese society takes an inferior position to ethics in civil life and political activities. In a traditional Oriental society influenced by Chinese civilization, the tendency to take less account of law is maintained, even after it is reformed under the influence of Western civilization.

The Oriental peoples did not regard the difference as a defect in their civilization. Arai Hakuseki, a Japanese intellectual in the Edo period (1603–1867), concluded that Western civilization might be superior to the Orient in practical fields, but remained inferior in the field of metaphysics.[5] The question is whether the conclusion

---

[4] Immanuel Kant, *Zum ewigen Frieden*, 1795, translated by W. Hastie, *Kant's Eternal Peace*, 1914, p. 88.

[5] Arai Hakuseki (1657–1725), an outstanding Japanese intellectual and statesman in the Edo period, examined, in his capacity as a government official, a Dutch missionary jailed for propagation of the Christian faith in 1708. He reached this conclusion at a time when contact with Western civilization was almost prohibited: *Seiyokibun* (date of authorship unknown).

is the same when all the merits of both civilizations are judged with a correct understanding of each. The answer will depend on how the Western civilization is evaluated, when physical development brings destructive conquests and war leads to the annihilation of the achievements of human civilization itself, including the achievements of that Western civilization.

b) The Westphalia Rule was an agreement between political authorities to end the Religious Wars in medieval Europe. It could, at the same time, be humanitarian since it gave peace precedence over each religious belief. This was possible so long as they remained tolerant of different beliefs.

The rule was prevalent among European civilized peoples as it was proven natural on the basis of the literature of learned people and state practices. Francisco de Vitoria (1480–1546), a theologian and jurist, argued that human beings naturally had different habits and cultures, so should be treated equally regardless of such differences. As far as the rules among the Europeans were natural, they would apply to any nation around the globe in transactions during wartime as well as times of peace.

"It would not be lawful for the French to prevent the Spanish from traveling or even from living in France, or vice versa, provided this in no way enured to their hurt and the visitors did no injury. Therefore it is not lawful for the Indians ...

"If it were not lawful for the Spaniards to travel among them, this would be either by natural law or by divine law. And if there were any human law which without any cause took away rights conferred by natural law or divine law, it would be inhumane and unreasonable and consequently would not have the force of law."[6]

Establishment of international law as the global legal system suggests that the Law of the European Family of Nations is "natural," beyond the local body of law. As a matter of fact, however, it was realized not by means of a natural process, but rather through forcible advancement of the former to the latter.

Japan had closed its doors to all Western nations except Holland from the seventeenth century until the advancement of the Western powers outwards. Aware that Oriental nations were falling under the domination of Western powers one after another, she abandoned the traditional closed policy in 1858 to conclude friendship treaties with several Western powers, namely, the United States, Holland, Britain, France and Russia.

During almost the same period, Turkey was forced to make peace with Russia through a treaty mediated by Britain and France which provided in one article that she was admitted to participate in "public law" and the European Family.[7]

Treaty relations between Western powers and some non-European ones did not signify the natural enlargement of the European Family. In concluding friendship treaties, European nations tended to treat non-Europeans as "honorary citizens" of

---

6 Francisco de Vitoria, *De Indis et de jure belli relectiones* (1532) in J.B. Scott (ed.), *Classics of International Law*, pp. 151–152.

7 Article 7 of the Treaty for Re-establishing Peace signed at Paris, 30 March 1856, between Turkey and the five powers: Parry, 114 *Consolidated Treaty Series*, p. 414.

their Family. Consular jurisdiction and tariffs were applied to non-Europeans in a discriminatory manner.[8]

It was necessary for the non-European partners to "westernize" themselves in order to amend the discriminatory treaties. The Meiji Government of Japan urged changes in that society and culture along the lines of Western nations from the time of the Restoration in 1868 in the belief that it would enable them to renegotiate "unequal treaties" with the West. In the course of the Sino-Japanese War (1894-1895) and the Russo-Japanese War (1904-1905), Japan strove to make her belligerent actions accord with the law of war in the hope of being recognized as a member of the family of "civilized nations."[9]

As far as international law is a system of tolerance, membership is an assurance of independence from Western domination. No state falls into total subjugation (though it may be forced to transfer a part of its territory) so long as it acts in accordance with the law of European nations in taking belligerent action even against such nations.

This is not to say, however, that Japan was consistent in promoting the system of sovereign equality. After the expulsion of Chinese and Russian powers from adjacent regions, Japan annexed the Korean Empire by following the example set by European powers in subjugating non-European nations. Moreover, Japan joined the European powers in driving China to the brink of destruction.

Judging from her behavior after opening the country, Japan accepted Western civilization or the Law of the European Family of Nations for the purpose of defending herself from external threats. In accepting the Law, she followed the precedent of the adoption of Chinese codified law in the seventh century, as a means of unifying the country after devastation from wars on the Korean Peninsula and civil strife.

Customary law of the Shogunate governments, which had held power since the late twelfth century, gradually replaced the codification adopted by the Imperial Government. When the Imperial Government restored power in 1868, it chose to introduce Western law rather than revive the codified law adopted over a thousand years previously.[10]

However, she did not anticipate the moral effect of law in society, whether it be municipal or international law. It is a tradition of East Asia that ethics is accorded the most important status in the normative order in society. As long as they follow

---

8 From a European perspective, these were episodes in the process of generalization of "the Law of the Christian Family of Nations": see List, Von Franz, *Völkerrect*, 1898, S3.

9 Nagao Ariga, *La guerre Sino-Japonaise au point de vue droit international*, 1896 and *La guerre Russo-Japonaise au point de vue droit international*, 1908. The "unequal treaties" were revised in 1911 after the successful conclusion of the Russo-Japanese War. It is interesting to note that the Declaration of War against the United States and United Kingdom in 1945, unlike that against Russia in 1904, did not refer to her intention to obey international law.

10 Immediately after the Restoration, the Imperial Government sought to adopt the codified laws of the recent Ming and Ch'ing dynasties in China as its own. It later chose Western law in preference to Chinese, but maintained some terms and concepts originating in the codification modeled after China in the seventh century in some parts of the modern system of law borrowed from Western countries.

the tradition of Oriental civilization, they will not adhere to law in their behavior in international society. They would not be persuaded to behave in complete accord with international law in view of the fact that Western powers had adopted a double standard in accommodating non-European nations.

c) The role taken by Japan in developing international law into a global order was a model for the adoption of the Western legal system by Eastern nations. It recognized the fact that nations civilized in different ways could commence friendly relations with one another by making agreements in accordance with international law instead of engaging in wars of subjugation. On the other hand, it does not necessarily mean that the Law of the European Family of Nations should naturally be the universal standard of behavior for all nations.

If the Europeans had dealt with nations with foreign civilizations in the same way as they did with each other, the Law of the European Family of Nations might naturally have progressed to a common body of norms of global society long before the Great War broke out. In this context, it was the European civilized people themselves who disgraced the achievement of their civilization – the legal system, including international law, inherited from the Romans – by preventing it from being accepted naturally as it deserved to be.

At the same time, however, it cannot be denied that the Europeans propagated international law as the common norm of international society. Originally, it was conceived and practiced among European civilized nations. Later, it was accepted by differently civilized nations, albeit reluctantly. Nations deduce the value of each form of social activity from works of ethics, religion and such. If they continue to adhere to each value standard, peace among different nations will be impossible.

International law has freedom of conscience as one of its principles. International society could not be orderly after unprecedented devastation unless nations accepted the principles of international law. There could not be a peaceful international legal order after the Second World War conceived differently from the rehabilitated international law. Apart from problems regarding its generalization, international law has proven only to be a normative body deserving to be a general legal order in human society.

(3) International law rehabilitated in the postwar order

a) The First World War, beginning in 1914, ended a century of peace among European nations following the conclusion of the Napoleonic War in 1815.[11] The Second World War, which followed after an interval of about twenty years, was epoch-making in means, scope and casualties to the extent that it was incomparable to any war in history, including the First World War. "Direct civilian losses were

[11] There was a war of subjugation between the European nations during this period. The Boer War in South Africa from 1899 to 1902 resulted in the annexation of a defeated nation of European origin to Great Britain.

apparently greater in World War I than they had been in European wars since the seventeenth century, but they were much greater in World War II, apparently twice as greater as military losses, considering the losses of the belligerents as a whole."[12]

The unprecedented destruction in the Second World War was due to the advances made in war technology through the application of modern science. However, it could not have become a reality had the belligerents not been convinced that they had reason to engage in such destruction. Although technology was practicable to wreak physical destruction, it would not lead the belligerents along a path to cause mass destruction to the enemy, to annihilate a race or take similar actions, unless they were released from the qualms of conscience.

While the First World War was unprecedented in many respects, it still had the characteristics of a classic struggle between newly risen powers and existing ones for leadership in international society. As far as the main participants other than the United States were concerned, the Second World War was also a classic struggle for hegemony in international society.

Germany, which was unified under the leadership of Prussia, and Japan, which commenced her process of modernization at almost the same time as German unification, became allies to challenge the existing hegemonies. Italy, which took similar action as the Germans in uniting the Italian Peninsula into a single country, aligned herself with the "latecomers" in the early stages of the War.

Great Britain had ideological reasons for joining France in opposing the alliance of Nazi Germany, militarist Japan and Fascist Italy. These two allies both possessed a large number of overseas colonies and were regarded as enemies by the Axis, which demanded a redistribution of those colonial interests.

The Soviet Union came into existence in the last stages of the First World War as a result of revolution against the Tsarist regime. The Soviets denied the existence of most Western values, such as individual rights to property, freedom of thought, and fundamental human rights, in order to facilitate the realization of a Communist world. As the Soviet Union was attempting world revolution, she could well have become allies with the "latecomers" or "have-nots" to oppose nations in "the propertied class" of international society. In the event, she became allies with the traditional European powers in order to defend herself from attacks by the German-Japanese Axis on both extremes of her territory.

It was the involvement of the United States that made the Second World War unprecedented in its character and consequences.

The United States differed from the others in that she was motivated to fight without the need to take defensive or offensive action with respect to such interests. She may have competed with Japan for some material interests in other continents, including mainland China. However, what motivated the United States to participate in the War was ideology rather than material interests. In fact, there was no expansion in the territory of the United States as a result of the War.

---

[12] Q. Wright, *A Study of War* (2nd ed.), 1965, p. 1541.

b) It is no coincidence that the main victors of the Second World War, the United States and the Soviet Union, were ideology oriented. In modern warfare, states must mobilize people to back up forces at the battlefront. Under the circumstances, victory in war depends on the successful mobilization of civilians. Belligerent states make ideological attempts to persuade civilians to act in accordance with their wishes. If propaganda reaches enemy states, the war potential of such states may be diminished by making their citizens doubt their own government's ideology.

The main belligerent states in the Second World War – the United States, Soviet Union, Germany and Japan – were all ideologically fortified in fighting it. In wars fought in such a way, civilians cannot avoid becoming targets of hostile action, including naval and aerial bombardments upon cities.

The fewer roles legitimate forces take in warfare, the less chance there is to arrange a ceasefire on the initiative of governments. Wars fought in the name of ideology end not in the surrender of material interests, including the transfer of territory, but rather in ideological subjugation, including a change in the polity and a revolutionary revision of the Constitution, on the part of the vanquished.

How the defeated states were discharged from responsibility for their acts during wartime, including the ill treatment of persons in occupied territory and destruction of personal property in the course of belligerent actions, was settled in peace treaties under traditional international law. In the case of wars fought by civilians as well as legitimate forces, government officials cannot escape personal responsibility for wars fought in their official capacity despite the privileges and immunity enjoyed under traditional international law. Even the government's responsibility for the loss of private interests is pursued through lawsuits brought by individuals after the conclusion of peace treaties.[13]

The First World War may have been unprecedented in some respects, but was mostly fought in accordance with traditional international law. It was fought by fully utilizing the most advanced technology available at the time, so involved greater participation by civilians than any previous war had done. However, it followed precedent in ending warfare through the conclusion of a peace treaty at a conference attended by all the belligerent states. The peace treaties, including the Versailles Treaty with Germany, were legal confirmation by all the participants of the restoration of peace. Every claim was settled politically and legally at the conference so as to bring hostilities to an end.

By contrast, the Second World War was not declared over by all the belligerents

[13] The Peace Treaty with Japan provides that Japan will, upon application, return the property and all rights or interests of any kind of each Allied Power and its nationals that were within her territory at any time between 7 December 1941 and 2 September 1945 (art 15). In accordance with this provision, the Japanese Government has compensated the loss of such property, even where caused by Allied action, including the bombing of Japanese territory. In return, the Allied Powers have, except as otherwise provided in the Treaty, waived all reparations claims by them and their nationals arising out of any actions taken by Japan and her nationals in the course of the prosecution of war (art 14(b)). In spite of this provision, nationals of the Allied Powers have repeatedly brought actions against the Government and enterprises of Japan.

concerned due to the impossibility of convening an ordinary peace conference with the main Axis states. Rather, war was renewed in the form of the Cold War and wars for national liberation immediately following the armistice between the legitimate forces of the belligerent governments.

Reoccurrence of belligerent action is not prevented by agreements between governments when taken by individuals. That situation is the same as the medieval religious wars in Europe in which endless hostilities took place to annihilate heretics. Now that the physical destruction of human beings is technologically possible, we are dependent upon normative restraints effective enough to make those parties refrain from taking such action, if we are to survive the coming centuries.

The religious strife in medieval Europe was brought to an end by the parties agreeing to compromise their beliefs at Westphalia, recognizing freedom of conscience as the principle of their relations. This was systematized into "international law" with a view to perpetuating the compromise. It was hoped this would prevent total destruction as ideological differences were no longer a valid reason for allowing states to take whatever action they desired.

The French Empire lost the Napoleonic War, but avoided collapse by being integrated into a system agreed to by all the belligerents at Vienna. Smaller political units were brought forth under the Vienna system, the independence of which were achieved by the system of international law. Such a small political unit as the Federal Republic of Switzerland could not survive the following centuries without a system of "permanent neutrality."

It was by virtue of this system that European civilized nations enjoyed peace thereafter for the next century. The First World War broke out and was fought on a greater scale and inflicted more damage than ever before, but ultimately strengthened the system by increasing the number of sovereign states.

The Second World War invalidated the traditional system of international society by being fought with weapons of mass destruction and resulting in the total destruction of most belligerents. No nation could escape destruction, whether they won the War or not. The balance of power in international society could not remain stable because the vanquished possessed no powers at all.

c) Despite all the confusion, signs of a new order became apparent during the course of the Second World War.

The Allied Nations expressed in documents issued during the War their intention to rehabilitate international law. However, what came to pass was not a rehabilitation of international law, but rather a United Nations structured differently from traditional international law. Traditional international law could not be rehabilitated in any case, whether they desired it or not, for the following reasons.

First, international law had become too confused by the practices during those decades to be restored to how it had been previously. Even if the Allied Nations wished otherwise, it had been violated so widely as to remain valid, especially through contrary practices during the War, including those of the Allied Nations themselves.

Secondly, the Second World War was fought with civilians, including people under colonial domination. In postwar international society, nothing could continue without striking the sentiments of people afraid of a recurrence of war and colonial domination. They would not adhere to a system under which they had suffered war casualties and foreign domination. Rather, they would claim that traditional international law should be declared obsolete. Newly independent states had long cultivated their own civilization quite distinct from European legal civilization. They would remain indifferent to the international legal order if it was a continuation of traditional international law of European origin.

Thirdly, the Allied Nations included as an integral member the Soviet Union, which was a state extraneous to traditional European civilization. The postwar international order could not be constructed as a reconciliation of the opposing belligerents, but rather as a compromise between the Soviet Union and other Allies. The ideology of the Soviets was fundamentally different from traditional Europeans'. It would be too difficult to integrate such ideology into the traditional doctrine for rehabilitation as the doctrine of the postwar international order.

Fourthly, the Allied Nations' ideology, like their war doctrine, was too confrontational and revolutionary to be the principle of a postwar order based on traditional international law. Nevertheless, the postwar international order could not be established without incorporating such doctrine in it. The defeated nations could not raise their voices in founding the postwar order, but the majority of the Allied Nations had also been dissatisfied with the existing order, and their voices must surely have been heard when the wartime Allies' ideology was created.

d) In view of the difficulties of rehabilitating international law as it had been, a solution was found in giving it secondary status among normative orders in international society. This was a practical solution since any postwar international order should be based on the unified ideology of the Allied Nations, which was not necessarily consistent with traditional international law.

Traditional international law was based on a society composed of actors homogeneous in race and civilization, but premised mutual recognition of the relative truth of their ideologies from the time of its conception. The actors were positioned equally within the system under the principle of sovereign equality. As the Allied Nations recognized the validity of international law, so an approximation of sovereign equality could be recognized as the principle of the postwar international order.

In spite of the policy-oriented affirmation by the Allied Nations of the validity of international law, it was undeniable that states could not claim substantially equal rights on the principle of sovereign equality. The postwar international order could be distinctive when it departed from the traditional principle of sovereign equality. The practice taken into the United Nations was that of sacrificing each state's sovereignty to the benefit of powerful nations. They asked other members to accept the practice as their contribution for having escaped destruction.

We must question how an international system conceived from such a practice protects human beings from total destruction by belligerent action thereafter. It also begs the question as to what legal device other than freedom of conscience – the principle upon which traditional international law developed – imposes an effective check on inhumanity and destruction.

No ideologies in conflict with those of the Allies stand after the War, but political and social ideologies remain practical, opposing rather than integrating with each other. Co-existence of civilizations may be possible, based on the assumption of the equality of each civilization, but co-existence of ideology is impossible insofar as each asserts its innate superiority over the other. A "general international order" must, in any event, be a system of co-existence insofar as it is a system of peace in international society. It is in this sense that postwar international society can be nothing other than a rehabilitation of traditional international law.

As a matter of fact, however, the international order was restructured on the general foundation of the Allies' doctrine instead of individual, regional and other centrifugal ones. This seemingly contradicts the way of international law, which has claimed to be positive toward the practice of compromise, tolerance and co-existence. It is in this sense that the system of peace was lost in international society following the unprecedented destruction of the Second World War, which was fought with little reference to traditional international law and practice.

2. The International Legal Order in Changed Circumstances

(1) International society transformed into multiple civilized societies

a) International society was originally constituted by nations with different ideologies, religions, customs and cultures. Any differences created barriers to assimilation. The European nations fought wars with each other in the name of their religious beliefs in medieval times, and fought wars against non-European nations due to differences in civilization in the process of advancing east.

Among the original members of international society, however, the differences did not cause serious conflicts. Under the rule of international law based on traditional international society, there could be no great war involving the rise and fall of superpowers. In fact, the Europeans, including the emigrants to America, enjoyed peace for about a hundred years before the Great War broke out. Multiplicity of the members of international society drives it into different situations from before, and the repetition of great wars since then is indicative of the fact that the system of international law has been almost ineffective for half a century.

Wars of annihilation were legalized on the ground that "uncivilized" nations were not qualified to enjoy the rights of international law. If the total destruction of warring parties was generalized, there could not be any criteria of "civilization" to distinguish qualifications for enjoyment of the rights of international law, including the right of sovereign equality.[14]

It is little wonder then that international law did not solve the most serious clash

---

[14] The Statute of the Permanent Court of International Justice enacted under the auspices of the League of Nations provides that "the general principles of law recognized by civilized nations" are a source of international law (art 38, 1 c). It is historic evidence of international law originating in Christian European nations and contemplating non-European civilized nations, such as Turkey, and Japan.

of ideologies, namely, the conflict between liberalism and Communism. On the contrary, international law narrowly survived the conflict by being content with law of "peaceful co-existence." There were, indeed, contrary arguments of Western writers as peaceful co-existence was advocated by Soviet writers to make a temporary compromise with the capitalists until completion of "the world revolution."[15]

The Cold War was no exception in limiting international law to be a system of conciliation. Now that the Cold War is over, the natural cause of international conflicts is "civilization."[16] That does not mean, however, that international society faces a new situation, because the clash of civilizations can be traced back to the Age of Great Navigation and medieval times in European history.

International law has survived many hardships, including great wars leading to the Cold War and subsequent wars for national liberation. This means that international law is flexible enough to be a system adaptable to every stage of international society. It also means that international law is tolerant of new subjects as a number of newly independent states have come under regulation in addition to the original ones. Notwithstanding that, international law is too inflexible to be a system of conciliation on the basis of the doctrine of freedom of conscience.

Owing to these characteristics, international law has managed to survive various crises of invalidation, and is believed to address clashes of civilizations other than those between the Europeans and non-Europeans and between capitalism and Communism.

b) Japan entered into diplomatic relations with major Western powers prior to the restoration of the Imperial Government in 1868. Under the Government, she commenced modernization on the basis of the Western model. This was intended to avoid offensive action from Western powers against the nation on the basis of differences in civilization.[17]

Integrating such non-European nations, international society continued to be a "Family of Civilized Nations" for some time. However, Japanese "westernization" would eventually become a cause of change in international law and society. After being accepted into the society of Western powers, Japan rose to power in East Asia by annexing Korea following the war against Russia, participating in the First World War, and engaging in a series of battles against China. By contrast, the other non-European civilized nations did not follow the example set by Japan, and mostly remained subjugated until the 1950s.

As Japan rose to become a great power, she came to consider international law an

---

[15] E.A. Korovin, *International Law of the Time of Transition*, 1925. See also O.J. Lissitzyn, "International Law in a Divided World," *International Conciliation*, no. 542, March 1963, p. 16. On the other hand, it cannot be denied that treaties of general character concluded in that period were possible by means of a compromise between East and West.

[16] Samuel P. Huntington, "The Clash of Civilizations," *Foreign Affairs*, Summer 1993, p. 22.

[17] The series of reformations following abolition of the feudal regime is called the Meiji Restoration after the name of the era of the Meiji Emperor's reign.

obstacle, especially with respect to her invasion of mainland China. The move reinforced similar movements in other regions. Germany took the same position as Japan in understanding that the existing order did not benefit the "latecomers" to international society, who made a later start in national unification and modernization. This view was shared by Italy, which came to be unified at almost the same time as Germany and Japan.

On the other hand, international society strengthened its innate structure by accepting "newcomers." Furthermore, it could be an impetus to the drive for independence by nations still colonized. In fact, their challenge broke the *status quo* guaranteed by the existing order, which ultimately resulted in the dissolution of colonial rule.

The First World War broke out between the newly-risen Germany and the anti-German powers and ended in the defeat of Germany and the birth of the Soviet Union. The Second World War was more typical (apart from the behavior of the Soviet Union) in that it was fought between newly rising states and traditional powers.

The ultimate cause of disturbance in international society leading to great war was the multiplicity of civilization commencing with the advance eastward by the European powers. However, the direct cause of it was challenges made by the newcomers to international society against the vested interests of the existing powers. Japan's role in the change in international society was unique in that she "westernized" to become an accepted member and then challenged that society, leading to the outbreak of a great war.

c) Japan is assumed to have had a centralized political system in the fourth century, but had an organized government in the seventh century modeled after the Sui and Tang Dynasties in China. Her geo-political circumstances made it possible for her to remain independent throughout history, although she was placed under the cultural influence of the Continent. It made Japan familiar to the centrifugal view of international society, which accounted for her willingness to be integrated into the Western legal system, including the sovereign state system, in the nineteenth century.

In contrast, China had taken the view that the world enjoyed the benevolence of the Chinese Emperor who personified virtue as proven by sages such as Confucius and his followers. Those who would not accept the benevolence were not qualified to be legitimate members of international society. In other words, the world consisted of civilized nations that were obliged to the Chinese Emperor on the one hand and "barbarians" on the other. The non-legitimate members could not live peacefully in the world as non-civilization was a just cause of war to be waged by the civilized.

The Chinese view of the world is cultural rather than political. It was because of this view that China under the rule of the Ch'ing Dynasty was almost indifferent to the invasion by Western powers in the nineteenth century, understanding them to be too barbarous for dealings with cultured people. This forms a stark contrast with Japan, which was driven to political reformation to avoid the perceived danger of losing political independence through infiltration by Western powers.

According to the view of the nationalist school prevalent in the late Edo Era

(1603–1867), Japan should be the center of the world. This was because the Japanese Emperor was higher in virtue than the Chinese, which was proved by the coherency of the dynasty since the foundation of the state, presumably in the fourth century.

According to them, the conception of international society originating from Hugo Grotius was erroneous in taking a centrifugal view of international society. In spite of its theoretical irrelevancy, the concept should be accepted for the present as membership of the Western family of nations was a stage in the realization of the right view of international society as conceived by them. Westernization was a compromise to be made temporarily as a means of realizing a world under the reign of "the true Emperor."[18]

Since the late feudal era, Western civilization had been studied in the language of The Netherlands, the only nation with which Japanese people were authorized by the feudal government to make contact. According to Yukichi Fukuzawa (1834–1901), who was a scholar of Western sciences in Dutch, the Western states were strong and wealthy because people were independent:

"Human beings are equal in enjoying rights, whether they are rich or poor, strong or weak, civilian or official. Relations among nations are comparable to relations among human beings. As a person has no right to injure other persons, so a nation constituted of persons has no right to injure other nations. Powerful nations are equal to weaker or poorer nations in recourse to rights. The former have no right to persecute the latter, for the same reason that a wrestler has no right to hurt the body of a sick person."[19]

He encouraged people to be independent, to enrich the nation as well as themselves, because the more independent people are, the stronger and richer the nation becomes. The general trend in the Meiji Era was affirmation rather than negation of his argument, which made them accept westernization, whether willingly or reluctantly.

In spite of the argument developed by Fukuzawa, the fact was that membership of the Western Family did not necessarily make the nation equal to the rest of the Family, but placed it under a ban on aspiring to predominant status within the Family. It supported the long-term view of the Japanese nationalists that entry into the Western family was a "necessary evil" to be withdrawn sooner or later.

So long as Japan strove to remain a faithful member of Western society, there could be no challenges to the existing international order, aspiring to hold the hegemony of East Asia. In expanding overseas forcibly, Japan left the Western family under the rule of international law, being encouraged by the theory of the nationalist school once set aside in the course of modernization or westernization.

Amid these circumstances in the 1920s and 1930s, Japan was joined by "latecomers" who were convinced of the disadvantage of being under the existing legal order. The Second World War broke out in an international society where members were in disunity in ideology, civilization and economic dependency. The situation was

---

[18] Takamasa Okuni, *Shin shin kohoron* (New and True Public Law), 1867.

[19] Yukichi Fukuzawa, *Gakumon no susume* (An Exhortation to Learning), 1873, Book III.

intensified by Japan, an "accepted member" of the European Family, as a main challenger to the existing order which found encouragement in traditional ideology.

d) According to the German theorists of that period, Germany had reason to challenge the existing powers because traditional international law, on which the old powers based their rights, had been superseded by international law particular to each region. Just as there was international law for the American region established on the basis of the Monroe Doctrine, so there was international law particular to central Europe, in which Germany was an indispensable member. They had already replaced the traditional international law on which some leading states sought to base their rights and interests.[20]

According to this theory, international law was invalid in a region in the absence of consent by the key nations in it. As American international law cannot be valid without the consent of the United States, so European international law could not be so without the consent of Germany.[21] The theory of the Greater Asia Co-prosperity Sphere advanced by Japan during the Second World War was a counterpart to this German "regional theory."

The regional theory is too simple to be a theory for the replacement of a general order of international law by a particular race or culture. The theory was politically oriented rather than legal, reiterating the absurdity of the Versailles peace system forced upon Germany after the First World War. More than anything, it was behind the times when the world was moving to become a single entity in every field, including law and politics.

On the other hand, it is realistic in discussing an international society divided, as it was at that time, into several blocs. It indicates that international order is positive when present in every region under the influence of a specific state or states which is/are less influential globally. As a matter of fact, the United States pursued regional unity in the face of threats from Europe. After their loss of hegemony over world affairs, the West European states often sought regional consensus beforehand, as they did with respect to Germany's admission to the League of Nations.

The German theory is unacceptable in that it takes advantage of regional practices to cover the irrationality. The Japanese theory is also unacceptable in that is reinforced by the German regional theory, but is somewhat unique in invoking civilization to point out the deficiencies of the existing order. These theories did not play any part in the conception of the postwar international order as a result of their countries having lost the War. In spite of everything, they might have been more persuasive if supported by Communist theory from the Soviet region, which became a reality in international society after the War.

---

20 This was the so-called "Grossraumtheorie." See, for example, Carl Schmitt, *Völkerrechtliche Grossraumordnung,* 1941.

21 The theory reiterated regionalism in resistance to generalism on the ground that traditional international law had been wrongly developed in ignorance of regional values: C. Schmitt, Grossraum gegen Universalismus: Der völkerrechtliche Kampf um die Monroedoktrin, 6 *Zeitschrift der Akademie für Deutsches Recht,* Heft 10,1939, S 333.

e) Russia is a regional state extending from Europe to the eastern extreme of the Asian Continent. From an historical standpoint, it has been a region rather than a state, where eastern powers come into contact with western ones.

The Communist revolutionary regime was established in Russia amid the confusion following the First World War. It was a realization of the Marxist-Lenin doctrine advocated against capitalism. Economic crisis following the Great Depression in the 1930s seemed to certify the truth of the doctrine. Under these circumstances, Fascists and militarists rose to power to resist the Communists in some leading nations, including Germany, Italy, Spain and Japan.

Until the end of the Cold War, the Soviet Union was the most radical in recognizing herself as the only Socialist state distinguishable from "the capitalists" constituting the rest of the world. She did not hesitate to justify herself by value standards inconsistent with traditional Europeans'. Apart from the particularity of the theory, the Soviet Union was distinctive in that she was a self-sufficient region state having little necessity to come into contact with other ones.

Challengers to the international legal order often sought to escape from their obligations by claiming that the order should be, or had already been, dissolved into several regional bodies of normative order. Their allegations might be justifiable if they implied a reproach to the existing status of regions under colonial domination. In any case, the Soviet Union was the only challenger to survive the Second World War as an integral member of the Allied Nations.

f) In establishing the postwar international order, the United States, United Kingdom, Soviet Union and China adopted the Moscow Declaration on General Security on 1 November 1943, stating that they agreed to establish "a general international organization for the maintenance of international peace and security" (para 4). According to the Charter of the United Nations, which is the realization of the Declaration, maintenance of international peace and security is purported by the organization, "in conformity with the principles of international law" (art 11).

As the Allied Nations planned "an international organization," so it was characterized by the great war they fought. As far as they conceived it as a practical institution, they could not be free of the practice of cooperation among the Allied Nations, including the Soviet Union as a necessary collaborator. Under the circumstances, an international organization would be inoperable without some compromise between democracy and socialism, traditionalism and revolutionary thoughts, individualism and doctrine for communal interests, and so on, and the Soviet Union was in conflict with the other members in supporting the latter.

A "general international organization" was established in the midst of hostilities against the enemies, without taking the voice of the enemies and neutral states into consideration. This situation meant the international organization was planned with little regard to the foreseeable differences in opinion between the main Allies. It also made the drafters fail to give much thought to the particularities of regions in planning the future operation of the mechanism.

Before the United Nations Conference on International Organization was convened in San Francisco, the Inter-American Conference on Questions of War and Peace was held in Mexico City in February and March 1945 to reconcile the inter-American system with the proposed general international organization. It was not self-evident under the Proposal how a general international organization was related to a regional one. The logical consequence of it, however, is that there is no "general" international organization, but rather, a league of regional organizations, unless the regional organization is subject to the general one.

Indeed, the Axis powers were suppressed together with the regionalism supported by their theorists and governments or military authorities. However, the Second World War caused conflicts between political and economic blocs. It is also a fact that most states were motivated to fight to defend each regional interest rather than the general one. The Allied Nations were composed of a balance between the Soviet Union and the rest. If they opposed each other, there could be no general international organization as declared in the Moscow Declaration in 1943.

g) There could hardly be a general international organization, bearing in mind the fact that a considerable part of international society was under colonial domination. If a general international organization replaced the general order of international society, a large part of which consisted of international law, it should have addressed the situation properly by restoring that part of the world to its due position.

The Charter met the requirement providing for a "Declaration Regarding Non-self-governing Territories" and an "International Trusteeship System" (chapters XI and XII). Areas under Trusteeship will disappear once they attain independence, as anticipated by the Charter (art 76 b). Non-self-governing territories will also become independent if they are changed in nature from what is provided for in the Charter.[22] Such territories have in fact disappeared as self-determination rises to become a basic principle of the United Nations.

The situation after the 1960s indicates that the fundamental character of the international legal order – that is, the system of sovereign equality – remains unchanged, but international law may possibly lose its core position within the international legal order. That is partly because sovereign equality has become a nominal principle, with many newly independent states having an antagonistic attitude toward international law.

According to the representative of India to the United Nations, in the discussion of the General Assembly on the status of Goa placed under the domination of Portugal, international law written by European writers, including Grotius, is regulating international life today, but the tenet in support of colonial powers is no longer acceptable. "It is the European concept and it must die. It is time, in the twentieth century, that it died."[23] They will be even less inclined to remain faithful to it in view of the practice of the European members not to act in conformity with it.

The acts they took in the process of the struggle for independence make the

---

[22] There is no clear distinction between international Trusteeship and "non-self-governing territories." The former is aimed at independence (art 76), while the latter is not (art 73). Both of these are in fact treated the same way in gaining independence, but this is not endorsed by any Charter provision.

[23] SCOR 987 mtg, 18 December 1961, 47.

destruction of traditional international law complete in the field of the law of war. "Wars of liberation" have broken out in the aftermath of the Second World War and are fought by guerrilla forces in disregard of the principle of regular armies. It may violate, among other things, the fundamental principle of no use of force in the UN Charter as well as traditional international law.

As far as the Charter provisions are concerned, self-determination is not found among the key concepts, but is mentioned sporadically in two provisions (arts 1(2), 55). By exempting "war of liberation" from the principle of no use of force, self-determination in the Charter is too abstract and hollow.[24]

In April 1955, all newly independent states from Asia and Africa held a conference in Bandung, Indonesia. They numbered thirty, including China and Japan. Ten principles, consistent with the UN Charter, were adopted at the Conference. As members of the United Nations, they exerted influence over the policy by grouping themselves as the Afro-Asians in the General Assembly.

This formed the background of the International Covenant on Economic Social and Cultural Rights and the International Covenant on Civil and Political Rights, adopted on the basis of a draft of a commission of the United Nations in 1966, confirming that "the non-self-governing territories" are related to "independence" (each Covenant, art 1(3)). In the same way, the General Assembly adopted a series of resolutions emphasizing the right of self-determination, including the Declaration on the Granting of Independence to Colonial Countries and Peoples on 14 December 1960 and Principles of International Law concerning Friendly Relations and Cooperation among States on 24 October 1970.[25]

As international society is the counterpart to the United Nations, so it may be divided into two groups of the former colonized nations and colonizing ones, which have different interests in the international legal order. The newly independent states would not adhere to traditional principles of international law in rehabilitating the international legal order. They would not necessarily depart from international law with its principle of sovereign equality, but make use of it by taking a double standard to be applied to each group member of international society.

The situation is not an eradication, but rather a gradual deterioration of the sovereign state system on which traditional international law has developed, notwithstanding generalization of the jurisdiction beyond the original part of the exercise, the European civilized region.

---

[24] The Soviets proposed that the phrase "self-determination of peoples" be inserted in the Charter. This proposal was accepted, but the relationship between the phrase and Charter provisions regarding colonial matters and trusteeship was left unchanged: R.B. Russell, *A History of the United Nations Charter : The Role of the United States, 1940/1945*, 1958, p. 810. The relationship was subsequently clarified, after the practice of "wars of liberation," by the two International Covenants on Human Rights adopted by the Commission on Human Rights in 1966.

[25] The resolutions go beyond the terms of the Charter, however liberally construed. The General Assembly assumed the legislative power regarding this matter, despite having no general law-making capacity to do so under the Charter: J.Crawford, *The Creation of States in International Law,* 1979 p. 89.

h) Economic difficulties in the 1930s led states to choose protectionism over free trade, under the principle of which the international economy had been balanced globally. The world was divided into several regional economic blocs, in the center of which leading states were situated. The United States was centered in the dollar bloc; Great Britain, in the sterling; Germany, in the mark; and Japan, in the yen.

The Second World War was, so to speak, a clash between such blocs. They made a war against rivals in an attempt to overcome the hardship of each country in the fields of politics and economics, aside from the temptation towards ideological propagation and territorial expansion. The apparent cause of the War was in such circumstances, but the ultimate cause was in the loss of the system of conciliation to be employed in such a crisis to avoid an all-out conflict.

Disorder in the fields of thought, economics and politics had developed since the decline of common standards in international society, which was accelerated by "the heretical doctrine" from the standpoint of the traditional Western civilization. Under the circumstances, economic and political difficulties were based on ideological differences between rival states. The difference in interests was emphasized in the differences between civilizations, as was the case with Japan confronting the traditional European powers.

Instead of reconciling different thoughts and civilizations, the Second World War practiced the destruction of people and nations on the grounds of such differences. No normative order was foreseeable to replace international law to conciliate views, the differences of which were likely to lead to other inhuman atrocities.

Indeed, theories propounded by Germany and Japan might be extinguished, but the Communist theory claimed to be the legitimate ideology of postwar international society. The Soviet regime had the universal perspective of world revolution by the proletariats against the bourgeoisies, but was ultimately dissolved by the declaration of its head in 1989.

If other challengers are possible in international society after the fall of the Soviets, they will be among the newly independent states. They share in common the fact that they were excluded from the international legal system on account of the differences between their civilizations and the Europeans'. They also share economic and social hardships due to their long colonial domination.

Since the Conference in Bandung, a group of newly independent states has been recognized. They have supported a series of resolutions of the General Assembly of the United Nations to encourage their "regional" preference.

Regional integration in Europe started by the West European nations in the 1950s, several years after the end of the War, suggested the reality of the regional conciliatory system. Unity of the American states was consolidated during the War. Notwithstanding the advocacy of philosophers, "the World Government" has proven impractical, even after the War. Instead, regional integration progressed in parallel with globalization in every field of human endeavor. "International government" will be realized on a regional basis in international society.

It is unlikely that a group of newly independent states will establish their own region in order to reap the benefits of a New International Economic Order. The postwar international order must not be threatened by other newcomers or have-nots, but there is a danger that it will be invalidated as a general order. It should be appreciated that regional integration may be a realization of the World Government. On the other hand, regional disintegration is also a reality, as seen in the conflicts following the Cold War.

Whatever situation may be taken into consideration in conceiving the international order, the traditional function of international law originating in European civilization must necessarily be part of it, since the doctrine of freedom of conscience is so distinctive of the conciliatory function. After the experience of intolerance on the basis of differences in civilization, ideology and religion, it is clear that a system of conciliation is needed most.

(2) An international order balancing world government and sovereign equality

a) According to Immanuel Kant, complete abolition of war or eternal peace could be realized by a pacific federation (*foedus pacificum*) rather than by a peace treaty (*pactum pacis*). He did not believe that international law imposes the renunciation of war upon states. It is "reason" that makes people feel a sense of duty to prevent human annihilation. International law is proof that human beings have reason. It drives them to realize "the world government" by taking advantage of the opportunities presented by great war.[26]

It cannot be denied that most "Peace Plans" are discussed in relation to great war.[27] World government may hold great appeal to people who never want to suffer the devastation of war again. The Second World War was no exception in providing an impetus for calls for a world government.[28] However, the reality of the argument stems from the fact that the world is becoming unified on the basis of the victors' alliance. In other words, a Peace Plan has a positive basis when discussed at the time of the occurrence of a great war. The general international organization of the Allied Nations is in fact believed to be "the government" of postwar international society.[29]

---

[26] He argues that the law of nations, developed by Grotius, Puffendorf, Vattel and the other "miserable comforters," cannot have the slightest legal force. Nevertheless, every state pays homage to law, which proves that there is a higher and greater moral capacity in man: Immanuel Kant, *Zum ewigen Frieden*, 1795, translated by W. Hastie, *Kant's Eternal Peace*, 1914, esp. pp. 82–84.

[27] See, among others, S.J. Hemleben, *Plans for World Peace Through Six Centuries*, 1943.

[28] In the 1940s, the proposal to establish "world government" in place of sovereign state systems appeared to gain popularity: E. Reves, *Anatomy of Peace*, 1945. However, sovereign state systems were in fact reinforced by the increasing number of independent states in the 1960s: see also Maurice Bertrand, *Refaire L'UNO*, 1991, ch. 3.

[29] The Japanese translation of the "United Nations Organization" into *Kokusairengo* does not imply an organization of the Allied Nations or the United Nations, but rather connotes a "federation of states" or "international government." It is believed that a tentative translation by Professor Yokota, who studied the Dumbarton Oaks Proposals during the War, was officially changed later: *Kokusaihogaiko zasshi* (*The Journal of International Law and Diplomacy*), 1944, p. 907. In selecting this particular translation, the tone of war alliance was set aside and a call for "world government" embraced. It differs from the translation for the United Nations meaning the Allied Nations of the Second World War, *Rengokoku*. In contrast, the Chinese translation does not distinguish between the U.N.O. and the Allied Nations. See also Wakamizu Tsutsui, "Japan's Role in the International Organizations with Particular Reference to the United Nations", 25*Archiv des Völkerrechts*, 1 Heft 1987, p. 26.

The Allied Nations, however, did not aspire to world government, but adhered to the principle of the sovereign equality of states for the purpose of maintaining international peace and security (Charter, art 2 para 1). In the course of the Conference on its establishment, they made a compromise regarding the collective principle by deeming the right of self-defense to be inherent to each member state. The concept of a general international organization was also compromised in that they made its operation dependent upon the regional cooperation of member states.

All are recognition of the fact that international society is in disunity in ideology, region and civilization. As matters stand, the United Nations seeks to rehabilitate traditional international law rather than render it obsolete, by refraining from developing into an entity equivalent to the world government.

Rehabilitation of the international order after the practice of the "anti-aggression" campaign depends upon the willingness of individual states to give up their sovereignty. That is the basis of traditional international law, but has been invalidated through the practices of the Second World War. One aspect of the rehabilitation of the international order is the replacement of traditional international law with the "public function" of an international organization. In any event, international law cannot be rehabilitated to what it was traditionally.

In certain fields of international society, international organizations have been in the position of subjects of international law next to states through their activities since the latter half of the nineteenth century.[30] In this sense, an international organization is far more positive than a world government realized on the basis of "people's reason."

However, an international organization, consisting of states, cannot be so revolutionary as to outlaw a state from the international legal order. In fact, the general international organization of the Allied Nations does not claim to replace international law based on the principle of the sovereign equality of states.

b) No social order can be valid without adapting to social change. Any power could establish a valid system provided they based it on a society observed correctly.

International society has decentralized power, in contrast to a municipal society unified by central powers. If they attribute the instability of international law to the structure decentralizing power, then they fail to appreciate the fact that international society has long been stable among equally sovereign states sharing Western or Greco-Roman civilization in common.[31]

The problem is whether the recent instability is caused by changes in the power structure. If the answer were in the affirmative, then the international legal order could not be rehabilitated without being accorded a new power structure.

The First World War was exceptional in that it was fought by almost all states in

---

[30] See First Report by Mr. Abdullah El-Erian, Special Rapporteur of UN International Law Commission, Relations between States and Inter-governmental Organization, *Yearbook of International Law Commission* (hereafter cited as "YBILC") 1963, p. 159.

[31] J.L. Kunz, The Changing Law of Nations, *The Changing Law of Nations: Essays on International Law*, 1968, ch. 1.

existence at that time, including some non-European ones. Nevertheless, it was no exception from the preceding wars in that it was, for the most part, fought under the regulations of the law of war. The laws of war and neutrality had been codified at the Hague Peace Conference held on two occasions immediately before the War. The belligerents had a clear consciousness that they were acting legally so long as their actions accorded with the law of war. No states were impeached for infidelity for remaining outside the war so long as they accorded with the law of neutrality.

Unlike the First World War, the Second was fought only under the nominal validity of traditional international law. There was no distinction between the legitimate and the illegitimate in the war being fought by the belligerents. Few states remained neutral throughout the Second World War. After such practices, international law could hardly be valid unless it successfully gave them a convincing account of its own terms.

It would be successful if the doctrine of the Allied Nations implied a general value standard to correct every "illegality" practiced in the course of war. It would depend on whether the mechanism or the United Nations Organization included the concept to correct the past "illegalities."

Considering that the Allied Nations were a political and military alliance formed by putting aside ideological differences with the Soviet Union, any system of the Allies' organization could not successfully handle disputes between the Soviets and the rest after disappearance of their common enemies. The Soviets were a minority in the Allied Nations, though the powers were somewhat balanced by China joining the Communist bloc, so it would prefer a regional alliance to a general international organization as the basis of foreign policy.

In this situation, the Allied Nations decided to create a general international organization as the postwar international order. However, it could not present a general value standard to correct "illegalities" practiced in the past and future. More than anything, it is an organization established leaving serious ideological differences unresolved.

The only way the Allied Nations incorporated practices of their joint actions into the structure was by conceiving a "general international organization." This was an institutionalization of the preferential treatment of specific states. Any "illegal" practice in wartime was formulated in the UN Charter system without modification if taken by the main Allies. The result was that the organization resembled a power-centralized one, something akin to the government of a municipal society, rather than an arbitral tribunal in international society. In fact, it was institutionalized to confer privileges upon specific powers to the extent that it might well be regarded as a "ruling system" of super-states, including the United States and Soviet Union.

Since the Second World war, international society has needed to have public law to deal with international crimes, such as crimes against peace, genocide, apartheid, and environmental damage, which are contrary practices not corrected under traditional international law.

Multiplicity of civilization in international society is advantageous in publicizing international law. In contrast to the West, Oriental people and society are strangers to civil law, but familiar with public law.

Whether they like it or not, the postwar international legal order must be "public," departing from fundamental principles of traditional international law. The situation might not necessarily be unclear in the political circumstance where nothing went without compromise between the Soviet Union and the rest. Even under these circumstances, apartheid, colonialism, terrorism and mass destruction were cited in the United Nations as international crimes.

The collapse of the Soviet Union in 1989 removed the direct cause of the paralysis of the United Nations, together with the fear of a third World War. It was ascribed not to the achievement of a "public" international organization, but to the superiority of the "free doctrine" to the opposing doctrine including Communism.

Now that the crisis caused by ideological confrontations has seemingly passed, unforeseen casualties, including environmental damage and ruthless terrorism motivated by religious beliefs, will bring catastrophes to human society, not to mention the risk of nuclear warfare. On the other hand, there is the possibility that another ideological conflict will arise in the form of a "clash of civilizations." It is questionable whether a "public" international organization could address such crises successfully on a positive basis like the practices of the Allied Nations during the Second World War.

The Allied Nations won the War, but could not help making a compromise by amending the original policy and doctrine, especially in the fields of decolonization and disarmament. At the last stage of the UN Conference on General International Organization, the character of "a general international organization for the maintenance of international peace and security" was also amended in order to make a concession to the claim of some members for regional autonomy.

The success of General International Organization depends on how tolerant or prepared the members are to make compromises to resolve differences in any field so as to deal with other clashes after the Cold War. The answer will be found in rehabilitation of international law in essence, which originates in a system of compromise between different beliefs and ideologies.

The postwar international order was established to balance world government and sovereign equality, and the same balance would survive during the period after the Cold War. International law originates in a system of compromise, so it is reasonable that it be integrated into international organizations as an integral part of the postwar international order, which enforces the "public interest" for the benefit of international society.

3. The International Legal Order under the Principle of War Renunciation

(1) Invalidation of the traditional order through the practice of counter-aggression

a) A birth is one aspect of the annulment of things already in existence. A new legal order is born by an integration of illegalities in light of the existing order.

The First World War was believed epoch-making in some respects, such as the participation of almost every state in existence in the world at that time and the use of high-tech weapons, resulting in unprecedented destruction. However, it was not exceptional insofar as it was fought and ended in accordance with traditional international law.

The League of Nations was conceived as an embodiment of the international order after the First World War. It was discussed at the peace conference convened to end the Great War following the armistice. The peace treaties, including the Versailles Peace Treaty with Germany, had the Covenant of the League of Nations, the constituent instrument of the League of Nations, as an integral part of them. Owing to this integration, the majority of independent states at that time discussed the establishment of the League of Nations as a general international order after the Great War.

The conditions of peace were, in any event, imposed upon the vanquished by the victorious. However, they took the form of an agreement to end hostilities between them in accordance with the traditional international law of war. With respect to the peace treaties providing for the League of Nations, states other than the belligerent states were invited to present ideas for consideration. Germany and her allies also presented their views regarding it for discussion at the Paris Peace Conference, but they were not taken into consideration by the victors.[32]

The League of Nations may have been no more than an institution designed to perpetuate the power structure resulting from the Great War, as had been the case, for example, with the entente in Vienna, the alliance after the Napoleonic War. Be that as it may, there had never been an international organization as an entity distinct from a standing international conference before, let alone an entity comparable to a state in capacity and personality. It was a manifestation of the international movement towards an "international government," which had progressed since the beginning of the nineteenth century.[33]

Apart from the birth of the League of Nations, there were some other indications that international law and society were definitely changing. Few states remained neutral throughout the First World War, and Belgium abandoned her neutrality at the start of it. The rules of warfare already established and codified were helpless to prevent the damage caused by the use of high-tech weapons.

In spite of these indications, few recognized that the international legal order had departed from the traditional one. Most of the belligerents of the First World War were states of European origin, out of whose custom and practice international law had grown. There may have been a movement towards outlawing war as an institution in relations between states.[34] However, the value standard of the

---

[32] The German draft was rejected by the Committee as "unrealistic": Report of Japanese delegate to Foreign Minister, 25 May 1919. H.W.V. Temperley (ed.), *A History of the Peace Conference of Paris*, vol. VI, 1924, pp. 456–457.

[33] See, for example, C. Eagleton, *International Government* (rev. ed.), 1948.

[34] This movement began in the United States in the nineteenth century: F. Przetacznik, "The Basic Ideas of the Philosophical Concept of War and Peace," 66*Revue de Droit International de Sciences Diplomatiques et Politiques*, 1988, p. 291.

belligerents was not so divisive as to render the existing rules and practices of the law of war obsolete. Any nation might defy tradition, but would be less powerful to take the lead in belligerent operations as a result. The War may indeed have made them aware of the symptoms of change in international law and society, but by and large, it remained a war fought in the traditional manner.[35]

The League system failed not because it had any fatal flaws, but rather because the most powerful states attached little importance to its activities. The United States never joined it. Germany, Italy and Japan withdrew from it. The Soviet Union was admitted to it belatedly, but then ousted from it for aggression to a member state. No international organization could be "the world government," without the simultaneous participation of the main powers.[36]

In this sense, the League of Nations is not necessarily the predecessor of the United Nations.[37] Nevertheless, it cannot be denied that it has some features of a forerunner of the United Nations in terms of its concepts and structure.

The League of Nations was intended to establish "the understandings of international law as the actual rule of conduct among Governments" (Preamble), rather than supersede the preceding system of international society. On the other hand, the Covenant provided that any war, whether immediately affecting any of the members or not, was a matter of concern to the whole League of Nations (art 11). This provision represents the essence of collective security, which was inherited by the United Nations.

This does not mean, however, that the two collective organizations had the same system on the same basis of international society. Indeed, members of the League of Nations were deprived of full enjoyment of the right of sovereignty provided under international law to the extent that they were not free to resort to war as they pleased. Nevertheless, they did not go beyond the limitations of the traditional system in being regulated by the law of war in taking part in sanctions and being sanctioned. The provisions of the Covenant were enforced by deeming members who resorted to war in disregard of the Covenant to have *ipso facto* committed an act of war against all the other members (art 16-1). In other words, the violator would be sanctioned by being deemed to have made war against all other members of the League, who were overwhelming in number and force.

Under a system in which no states are freed from the obligations of *jus in bello* in taking sanctions, no problem arises as to how human rights are guaranteed in a war

---

35 See J.W. Garner, *International Law and the World War*, vols 1 & 2, 1920.

36 It may have been possible for the leading members of the Allied Nations who were central powers in the League of Nations – the United Kingdom and France, among others – to support the restitution of it as a postwar international organization. However, none of them could afford to promote such an organization. The most influential states in designing it, the United States and Soviet Union, were outside the League. Under the circumstances, it was not feasible for the League of Nations to be revived to become a general international organization after the Second World War.

37 The League of Nations was agreed upon in June 1919, came into operation on 10 January 1920, and was dissolved on 18 April 1946. The United Nations was agreed upon in June 1945 and commenced operations the following year, so there existed an overlap between "the two world organizations" for some time: F.P. Walters, *A History of the League of Nations*, 1952.

fought for just cause. They would take hostile action on condition of *jus in bello* in traditional international law, regardless of the "just" or "unjust" status of belligerents distinguished in the light of *jus ad bellum* or the Covenant.

The United Nations has quite a different system of sanctions in relation to war and the law of war.

In creating a postwar international system, what became the basis was not League practices, but rather the practices of non-members taken outside it. International law had undergone fundamental changes due to the practices of non-members of the League of Nations rather than those of it. The United Nations was thus based on the practices of the changed international law. The League of Nations might be in an intermediate position between traditional international law and the changed one by organizing the former, but the United Nations stood on the side of the latter by incorporating practices contrary to the former into its structure.

b) If the most important international affairs had been dealt with within the League of Nations, the international order after the First World War would have been organized in accordance with traditional international law. In reality, however, serious disputes between the two World Wars were settled outside the League of Nations with little regard to it.

In attacking China, Japan did not recognize that she was waging war, but instead described the act as an "incident." This characterization was not opposed by other states, including the United States and United Kingdom, who were assisting China with no intention of causing a rupture with Japan. If they sought the legalization on the Covenant of the League, they could not escape submitting the matter to the Council (art 15). If they sought it on the basis of traditional international law, they would find it was either war or in violation of the law of war and neutrality.

Japan did not resort to invoking the right to war, but instead invoked the right to self-defense, which was exempted by the War Renunciation Pact in 1929. The United States also found justification of its discriminatory attitude toward the dispute between the United Kingdom and Germany in "the ultimate right of self-defense."[38]

From the standpoint of traditional international law, Japan was at war with China, and the United States and United Kingdom should have abided by the law of neutrality if they wished to avoid entering into war with Japan. In the same sense, the United States violated the law of neutrality in relation to Germany, which was at war with the United Kingdom.

The acts of the United States and United Kingdom might be excused with respect to the prior violations of international law by Japan and Germany. Once one state had violated international law, the other could justify its reaction in the face of any reprisal.[39] The Resolution at the Budapest Conference of the International Law Association in 1934 argued that a deviation from the law of neutrality in a manner discriminatory to one party in a war was legitimate where it was a reaction to a

[38] C.G. Fenwick, Neutrality on the Defensive, 34 *American Journal of International Law* (hereafter cited as "AJ") 1940, p. 698.

[39] C. Eagleton, The Needs of International Law, 34 *AJ* 1940, p. 699.

breach of the agreement on the renunciation of war or non-aggression.[40] It was in accordance with this suggestion that the United States, while remaining neutral herself, transferred warships to the United Kingdom upon her entry into war with Germany in September 1940.[41]

"Reprisal" is a term excusing an act in violation of international law by reason that the initial act responded against was itself in violation of international law. It is rightly taken when a state responds to the injury for its own benefit. The Budapest Resolution was novel in excusing an act of a third state in relation to a conflict on the basis that it was a reprisal.

This novel conception was based on the War Renunciation Pact, concluded in 1928 and entering into force the following year. According to that argument, what is counteracted is a violation of the pledge of war renunciation or non-aggression embodied in the Pact. War renunciation is a matter of concern to every member of international society, so any state may take a counteraction, whether that responding state was injured by the violation or not. It depends on the definition of reprisal as to whether such an act may be called a reprisal or not. It could be a reprisal taken by a state, not in the capacity of an injured state, but rather in that of an "interested state."

Whether called an injured state or interested state, the state taking the reprisal is subject to the conditions of the injury inflicted by the wrongful act of the other state. Its unlawful acts performed by reason of reprisal will be excused provided they are not excessive and are proportional to the injury sustained.

With all the conditions, reprisal has been regarded with distrust because it is often used as an excuse for illegal acts, especially when taken by powerful states. Moreover, a reprisal by a third state will not be trusted because it is in fact freed from the condition of proportionality since it is taken by a state or states against which the wrongful act was not directed.

In view of the original meaning of reprisal, counteractions against aggression must be distinguished from acts taken to recover specific rights. They are taken to promote the ultimate purpose of international society rather than an individual one. They are not made unlawful for being excessive with respect to the illegality made by the aggressor since they are justified by the participation of as many states as possible, including powerful states. This was proven by the practices in the Second World War taken as counteractions against non-compliance with the pledge of war renunciation.

So long as the postwar international order followed the practice of counter-aggression or "the interested state," it would not accord with traditional international law, let alone the Covenant of the League of Nations.

---

[40] Report of the 38th Conference, 1934, p .4; 33 *AJ* 1939, p. 825.

[41] Q. Wright, The Transfer of Destroyers to Great Britain, 34 *AJ* 1940, p. 121. In the early stages of the Second World War, many states, including Italy, Turkey, the Soviet Union, Bulgaria, Egypt, Spain, Hungary, Romania, and later the United States, together with other American states, explained their policies through the use of similar concepts: Kisaburo Yokota, *Anzenhosho no Mondai* (Problems on Security), 1949.

c) Any forcible action might involve some degree of inhumanity, but be excused for being in defense of the acting state. The issue arose as to whether enforcement of an order of international society excused inhumanity involved in the action or not. Notwithstanding the practices of the Second World War, casualties involved in realization of the general principle of the renunciation of war were such that they should not be repeated further.

International society is, after all, composed of people, so any norm is evaluated so as to minimize human casualties. Modern war technology is such that any breach of the peace causes grave casualties, so forcible action should be kept to the absolute minimum, whether it is a counteraction to a wrong or otherwise.

The law on protected persons is an integral part of *jus in bello* under traditional international law, in discordance with which no state may fight war. Apart from the legitimacy of the war, *jus in bello* is effectuated in the light of *jus ad bellum*. This was true of the League of Nations, as a sanction imposed under article 16 of the Covenant was war waged in accordance with *jus in bello*, including the laws of belligerency and neutrality.

"Non-belligerency" or "intermediacy" is a violation of *jus in bello* on the assumption that traditional international law is not invalidated. It would be legitimated when it had positioned itself on any system replacing the traditional system in the name of non-belligerency. It would be made positive through contravention of *jus in bello*, including rules of neutrality, as practiced repeatedly prior to commencement of the Second World War.

It is a logical consequence that dissolution of neutrality brings war to dissolution. This does not mean disappearance of war on earth, but rather indicates the situation where no states would invoke the law of war and neutrality to defend their rights and interests. It is a result of the legalization of non-belligerency through the repeated acts of a number of states, including powerful ones.

It is justified as a sanction against violations of the pledge of war renunciation made by "assisting states" in the process of helping victim states. It was taken outside the League of Nations, but attempts were made to coordinate it with the League system by assimilating violation of the Pact with that of the Covenant and vice-versa.[42]

If an act in the Second World War was based on reprisal against violation of a principle of existing international law, it could not be an act taken contrary to *jus in bello*. On the other hand, if an act was based on the status of "assisting states," it could not be illegal by reason of being contrary to *jus in bello*. It is only in the latter case that invalidation of the traditional system of international law is evidenced.

The question is how loss of the system of humanity involved in the invalidation of the traditional system is compensated for, to the benefit of the belligerents and civilians in the course of the "sanction." It depends on the answer to the question of whether the system designed for the postwar international society deserves to be appreciated as an innovation of the system of traditional international law.

---

42 Walters, *op. cit.*, p. 387.

(2) Survival of jus ad bellum *in the practices around the time of the Second World War*

The international legal order is proved positive by counteractions to violations of it. Any legal system is merely a scheme on paper in the absence of effective means of execution. The international legal order is based on an international society composed of sovereign states, so executed by a state claiming to counteract the violation of individual rights.

The postwar international order is positive in that it was formulated after the practices of the victorious Allied Nations. At the same time, it is an order involving no use of force, quite distinct from the traditional international legal order effectuated by the use of force by individual states.

The prelude to the Second World War was joint opposition to the Axis powers, independent of the individual interests of the opponents. They based their acts on the international public order embodied in the War Renunciation Pact and other instruments. In acting on such basis, they were understood to be in a state of "non-belligerency" as opposed to war and peace.

The United Nations was based on such prewar practices, so is an institution of international public interest under the principle of non-aggression. Under this principle, members are prohibited from using force, except where expressly permitted to do so. A clear distinction is drawn in deeming acts of force either to be ones of aggression or counter-aggression, right or wrong, in light of the principle of no use of force.

Back in the classical era, war was discussed in accordance with the distinction between just and unjust in the light of *jus ad bellum*. The postwar situation is a resurrection of the system of just war or *bellum justum*, which was believed to have been defunct since the nineteenth century. It is a departure from the system whereby war is legal unless in disaccord with *jus in bello*. In the event, states are questioned as to the cause for which they are using force or fighting war. The postwar international order is a conversion of the system of *jus in bello* to one of *jus ad bellum*, or from a system of indiscrimination to one of discrimination in the light of the just cause of war, aside from the difference in substance of *justa causa*.

In the resurrected system of *bellum justum*, *justa causa* is a synthesis of instruments making war illegal, such as the Covenant of the League of Nations, Locarno Pacts, and the Renunciation of War Pact, institutionalized on the basis of the practice of counter-aggression. The United Nations Charter is, so to speak, an instrument restricting "just war" to "counter-war" with respect to violations against the principle of no use of force proved on the basis of such instruments.[43]

Violation against the principle is synonymous with aggression, so should be counteracted under the auspices of a public authority. In order to exert such

---

[43] H. Kelsen, *The Law of the United Nations*, 1951.

authority, the General Assembly and Security Council of the United Nations have repeatedly declared reprisal inconsistent with Charter principles.[44]

If states are deprived of the ultimate means of armed counteraction, international law will no longer be entirely positive. It will remain positive to the extent that correction of the contravention is possible in the just cause of collective security.

As far as the express provisions of the United Nations Charter are concerned, "just cause" is not specified. The Charter leaves the enforcement action to the discretion of the Security Council. It decides what action will be taken on the basis of the existence of a "threat to the peace," "breach of the peace" or "act of aggression" (art 39). It is not clear whether individual states may respond to a breach in international law in circumstances where the Security Council remains indifferent to the situation.

In the independence process of "non-self-governing territories" left to the "sacred trust" of some important UN members (art 73), it is recognized that forcible struggle for independence is consistent with the Charter principles. In the process of recognition, "self-determination" comes to be one of the fundamental principles of the UN Charter. A response to a violation against the principle has come to be regarded as a "just cause" to be added to the original cause of "non-aggression."

In the sense that self-determination results in an increase in the members of international society as well as the United Nations, international law is not adversely affected by the addition of the just cause of self-determination. The UN Charter assures that it is based on the principle of sovereign equality of all the members (art 1-1). So long as the decolonized nations hold membership of the United Nations, they would not prevent the principle from being incorporated into the Charter.

However, this situation would not necessarily be favorable to international law since nations colonized under traditional international law might well take an antagonistic attitude towards it once released from that status. Whether they intend it or not, the appearance of decolonized nations in international society is concomitant with a decline in traditional international law.

The newly independent states have been accepted as members of the United Nations, so the Charter is taken to recognize the cause of independence, the "war of liberation," to be consistent with itself. "War of liberation" is not exempted from the principle of no use of force in any explicit texts of the UN Charter, but has come to be regarded as consistent with it through the practice of the United Nations.

Resistance against the domestic government necessarily takes the form of irregular or guerrilla combats. Under the practice of war adopted by the Hague Conventions, the right to engage in war is enjoyed exclusively by the regular army. Most wars of liberation engaged in by irregular combats or guerrilla forces are a deviation from the conventions adopted at The Hague. In accepting the result of a

---

[44] For example, the Declaration on Principles of International Law concerning Friendly Relations and Co-operation among States in accordance with the Charter of the United Nations, adopted by the General Assembly on 24 October 1970.

war of liberation, the United Nations no longer adheres to the traditional principles of the law of war, including the rule of the "legitimate army."

It would be incorrect to say, however, that the law of war would be valid but for the practice of wars of liberation. The rule of the legitimate army had almost been invalidated during the Second World War through resistance activities against the occupying forces in Europe and Asia. Resistance activities and wars of liberation would not attain their object if they were fought in accordance with the normal rules of traditional international law.

Under the principle of *Ex injuria jus non oritur,* there could be no acceptance of the results of resistance activities or wars of liberation, that is, expulsion of the aggressors from the occupied area and attainment of national independence. Unless traditional international law was invalidated, neither could the United Nations have appeared nor suppressed nations become independent. The practice of "illegitimate combatants" was nothing more than a furtherance of the practices prevalent in the prewar period.

(3) Invalidation of jus in bello *in favor of enforcement*

War or armed combat develops without limitation when fought in the belief that the state is dealing with an enemy with a different civilization, ideology or legal status. The Europeans fought annihilative wars against non-Europeans, and the anti-colonial fighters did not hesitate to adopt guerrilla tactics in the belief that they were freed from all regulation in taking hostile action.

When making external advances, the Europeans would not invoke international law as a normative guard against conquest. Thus, it was only natural that the anti-colonial fighters would have no regard for international law in making wars for independence to recover their status lost in the course of destructive warfare with the Europeans.

Independence was sought at a time when the validity of international law was doubted by the Europeans themselves. Wars for independence were fought in circumstances where both the authority of international law and the predominance of the European powers had declined. It is no exaggeration to say that war for self-determination is motivated by the loss of authority by European civilization.

National liberation movements are characteristic of combats by irregular armies, known previously as "guerrilla forces." In European history, combats originated in resistance against the invaders led by Napoleon. Later, resistance fighters became active in occupied areas during the Second World War. Civilians in the occupied territories in France and Eastern Europe vehemently resisted Germany. Japan was unable to complete her conquest of China on account of steadfast resistance by Chinese irregular combatants.

According to Chairman Mao Tse-tung of the People's Republic of China, well-equipped invaders cannot be excluded without action by irregular combatants enrolled secretly, or guerrilla activities.[45] He pointed out that Japan erred in her

---

[45] Mao Tse-tung discussed guerrilla warfare in an essay written in May 1938.

conviction that she would succeed in conquering China through her predominance in legitimate forces. According to him, there would never have been the conquest of mainland China by the Manchurians who established the Ch'ing Dynasty, or the annexation of the Americas and India by Great Britain and Latin nations, and the like, had the native people in each area been skilled in guerrilla warfare.

Resistance movements, encouraged by the Allies' governments or domestic governments in exile to exhaust the enemy's strength, were no exception in deviating from the rule of legitimate warfare. It was thanks to such irregular activities that resistance movements during wartime occupation and liberation movements after the War successfully defeated well-equipped armies occupying those states.

The Geneva Convention III relating to the treatment of prisoners of war, signed on 12 August 1949, adopted the practice in the provision that "members of organized resistance movements" were qualified to become prisoners of war (art 4 A (2)). If the Convention had been based on the rules of the traditional law of war, it would have left such members liable to be punished for treason against the occupation authorities.

As the Mao strategy was reinforced by Communist ideology, guerrilla activities became vehement when taken for ideological causes. Participants in resistance movements believed they were fighting for freedom, and the national liberation front fought, for the most part, in the name of socialism or Communism as well as nationalism. They were assisted by people and foreign states that shared a common ideology and national policy.

The Second World War involved considerable loss of civilian life because it was fought, for the most part, by guerrilla strategies. Regular forces were compelled to attack civilians to counter their hostile actions. The problem is whether such fighting in the cause of national liberation compensates for the loss of human life and damage to property caused therefrom.[46]

If the cause justified non-compliance with international law, "enforcement" would be the same as war for national liberation in being liberated from *jus in bello*. The UN Charter has no answer to this problem because it is an instrument agreed to in the midst of the Allies taking action against their enemies or aggressors. There could be little doubt as to the legitimacy of actions against outlaws, whether taken during the War or after the establishment of the organization.

Instead of creating a new law of sanction, the United Nations encouraged conversion of the law of war into humanitarian law in armed conflicts. Approving national liberation activities as consistent with Charter principles, the United Nations took part in legislating the Protocols Additional to the Geneva Conventions

---

[46] Guerrilla warfare may be an effective means for people to resist invaders or aggressors, but entails the sacrifice of countless victims in a war fought by legitimate forces. In fact, General De Gaulle's government in exile recommended a temporary cessation of actions by the French Resistance in order to avoid an increase in the number of victims of retaliatory punishment by the Germans: see R.B. Asprey, *War in the Shadows: The Guerrilla in History*, 1975, vol. 1, pp. 471–472. A large proportion of the Chinese victims of Japanese invasion were involved in resisting the Japanese forces after the collapse of their regular armies.

of 12 August 1949, which were motivated by the inhumanity caused by a series of wars for national liberation.

According to the Protocols completed in 1977, the principle of self-determination was realized by discriminating against belligerents in favor of insurrections and resistances in occupied or colonized regions against armies of the government. In contrast to the traditional law of war, the Protocols provided that humanitarian treatment should be given to the captured combatants, regardless of the non-fulfillment of the condition of "legitimate armies" (Protocol I, art 44-4).

Self-determination has taken a central position in the UN Charter, supplementing key principles provided on it originally, including no use of force. Irregular combatant actions necessary to realize such principle are thus recognized as being consistent with the Charter. There could be no reason, therefore, why enforcement actions were not allowed to go against traditional principles of international law in realizing the original UN principle of no use of force.

The series of legislation on the law of armed conflicts may promote the principle of humanity in such conflicts, but leaves the problem unresolved as to how guerrilla activities are distinct from terrorism, which is generally accepted to be inhuman, with or without reason. The assimilation of war for national liberation and enforcement presents the unsolvable problem as to how enforcement taken contrary to traditional principles of international law is harmonized with the humanity principle, the key concept of the UN Charter, for which cause the Allied Nations fought the Second World War.

Protocols Additional to the Geneva Conventions of 12 August 1949, which were completed in 1977 on the practice of wars of liberation, were not acceded to by Western nations because they included too many contraventions of the traditional principles of the law of war, including contravention of the rule of the legitimate army, by giving favorable treatment to guerrilla combatants. Under traditional international law, which presupposes combats by regular armies, all captured combatants should be treated equally in a humanitarian manner, regardless of the state to which they belong. This rule is not necessarily applicable to combats by "irregular armies," much less to the combats fought in the name of an ideology inconsistent with the enemy's.

The end of a war born from ideological differences unveils another cause of conflict that may develop into another war. The end of the Second World War was the prelude to conflicts between Communism and capitalism, self-determination and colonialism, economic protectionism and laissez-faire, the developed and developing, democratic and totalitarian, not to mention between different civilizations.

War would not cease until the opponents became so incapacitated that they could no longer realize the ideology they believed in. It would be based on international law, including the principle of non-aggression or no use of force, in accordance with which collective security should act. It is the very function of collective security to bring aggressors into disfavor politically, legally and militarily.

There may be no reason why aggressors were treated on equal terms with the victims and collaborators in engaging in sanctions as freedom fighters against the suppressors. It would proceed under the circumstance that traditional international law was invalidated, while no legislation placed limitations on the belligerents engaging in enforcement actions. The question would be why an injury to humanity was excused for one cause, but not for another, when humanity was the ultimate purpose of collective security as well as international society.

Leaving aside the enactment of *jus in bello* prohibiting specific inhuman acts and weapons, the question may be answered by placing every act under equal regulation by international law. This is the approach taken by the traditional law of war, the mutual guarantee of rules of belligerent action. However, it could not be the solution in recent warfare because ideological differences were too serious, in most cases, to tolerate the opponents being placed on an equal legal footing.

In view of the fact that an act is deemed to be an aggression on the basis of existing law, an act against an aggressor is not assimilated with a war of liberation fought to overthrow the existing legal situation. In this context, self-determination could not be deduced from the collective doctrine, including the doctrine of the Allied Nations or the UN Charter, which was a formulation of the practice of counter-aggression. In fact, there is no authentic evidence of tolerance of wars of national liberation in the UN Charter.

(4) Humanity as the higher norm of international society

a) The membership of a general collective organization comprises states, which are different in powers and privileges, but equal in their capacity as sovereign states. In contrast, members of regional organizations, such as the European Union, Organization of American States, and Organization of African Unity, are homogeneous in almost every respect.

The principle of sovereign equality is conceived on the model of civil law, under which civilians stand equally in legal qualification. In a municipal society, members of that society make contracts with each other to keep their relations orderly and stable. This was also the situation in international society back in the era when the European civilized nations and accepted members predominated over the rest.

The question is how an international society composed of members with different civilizations can be "civil" in the true sense of the word, as one composed of European nations is. Oriental civilization has little to do with civil law traditionally, and the developing states, including the Communist ones, attach more importance to public law as a means of promoting the social policy fixed by each ideology. In this situation, they tend to act as if they have little understanding that they are in an equal position in transacting with each other. An armed conflict is affected most by this situation as they fight it in the name of each ideology, drifting into intolerable actions against their opponents. The question must be whether members of the postwar international society are persuaded to follow an order based on various value standards so as to address this common danger to humankind.

Self-determination bases the struggle for release from subjugation on the differences between civilizations. It is not realized until the struggle for independence results in the victory of the national liberation front, as collective security is not accomplished until the aggressor is suppressed. They will not finish in conciliation with doctrinal antagonism dissolved. They will reach a compromise if human rights arguments are persuasive enough to make them set aside their ideology in the interest of achieving such rights.

Jus in bello was invalidated in the process of collective action against the aggressors before and during the Second World War. It was rehabilitated in the situation that enforcement action was not practicable under the United Nations in the face of disagreement between the East and West. In rehabilitating *jus in bello*, it also had to be borne in mind that the key concept of the UN Charter was human rights.

The ultimate purpose of international law is the realization of human rights, conditional upon freedom of conscience. So long as humanitarianism is sought through international law, it is expected that conflicts will end in conciliation between the disputants.

The United Nations is a result of the Second World War being fought in the name of the Allies' ideology. Public law, including criminal law, social legislation and laws regulating economics, is the natural basis of the Allies' organization consequent upon the circumstances of its birth. In this respect, a struggle for national liberation is consistent with the Charter doctrine.

The United Nations is a public organization enforcing doctrine, rather than an arbitral tribunal adjudicating conflicts between equal parties in a legal capacity. The disputants differ in capacity in light of the public doctrine of the United Nations. In contrast, the League of Nations was an arbitral tribunal in function, adjudicating conflicts on the basis of traditional international law. Under the Covenant, a peace breaker is a violator of the instrument to which it once agreed, rather than a criminal who has committed a crime against the interests of society.

The United Nations is an order formed on the basis of the practice of counteraction against aggression. An order on the principle of war renunciation is paraphrased as an order of *jus ad bellum*, supplemented a little by *jus in bello*. International society with multiple ideologies, cultures, and stages of economic development could hardly be ordered unless it had the means of conciliation. This situation is particularly serious in a world where technology has developed to the stage where the physical destruction of opponents with different ideologies, civilizations and the like is now possible.

b) A system of law must be effective enough to impose some disadvantage upon its violators. To make the principle of war renunciation practical, what is necessary is not so much the existence of collective forces as the certainty of response to violations.

Collective security was sought on the basis of the principle of war renunciation "to save succeeding generations from the scourge of war" (Charter Preamble). The effect of the principle is dependent upon whether human beings avoid the inhumanity caused by the physical destruction of war. There is also the question whether an international order based on the doctrine of *bellum justum* is naturally conjugated with *jus in bello*, both of which are integral parts of traditional international law. The answer depends on whether the situation necessarily renders "freedom of conscience" or "tolerance for different ideologies" obsolete as international society comes to be united to give effect to "the public interest."

However, international society has not yet come to be united with a common ideology or civilization. On the contrary, the unitary basis of the civilization has been lost even among the European nations and people since the twentieth century. Diverse political views have developed from ideologies inconsistent with one another.

It was expected that the world would be unified under the ideology of the Allied Nations. This turned out to be elusive as the Soviets dreamt of the realization of a unified world under Communism, resulting from the victory of a struggle of the proletariat. The situation deteriorated as the struggle for the Communist world was conjugated with the struggle for release from colonial rule.

World peace under any unified ideology has proven elusive, so there cannot be any system other than one of conciliation between sovereign states, however "heretical" or ideologically inconsistent the dissidence may be.

Originally, international law was conceived to be a system of conciliation between different beliefs. It lost that confidence once by justifying discrimination against "the uncivilized." At the same time, it was accepted by some non-European civilized nations through peaceful intercourse between the Europeans and themselves.

The gist of the problem is whether the postwar international order has been rehabilitated on the intolerance of different ideologies, on the basis of sanctions against the Axis aggressors, the struggle for national liberation as a result of them, and opposition between totalitarians and democrats. The answer may be in the affirmative, bearing in mind the fact that the right to self-determination has established itself by co-relation with human rights (International Covenants on Economic, Social and Cultural Rights and on Civil and Political Rights, art 1).

The greater role international law plays in the international normative order, the more importance it places upon the system of conciliation, through which humanitarian treatment is practicable. On the other hand, it weakens the effect of collective security, discouraging ideologically motivated enforcement actions. However, the collective security of the United Nations is distinguished by the promotion of human rights, so it is unavoidable that it should be more or less inefficient in the interest of humanitarian treatment. The happy medium will be found in international law balancing *jus ad bellum* and *jus in bello* on the original principle of freedom of conscience.

4. The United Nations as the Positive Order in International Society

(1) The concept of a general order after the invalidation of international law

No international system could remain adverse to pre-established practices if it intended to be positive in international society. The postwar legal order in international society could not be anything other than what had been consolidated on the prewar practice.

A "wider and permanent system of general security," declared to be established by two main Allied Nations, the United States and United Kingdom, on 14 August

1941, and to which the Soviet Union and China joined in Moscow on 1 November 1943, was realized as the United Nations in October 1945. If it intends to be positive in postwar international society, it must be a counterpart of the prewar practice of non-belligerency.

As non-belligerency is the institutionalization of counteracts against violations of the War Renunciation Pact, the fundamental principle of the Charter must be no use of force. According to the United Nations Charter, members shall refrain from the threat or use of force at their discretion (art 2-4) on the one hand, and take part in enforcement actions "by all the Members of the United Nations or some of them" (art 48) on the other.

All members shall give the United Nations every assistance and refrain from giving assistance to any state against which the United Nations is taking enforcement action (art 2-5). It is a deprivation of the right of a state to choose one status out of belligerents and neutrals at its discretion to fulfill the needs of an enforcement action. It is just a reproduction of the state of non-belligerency, under which the neutrality agreement is nullified in the interest of the Allied Nations before the term is expired.[47] The collective obligation in fact prevails over the obligation, including that of neutrality, in the agreement with other states (art 103).

The Covenant of the League of Nations provided that members undertook to sever financial, commercial and personal intercourse with the covenant-breaking state (art 16). This may be deemed to invalidate neutrality by forcing members to comply with the collective decision. However, it did not altogether nullify the system of law of war and peace, but presupposed the system, since the decision would be carried out through the war action of member states. No one imagined that action could be taken without the limitation of *jus in bello*.

The system of the United Nations differs in substance from that of the League. The sanction in article 16 of the League Covenant seems to be followed by the UN Charter in being incorporated in non-military enforcement, including complete and partial interruption of economic relations (art 41). However, any enforcement under the Charter is not conditional upon *jus in bello* insofar as it does not presuppose war as a legal status. It is characteristic of the United Nations that an "enforcement action" taken under the articles in Chapter VII and a "joint action" under article 106 of the Charter are not conditional upon *jus in bello*.

To systematize military counteraction against violation of the obligation of war renunciation taken by the Allied Nations, the armed forces necessary for such actions are contributed in accordance with "a special agreement or agreements" (art

---

[47] Japan sought mediation by the Soviets, with whom she had enjoyed neutral relations under the Russo-Japanese Neutrality Treaty concluded in April 1941. The Soviets did not oblige and instead invaded Japanese territory after declaring war against her. Seven days after the invasion, Japan surrendered. The Soviet Union had been neutral in relation to Japan when the United Nations Conference on General International Organization was convened in San Francisco in April 1945. All of the circumstances indicated that this neutrality could not be valid, even though it had been engaged in through the correct procedures of traditional international law.

43). The armed forces are composed of "national contingents" of member states contributed by special agreement (art 45).

Pending the coming into force of such special agreements, permanent members of the Security Council may take "joint actions" on behalf of the Organization (art 106).

"Enforcement actions" may be war in substance, but such war has no legal status since it is outlawed under the Charter system. The law of war had come almost to be identified with *jus in bello* by the end of the nineteenth century, as the Hague Conventions in 1899 and 1907 stipulated *jus in bello*. In light of the practice of the Second World War, what is invalidated is the traditional system of law of war as a whole, consisting of *jus ad bellum* and *jus in bello*.

It is the logical consequence of invalidation of the traditional system that members of the United Nations are freed from *jus in bello*. It is proven by the practice of the Second World War as well as the logic of the United Nations. Selective validation of *jus in bello*, by excluding the humanitarian part from invalidation, cannot be found in the Charter, which is a reproduction of the practice of the Second World War. If they intended to avert casualties as experienced in the War, "enforcement actions" had to be based on legislation departing from precedents of that War.

In conceiving a system of postwar collective security, the League of Nations could not serve as a model since it provided *jus in bello* as the basis for an action. The sanction under the League system was war against a covenant-breaker engaged in by the other members. The theory of *tabla rasa* with respect to *jus in bello* is possible when an enforcement action is a development of the "assistance" given to the victim under a state of non-belligerency, as practiced prior to the Second World War.[48]

Legislation cannot necessarily lead the age, but may provide a mere compilation of past practice until that time. The series of treaties of the law of war adopted at the Peace Conference in The Hague was applied in the First World War, which broke out immediately after it. Some parts proved positive, but other parts were rendered ineffective by contrary practices deriving from the newly invented weaponry and related strategies.

This also holds true with respect to the United Nations Charter, which is a compilation of the practices before and during the Second World War. The members would not deal with problems after the War on the basis of the Charter because the situation had changed considerably since the time of its drafting. The relations of the Allied Nations changed from ones of close cooperation to staunch opposition. Nuclear weapons were used between the Charter's finalization and entering into effect.

These circumstances indicate that the situation understood in the UN Charter does not represent the reality of postwar international society itself.

While neutrality is not sustainable in light of the Charter provisions, occupation

---

[48] It was once answered in the affirmative to *tabla rasa* at an early stage of the UN activities in the Korean War: see *Proceedings of American Society of International Law*, 1952, pp. 216–220.

forces in Austria were withdrawn in 1955 on condition that she retained her neutral status. In the midst of the Vietnam War, the United States invoked the right of neutrality to justify acts in violation of the territorial sovereignty of Cambodia.[49]

Seeing that *jus in bello* was an inevitable basis of humanitarian treatment to be afforded all persons, whether belligerents or civilians, in wartime, it could not be invalidated, even though an "enforcement action" could be taken for any just cause.

Conventions concluded before the outbreak of war on the limitation of weapons, including chemical weapons, could not be invalidated after the development of high-tech weapons, such as nuclear ones. The Charter gives a minor position to disarmament to be discussed in the General Assembly (art 11). This fact is reaffirmation of the validity of prewar conventions, including the Geneva Protocol for the prohibition on the use of poisonous gases in 1925, and additional legislation on the prohibition on biological and chemical weapons.

This situation proves that international law has not been altogether invalidated, even after the consolidation of a general collective organization based on the contrary practices of the Second World War.

(2) Practical compliance with social realities becoming a positive order in international society

a) The emancipation of colonies was propagated by Japan as a just cause for opposing the Allied nations, especially the United States, United Kingdom and Holland. The Joint Declaration on Greater Asia issued in Tokyo on 6 November 1943 in the name of seven Asian nations declared that the Asian nations should be released from Anglo-American domination for the sake of world peace and prosperity.[50]

The Cairo Declaration made public by the United States, United Kingdom and China three weeks later on 27 November 1943 and stating that the Allies coveted no gain for themselves and had no intention of territorial expansion, was presumably a response to the Joint Declaration. In contrast to these instruments, the UN Charter sets aside colonial matters for future solution, leaving them under the Declaration Regarding Non-self-governing Territories (Chapter XI) and the International Trusteeship System (Chapter XII).

As long as colonial territories fall under the rules of either of the two systems, they will not be discussed seriously in any UN organ. They are all under the domestic jurisdiction of the respective member state, though Trusteeship differs from the Declaration in having the goal of "independence" (art 73).

Colonialization represented the past under the traditional international law

---

[49] The United States sent combat forces to Vietcong sanctuaries in Cambodia: J.N. Moore, *Neutrality Law and the Indo-China War*, 1972, ch. X, p. 479.

[50] The Joint Declaration on Greater Asia comprised the following points: joint efforts to establish an order for co-existence and prosperity; respect for mutual independence; respect for each tradition; cooperation for economic development; and contribution to world development by access to natural resources in the spirit of friendship on the principle of no racial discrimination.

system and was to be liquidated under the new one. It was the outcome of discrimination on the basis of civilization. If the United Nations adhered to the domestic jurisdiction of each member state, a corollary of state sovereignty, it would hardly work as a general international organization in postwar international society in place of traditional international law.

The year 1945 may have brought the conclusion of war in the sense of a regular combat coming to an end, but it also heralded the beginning of wars of liberation in areas where a power vacuum had been produced by the withdrawal of the Axis nations. In a broader sense, the Second World War did not end with the surrender of Japanese forces, but continued illegitimately in the form of popular insurrections in suppressed areas. What augmented the postwar crises was the link between anti-colonization activities and the class struggle against the capitalists led by the Soviets and their affiliates.

Commenting on the Conference of the Allied Nations on General International Organization in San Francisco, a Japanese newspaper foresaw that the Organization led by the Anglo-Americans could not prevent international society from falling into catastrophe due to its failure to settle problems with their enemies, the Soviet Union and colonialized people.[51] If the United Nations were taken as the Charter provided, it would be a forum to unveil the disunity of the Allied Nations, in the same way that opposition between the United States and Soviets paralyzed its activities.

b) The first item on the agenda of the Security Council was the war of independence in Indonesia and the counteraction to it by The Netherlands with British forces, which was brought to discussion by a member in the Soviet Bloc.[52] The Security Council would not intervene in the matter under Chapter VII of the Charter because there was little support for the holding of such discussions among the permanent members who had direct connection with it.[53]

The Charter authorizes the Security Council to decide any matters that are "a threat to the peace" under Chapter VII of the Charter, whether it is within domestic jurisdiction or not, so far as it is not a matter of any permanent member state (art 2 para 7, art 27). No international organization could be effective in postwar international society if it remained aloof from a liberation movement on

---

[51] Editorials of the *Asahi Shimbun*, 27 July 1945.

[52] The Ukrainian SSR drew, at the second meeting, the Security Council's attention to the situation in Indonesia, pointing out that regular British troops as well as Japanese forces were engaged in action against the local population, which constituted "a threat to the maintenance of international peace and security." The Council included the question in its agenda on 25 January 1946: *Repertoire of the Practice of the Security Council 1945–1951*, p. 302.

[53] France resorted to its right of veto in the Indonesian case, which was the first time this right was used by a member other than the Soviet Union to defend an internal matter from UN intervention (194 mtg, 25 August 1947). It was foreseeable that her overseas territories would be brought up for discussion by the Security Council after the Indonesian case. Throughout the 1940s and 1960s, "a good many of the vetoes arose directly or indirectly from the process of decolonization (for example, Syria and Lebanon, Indonesia, the Congo, Goa, and Southern Rhodesia)": S.D. Bailey, "Veto in the Security Council," 566 *International Conciliation* (hereafter cited as "IC"), January 1968, p. 43.

the ground that it did not intervene in the domestic jurisdictions of member states. In the case of Indonesian independence, the United Nations concerned itself with the issue as a "domestic matter," recommending that The Netherlands and insurgent troops enter into a ceasefire, rather than intervening in the affairs under Chapter VII of the Charter. It was not the way anticipated by the exact provisions of the Charter, but a practical way of avoiding a deadlock in the deliberations of the Security Council.

Hence, a solution was found to the Indonesian problem, not through enforcement under Chapter VII of the Charter, but by mediation and observation by the United Nations, which later came to be called "peacekeeping."[54] From the beginning of deliberations, the Security Council settled the issue on the basis of no specific articles of the Charter despite the existence of relevant provisions in Chapter VII.

At the very beginning of the deliberations, the United Nations acted differently from what was anticipated by the Charter provisions with respect to the maintenance of international peace and security. In dealing with the Indonesian problem, the United Nations made a precedent to be followed at subsequent deliberations. According to the practice, the struggle for liberation in any member's territory fell under the jurisdiction of the United Nations. It intervened in the matter, not by action under Chapter VII of the Charter, but by mediation and observation to be termed "peacekeeping" thereafter.

Peacekeeping has been accepted as a practical way of maintaining international peace and security, notwithstanding the absence of any provision in the UN Charter. With the clear intention of peacekeeping, the United Nations sent observation "forces" to the area of dispute in the Suez Conflict in 1956. During the Cold War, when the Security Council was in constant paralysis owing to the repeated invocation of veto powers, the United Nations acted as a collective organization on the understanding that peacekeeping coincided with collective action.

c) The United Nations provides membership by all independent regimes as the practical solution to the problem of liberation movements. It does this by setting aside doctrinal ambiguity about the relationship between self-determination and the Charter, two articles of which mention "self-determination" sporadically (art 1-2, 55).

From the standpoint of procedure, the solution is easier as it relates not so much to the maintenance of international peace and security as it is done to promote "cooperation in solving international problems of economic character" (art 2-3). In response to the economic hardships faced by newly independent members, the General Assembly encouraged the other members to give them preferential treatment (Charter of Economic Rights and Duties of States, Res. 3281, XXIX,

[54] The Good Office Committee, established in 25 August 1947, developed into the UN Commission of Indonesia (UNCI) on 21 November 1948, through which the independence of Indonesia was recognized by The Netherlands. Observance of the truce following the ceasefire in Indonesia was the first practice of peacekeeping, but is not included as an example of it in documents of the United Nations: see UN Department of Public Information, *The Blue Helmets: A Review of United Nations Peace-keeping*.

12 December 1974). Economic relationships in accordance with the resolution are termed the "New International Economic Order."

The New International Economic Order had no practice before it was conceived and declared by the General Assembly. Newly independent states or developing countries had the experience of colonization, or the attempt of it, by foreign countries in common, but had no practice of combined acts based on common rules and interests. They were incomparable to the West European nations uniting their market on the basis of a common culture and history.

Any legal order must to some extent be a reproduction of practice consolidated at the time of its establishment in order to provide guidelines over the coming years, notwithstanding that states are required to depart from such prior practice. In conceiving the New International Economic Order, the General Assembly of the United Nations would not pay regard to the fact that most economic cooperation is regional. Preference in economic transactions is limited to some specific regions approved by the General Agreement on Tariffs and Trade (GATT) (art 1 para 2). If the NIEO followed past practice and legislation, it would not, in principle, give preference to developing countries.

Seeing no conspicuous results of the NIEO, a number of investment protection agreements have been concluded on a bilateral basis between the developing and developed nations. Such agreements have provisions recalling the traditional system of foreign investment, the conditions of which are inconsistent with the resolutions of the General Assembly adopted in relation to the NIEO.[55]

d) The failure of practical compliance with social realities was fatal for a general international organization taking the lead in formulating the postwar international legal order. In some fields, it has succeeded at practical compliance, but in others, it has failed. To address the activities of national liberation movements, the United Nations made self-determination one of its fundamental principles. In the field of maintenance of international peace and security, it focused on observation activities in the name of peacekeeping. To lessen atrocities in armed strikes, it ascertains the validity of *jus in bello* in the name of humanitarian law in armed conflicts.

The UN General Assembly failed in its conception of "the new order" because it overlooked the realities of regional integration in the field of economics. Economic collaboration among nations is successful at regional level, as evidenced in Europe and North and South America. Southeast Asian nations are moving to create a free trade area following China's admission to the World Trade Organization. What the General Assembly adopted was a preference towards the developing countries on a general basis instead of a regional one.

Originally, the United Nations was conceived and structured as a general international organization based on the doctrine of the Allied Nations as declared in their instruments, including the Atlantic Charter and the Moscow Declaration.

---

[55] They have sought to develop their economies by concluding investment protection agreements with developed countries on a bilateral basis. The preferential legal system ultimately failed in 1980: R.E. Hudec, *Developing Countries in the GATT System*, 1987.

However, the original proposal was amended in the adopting conference to balance it with regionalism by inserting an article ascertaining the "right of self-defense." If the United Nations is to adjust to the realities of regionalism in international society, it must be interpreted to be a league of regional organizations based on the right of collective self-defense.

In this context, it is a matter worthy of reconsideration as to whether the postwar international order has been general from the beginning. Taking international law as the integral part, an international legal order can be a system of compromise among different ideologies in the world. It is positive not on general consensus, but on the autonomy of each ideology and region in one sense or another.

This holds true with respect to relations with "enemy states." The postwar international order is not accomplished unless such states are placed in their due position. They will be settled in "a general international organization" of the Allied Nations when it is balanced with regionalism in both the theory and practice of the organization. To make it balance with regionalism, they added a provision on self-defense to the Charter. It evolved into a practical institution thereafter on the concept of self-defense, which deserved more attention to realize the legal situation of the postwar international order originally designed by the Allied Nations.

(3) Regional amendments becoming a positive order in international society

a) Considering that the Second World War was caused by conflicts between economic blocs, leading to the loss of laissez-faire, economic stability is a prerequisite to peace in international society.

In the final stages of the activities of the League of Nations, it had the notion that economic and social matters should be separated from peace and security.[56] It appears that the Economic and Social Council was placed in the machinery of the United Nations in keeping with this idea. It is one of the principal organs of the United Nations (art 7), but does not deal with every problem in economics and society. Instead, it has taken on the role of coordinating the activities of "the Specialized Agencies" (arts 57 and 63) as "the economic center" of postwar international society.

The International Trade Organization, a specialized agency, was not realized on account of the Congress of the United States failing to accept its Charter. It would have had a general jurisdiction with the intention of rehabilitating the postwar international economy under the principle of free trade. It was replaced by the General Agreement on Tariffs and Trade extracted from the ITO Charter, which was reformed into the World Trade Organization in January 1995.

GATT had not substituted the ITO because it was an organization of the Western region between two politically opposing regional blocs. It might succeed in making

---

[56] See the Bruce Report on the Development of International Cooperation in Economic and Social Affairs, 22 August 1939, which was adopted by the Assembly in December 1939.

economic relations between Western nations closer, but not in bridging the gap between East and West corresponding to the Communists and Capitalists, and between the North and South corresponding to the developed and developing nations.

Apart from laissez-faire economics in the nineteenth century, no general system has been successful in regulating the international economy. Historically, successful precedents of economic cooperation were found among regional attempts. Customs unions have been positioned harmoniously between laissez-faire and regional systems, though they imply a political affiliation, as, for example, the customs union in German districts was a prelude to the unification of the German Empire. As a matter of practice, customs unions have been recognized as compatible with political neutrality.[57]

Regional organizations in Europe, including the European Economic Community based on the Treaty of Rome of 25 March 1957, have had customs unions as their core, in a way compatible with GATT (art 24). It developed into a European Union with more general purposes, including the maintenance of peace and security, on the basis of the Maastricht Treaty signed on 7 February 1992.

Despite their significant effect upon international peace and security, regional economic organizations are neither subject to the Security Council nor the Economic and Social Council of the United Nations, as they are neither included in "regional agencies" provided in Chapter VIII of the Charter, nor "specialized agencies" to be brought into relationship with the United Nations in accordance with article 63. As is the case with regional arrangements against renewal of aggressive policy by enemy states, "regional arrangements," including those on economic integration, are placed outside the jurisdiction of the United Nations.

b) "Enemy states," having been destroyed militarily, would be rehabilitated in other fields, including economics, to the same level of influence they had enjoyed in the political and military fields in prewar international society. At that moment, however, they would have no grounds for acceptance as major powers of the United Nations with privileges, including the power of veto in the Security Council, which was conferred exclusively upon the main Allies.

On the other hand, they could be indispensable members of regional organizations established for the purposes of defense or economic cooperation. Such organizations or agreements would have enemy states as indispensable partners within their regional base.

In the event that war ended in compromise, the victorious and the vanquished would be sufficiently equal to take steps to agree on the conditions of peace. However, where nuclear weapons had terminated the hostilities, the vanquished had no voice regarding the conditions of peace, whether in formality or substance, not to mention the ways of the postwar order.

The Second World War was caused by a violation of the peace conditions of the

---

[57] The Customs Union in German districts brought political unification in 1871: see J. Viner, *Customs Union Issue*, 1950.

preceding war on the part of the defeated Germany, and by a challenge to the agreed order on the part of the victorious Japan. They claimed that the international order should be divided into several spheres in which they were recognized to be hegemonic. The claim was suppressed militarily and ideologically, but the existence of such states could not be negligible in each region, even after their defeat, in economics, culture or history.

As the Allied Nations had opposed the Axis nations' claim for regional hegemony, the postwar international order would need to be general in doctrine. Nevertheless, the international economy was left regulated in each region as far as the system of the United Nations was concerned.

The practicability of a general international order soon came to be doubted amid the conflict between the Soviet Union and the other former allies. It was doubted even more once a group of states, which had attained independence as a result of their struggle for national liberation, stood outside both blocs.

Now that the struggle for superiority between Communism and Capitalism has ceased, and some liberated nations have almost attained the status of developed countries, international society might well be regulated under the general system conceived originally. However, what is sought is not unification of international society in every aspect, but harmonization to bring every nation and group of nations to equal status in a truer sense.

The fact is that international society faces the danger of clashes between different doctrines, races and religious beliefs. It began with the disunity of the Allied Nations immediately following the liquidation of their common enemies.

Peace has been maintained for over a half century since the end of the Second World War, not because of the effective enforcement of one ideology, but because of a compromise between regions with different ideologies. From the standpoint of the normative order of international society, the United Nations system has not replaced international law altogether.

(4) The United Nations as a system inclusive of "enemy matters"

Collective security differs from the traditional system of international law in seeking to enforce peace from a specific ideological standpoint, including the doctrine of the Allied Nations. It is not a breakaway from the system of international law, but rather a restoration of the classical element of *jus ad bellum* in the system by institutionalizing acts of "enforcement" in a discriminatory manner against "the aggressors."

It is not, on the other hand, a mere restoration of *jus ad bellum* in that it has a positive ground of evaluation of just cause evidenced by the Covenant of the League of Nations, Renunciation of War Pact, United Nations Charter and so forth. In this sense, collective security has evolved rather than been restored in the process of development of international law.

In view of this nature, collective security must be a system exclusive of the matters of the enemies against which the enforcement is directed. As far as the United Nations is concerned, it is the system of the Allied Nations exclusive of the Axis nations. If it was intended to be a general international organization in the true sense of the word, it should have been organized to be flexible enough to cover every situation including enemies' matters, which was not taken into consideration at the time of its establishment.

As far as the United Nations is concerned, the status of its enemies is none other than outlawry. However, the Atlantic Charter, declared by the heads of the United States and United Kingdom on 14 August 1941, includes the following phrase: "They will endeavor, with due respect for their existing obligations, to further the enjoyment of all states, great and small, victor or vanquished, of access, on equal terms, to the trade and to the raw materials of the world which are needed for their economic prosperity."

If they ended the war in accordance with the ordinary procedures of traditional international law, any states could claim rights even after defeat on the occasion of the conclusion of a peace treaty negotiated between all the belligerent states. In contrast to the First World War, the Second did not end with the conclusion of a peace treaty in relation to the main Axis nations, Germany and Japan. In this situation, there was no place except the United Nations where the enemies' rights and interests could be multilaterally disposed of. However, no principles of such disposal were found in the Charter, as the United Nations excluded enemy matters from its jurisdiction in order to reserve them exclusively for the main Allies.

If an international organization of the Allied Nations aspires to be a general postwar order, there is no reason why enemy matters should be placed outside the discussion. It is unreasonable to outlaw enemy states from the postwar international order, contrary to the assurance of the Atlantic Charter.

France, the United Kingdom and United States brought the Berlin problem before the United Nations in 1948 after failing to reach a political compromise between the four occupying states.[58] A majority of the Security Council placed the issue on the agenda in October 1948 despite the Soviets' contention that it would violate article 107 of the Charter since the problem related to peace with Germany.[59]

Japan had some overseas territories and the spheres of her influence were to be detached to benefit the Allied Nations. The final status of the territories should be discussed at a peace conference. If the problem of territories was settled without a peace conference, the vanquished could not help but accept the principle of *uti possidetis*, that is, the detachment of the territories as they were occupied.[60]

The United Nations was involved in the Korean War after that country's detachment from Japanese rule. This developed between the northern and southern regimes established temporarily in their respective occupation areas from June 1950

[58] The Soviet Union blockaded the enclave of the West Zones of Berlin in 1948, leading to a massive airlift by the Western Allies: *Repertoire of the Practice of the Security Council 1945–1951* (hereafter cited as "Repertoire"), p. 354.

[59] The exact interpretation of the article might be that it was directed against a renewal of aggressive policies by the enemies: I. Brownlie, *International Law and the Use of Force by States*, 1963, pp. 336–337.

[60] Japan has consistently sought to hold peace negotiations with Russia and denies the principle of *uti possidetis* in relation to the Northern Territories, which have been under the belligerent occupation of Russia since her invasion following Japan's surrender.

until the armistice in July 1953. The United Nations did not base its actions in Korea on any articles of the Charter, but the Security Council decided that the situation was a "breach of the peace," which is a term found in article 39, Chapter VII.[61]

During the Second World War, Iran and Greece could not resist the Allies' demands for the garrison of their troops in each territory. At the third meeting on 28 January 1946, Iran raised the issue in the Security Council that the Soviet Union, pending completion of withdrawal of her troops, interfered in internal affairs. She contended that the Soviet troops should withdraw from her territory in accordance with the agreement on which she authorized the Allies' garrison until 2 March 1946. The Soviet Union counter-argued that the United Kingdom should not interfere in the internal affairs of Greece with her garrison troops.[62]

These are examples of peace matters being discussed in the United Nations instead of at a peace conference. If the Charter had no jurisdiction over the matters at all, the drafters would be blamed for having lacked a definite vision for the replacement of traditional international law, including the procedures for the termination of war.

The solution was given, in effect, by modification of the enemy clause at the San Francisco Conference on International Organization. According to the latter part of article 53 inserted at the Conference, "regional arrangements directed against renewal of aggressive policy" on the part of "the enemies" are excluded from authorization by the Security Council. To balance the benefits from the insertion, a provision on self-defense was added to article 51, the last article of Chapter VII. Thanks to these amendments, member states came to be able to choose whichever means of the United Nations or regional arrangements they believed would be most practical for their defense.

Under the adopted text of article 53 of the Charter, members are immune from the Charter provisions in taking actions in regional arrangements directed against the renewal of aggressive policy by an enemy state of the Allied Nations. The practical effect of this amendment is that they may assimilate any UN members to "enemy state" to be immune from the Charter obligations, including the obligations placed upon them to accept and carry out the decisions of the Security Council (art 25).

This provision has the effect of positioning an enemy state with equal status to a UN member or members in a sphere placed outside the jurisdiction of the Security Council. It corresponds to the Charter provisions empowering the Security Council to add enemies to the original ones to be outlawed on a charge of breaching the peace.

Acts exempted from authorization by the Security Council, by virtue of the latter phrase of article 53 of the UN Charter, may be legalized as individual and collective self-defense under article 51. The right of self-defense is exercised, under the Charter system, against states that are regarded as equivalent to the enemy states.

---

[61] The Resolution of 25 June 1950 does not cite a specific provision of the Charter, but employs the terminology of article 39.

[62] *Repertoire 1945–1951*, pp. 300–301.

From an ideological perspective, regionalism is hardly consistent with the doctrine of any postwar security system, bearing in mind the fact that the Second World War was caused by clashes among opposing blocs in the 1930s. On the other hand, from a practical point of view, global organization cannot be effective without regional cooperation. In fact, the Allied Nations was based on regional security arrangements to resist the common enemies.

In concluding the text of the UN Charter, the Allied Nations did not fail to supply a positive basis to the doctrine by bestowing a right of self-defense on respective members. It also achieved this goal by taking both enemy states and regional arrangements into the system.

The United Nations has dealt, or is still dealing, with problems brought up for discussion instead of being referred to a peace conference. This is due to the invalidation of traditional international law developed on the basis of a balance of power, which proved inefficacious to secure any states in the practices of the Second World War. In this context, regional arrangements with "enemy states" on the right of self-defense could not altogether be beyond expectation in light of the Allies' original doctrine and related concepts.

CHAPTER 2

AN INTERNATIONAL LEGAL ORDER ACHIEVED THROUGH SELF-DEFENSE

I. The Social Characteristics of Self-defense in the International Legal Regime

(1) Self-defense under the principle of no use of force

a) The "general international organization" for the maintenance of international peace and security, which the main Allied Nations agreed in Moscow in November 1943 to establish, was based on the practice of imposing sanctions against enemies alleged to have violated the principle of "no use of force." This principle appears in international instruments of general character concluded in the period between the two great wars, including the Covenant of the League of Nations signed at the Paris Peace Conference in 1919 and the Renunciation of War Pact signed in Paris in 1928. The postwar international order is based on those instruments as well as the Charter of the United Nations insofar as it takes the international organization of the Allied Nations as its integral part.

These instruments prohibit the contracting states from using force except in certain instances. In the system of the League of Nations, members acted to preserve existing political independence from aggression (Covenant, art 10). This was understood to oblige the League members to act against aggression.[1] On the other hand, it could also be read to release them from their obligations under the Covenant for that reason. If the Covenant took a general concept as the basis for an act, self-defense might be the best choice.

The Locarno Pact, which was concluded in 1925 some three years before the Renunciation of War Pact, exempted an act of *légitime défense* or self-defense from the obligation. The Renunciation of War Pact had no provision on self-defense, but was generally believed to grant parties to it an exemption to take forcible acts for the purpose of self-defense.

---

1 Article 10, which President Wilson insisted to be a key provision of the Covenant, was one factor motivating the Congress of the United States to reject membership of the League: B. Williams, *State Security and the League of Nations*, 1927, p. 258. The Lodge Reservations to the Treaty of Versailles reserved this provision by reason that it interfered with the power of the United States Congress to declare war (para 2). If Congress was right in interpreting the provision in this manner, the article could not be a provision for self-defense.

The Pact system was an integral part of the international security order prior to the Second World War. The order developed from the traditional order of international society, which was based on the dichotomy of peace and war given legal status. Based as it was on the order that existed just prior to its establishment, the postwar international security order could be nothing other than a reproduction of non-belligerency.

This was deduced from acts against violations of the Renunciation of War Pact and brought into the system of enforcement of the United Nations. In drafting the Charter, however, they did not deem it necessary to define the system as having a cause for exemption as had been the case in other systems, including that of the Renunciation of War Pact.[2]

In municipal society, individual persons are excused from legal obligations on the basis of "legitimate defense" and "acts of necessity" conditional upon the presence of imminent danger.[3] If states in international society are analogous to nationals in municipal society, then an act corresponding to legitimate defense or an act of necessity may naturally be exempted from the prohibition on the use of force.

In international society, there are some cases in which an exemption is sought by reason of "necessity."

In destroying the Danish Fleet in Copenhagen in 1807, England was accused of violating the neutrality of Denmark, but argued that she was excused by reason of necessity.[4] The German Prime Minister attempted to justify violation of Belgian neutrality at the beginning of the First World War on the ground that there was a state of emergency.[5] Occupation of Greece by Britain and France during that War might also be excused by reason of necessity.[6] In 1981, Israel attacked a nuclear reactor in Iraq, claiming that it was a threat to her existence.[7]

In those cases, the "act of necessity," on the basis of which they legitimated their actions, was not always accepted.[8] This situation does not differ fundamentally from that in municipal society, where the legality of the act to be excused for necessity is often disputed. International society is different from municipal society in that it has no established procedure to clear doubts as to the legality of acts.

---

[2] In the course of discussions on the Dumbarton Oaks Proposal, the United States removed the doubts of the Chinese delegate by replying that no unilateral use of force could be undertaken without approval of the Council, except in the case of self-defense: U.S. Department of States, *Foreign Relations of the United States* (hereafter cited as "FRUS"), 1944, I, p. 862.

[3] The Japanese Criminal Code requires an "imminent and illegal threat" for "legitimate defense" (art 36), but only an "imminent threat" for necessity (art 37).

[4] C. J. Kulsrud, "The Seizure of Danish Fleet 1807," 32 *AJ*, 1938, p. 281.

[5] The German Government attempted to legalize its violation of Belgian neutrality by reason of military necessity: J.W. Garner, *op.cit.* vol. 2, 1920, p191.

[6] J.W. Garner, *op. cit.*, vol. 2, p. 255.

[7] U. Shoham, "The Israel Aerial Raid upon the Iraqi Nuclear Reactor and the Right of Self-defense", *Military Law Review*, 1985.

[8] It has been pointed out that the argument for necessity is supported by Anglo-Saxon writers, but not by Continental European ones: Jürgen von Kempeski, *Der Überfall auf Kopenhagen*, 1940.

There may be a reason innate to international society as to why an "act of necessity" has not been established.

Under traditional international law, a forcible action is legalized by reason of war, intervention or reprisal. They are means of redress for wrongful acts in place of lawsuits and prosecutions. In this situation, states would not take the trouble of basing the forcible act on any concept not yet established, such as act of necessity.

Until the principle of no use of force invalidated war, intervention and reprisal, concepts comparable to legitimate defense and necessity in municipal law were not practical for legalizing forcible actions. While the principle of no use of force was discussed in relation to the instruments and practice thereon, states did not dare to seek to justify their acts on those concepts.

The definite reason why those concepts were not established was that there was no concept that could be substituted for reprisal. In international society, an injury to a legal right is remedied by reprisal. If the principle of no use of force involves an invalidation of reprisal, then any means substitutable for reprisal must be established instead.

It depends on the definition of the term "reprisal" as to whether it is inconsistent with any system of municipal law or not. If reprisal is synonymous with self-help, then it is prohibited in modern municipal society. If, on the other hand, reprisal is taken as a means of recovery for a right in the civil law field, then it is consistent with the municipal system of law. In any event, no entity can be left without a means of recovery for its injured rights, whether in international or municipal society.

If the prohibition on use of force is assimilated with the prohibition on self-help, then any "public" authority must take the exact role of governments in municipal society. In this case, it will exempt certain acts from the prohibition for precisely the same reason that an individual person is excused for certain violations of legal principles in municipal society. The possible inference from municipal law in that case would be that a state's recourse to arms in an emergency would be tolerated.

In municipal society, individual persons are excused from their legal obligations on the grounds of legitimate defenses or acts of necessity conditional upon the presence of imminent danger. As far as the *traveaux préparatoires* at the San Francisco Conference on General International Organization were concerned, there is no evidence that any states participating in the Conference entertained doubts about the silence regarding the exception to the prohibition on the use of force. The Charter was driven towards the provision of self-defense, not by theoretical or practical necessity, but by the political necessity of balancing the rights of the members.

The circumstances in San Francisco do not mean that the General International Organization also claims to be the "government" of international society. The Charter confirms the validity of international law with the principle of the sovereign equality of states.

In light of the circumstances described above, the issue will be whether self-defense in the Charter may be assimilated with legitimate defense or an act of necessity in municipal society. To put it another way, the issue will be whether self-defense is possible in a society where no superior authority is prepared to supplement the actor's act. It is a question of whether a state is excused for its use of force on the same conditions as legitimate defense, assuming that international society has something akin to public law, though it has no authority like a government.

b) The War Renunciation Pact and other conventions stipulating "no use of force" as their principle have the character of public law in international society. However, they do not employ common systems to realize it. The Covenant of the League of Nations has an organization for its realization, but the War Renunciation Pact does not. However, the former proved ineffective in the face of developing opposition in the 1930s, whereas the latter was realized by an ad hoc alliance of individual states, without a proper organization for its realization.

The United Nations was created on the basis of the latter practice, the sanctions by the Allied Nations against the Axis states. According to the United Nations Charter, the first step to a response to a violation is a measure not involving the use of armed force, including interruption of economic relations (art 41), which is a copy of the principal sanction of the League of Nations. The next and final step of "enforcement" is "such action by air, sea or land forces as may be necessary to maintain or restore international peace and security" (Charter, art 42). "All members shall give the United Nations every assistance it takes," and "refrain from giving assistance to any state against which the United Nations is taking preventive or enforcement action" (arts 2-5). The second step is not found in the League system, but rather in acts under non-belligerency immediately prior to the Second World War.

As the system is modeled on the practice of non-belligerency, it is practical to meet aggressive actions. Notwithstanding the centralization of power among the nations taking permanent membership, the Security Council is not equivalent to the system in municipal society of executive power according to law. It acts in response to threats to peace, breaches of the peace and acts of aggression, which do not necessarily involve illegality.

Indeed, the United Nations aims to maintain international order by collective means, and would not take over the function of reprisal of each individual state. Under the system, states continue to act to defend the rights and interests of each in conformity with international law. It is they who execute the legal order of international society by use of armed force as a last resort. This is the natural way of executing international law in an international society unchanged in structure even after the establishment of a general collective organization.

In spite of this situation, the United Nations declares that reprisal is inconsistent with Charter principles.[9] A total prohibition on reprisal presupposes a capacity for collective action to suppress any use of unlawful force.

The Covenant of the League of Nations imposed some restrictions on the making of war, but did not prohibit the members from making war for any reason. Far from illegalizing war as a concept, the violation against the Covenant was sanctioned by

---

[9] See Chap. 1 note 44.

deeming it to be an "act of war" against all other members (art 16). Under this system, war is organized to function as a reprisal to a violation of the Covenant. War had the function of realizing international law when an individual state had recourse to it to recover a lost right. The League system of sanction turned the function of war into organizational use as the ultimate means of realizing the Covenant.

The United Nations is unconnected with war, while individual states continue to be power units without the obligation of complete disarmament, though they are subject to regulations of armament taken by the Security Council (art 26). When peace is broken, all or some of the members will deal with the situation by using their armed forces in accordance with decisions made by the Security Council (art 48). There arises the problem as to how they legalize their act in cases where the Security Council makes no definite decisions on the matter.[10]

In any society, a legal norm consists of public and private parts. International law lacked the public part until the 1930s. It now has both public and private parts of the normal legal order as a result of the practices of the Second World War. In this situation, states must use armed force to realize the public or collective interest as well as each private or individual right.

Unless the international normative order changed into a natural order, it must have been achieved through counteraction to wrongfulness. War was the ultimate means of counteraction to keep it positive. It was deficient not in legalizing war, but in failing to draw a distinction between a war fought to counteract wrongfulness and one fought in response to such counteraction. In view of the development of the international normative order, the principle of no use of force distinguished one as illegal from the other, leaving the means of differentiation unimproved.

Under these circumstances, self-defense is recognized to be the inherent right of all member states of the general collective organization. According to the UN Charter, use of force or war is prohibited, but response to an "armed attack" is recognized as self-defense. Between collective and individual acts, self-defense is individual. However, a state acts in the capacity of collective authority if it complies with the collective purpose. If the collective organization has established no means to distinguish a right act from a wrong one, it does nothing to improve the system of the War Renunciation Pact.

Viewed in this light, the collective organization takes an extremely cautious approach to self-defense, only regarding it as legitimate conduct under the principle of no use of force. In taking action against China, Japan invoked the right of self-defense to avoid censure for violation of the War Renunciation Pact. It was against such acts that the Allied Nations took action in applying the Pact.

The analogy of legitimate defense or act of necessity in municipal law is a simplistic way of finding the conditions of self-defense. The conditions under the

---

[10] A number of reprisal incidents have been discussed before the Security Council, some of which were condemned for reprisal and others not. As a guide to avoiding condemnation by the Security Council, the problem may be answered by applying the criterion of "reasonableness" of reprisal, although the Council maintains the general proposition that all armed reprisals are illegal: D. Bowett, "Reprisals Involving Recourse to Armed Force," 66*AJ*, 1972, p. 1.

postwar system must be sought in light of the essence of the system, embracing both collective and individual elements of the legal order. Efforts to find it would, however, be in vain because there is no practice of international law in the same circumstances as exist at present.

On the other hand, this does not necessarily mean that traditional international law is out of consideration in seeking the conditions of self-defense in present circumstances. The Charter of the United Nations itself recognizes that it acts in conformity with the principles of international law (art 1-1). When self-defense is disputed before an international court, it will be argued by the analogy of legitimate defense in municipal law, as was done before the International Court of Justice in the Nicaragua Case.

c) In most cases where individuals take legitimate defense, they defend their personal rights and interests without being conscious of the public function. In taking it, they only seek to be excused for the violation of law involved in the act. It is the government that pursues any social purpose in responding to the initial violation, that is, punishment of crimes, redress for injury, and so on.

A legal concept is positive so long as it is brought to constant realization. Legitimate defense in municipal law is positive in a system where the governmental organs never fail to respond to the initial violation.[11] Traditional international society was composed of sovereign states knowing no authority superior to them. There was no assumption that any entity other than the state took action on its behalf. In this situation, there is good reason for a state to take action on behalf of another state or seek to join the other state in performing the act.

Municipal law recognizes defense acts taken in aid of other persons. International law has reason to recognize similar acts as self-defense to a greater degree. Municipal law excuses such violations of law by reason of emergency, rather than the inefficacy of social organs. The situation differs in international society in the need to recognize such an excuse, so the reason may well be different with respect to the meaning of emergency as a condition of municipal law.

In concluding the Renunciation of War Pact, states reached a consensus on the exemption from the obligation not for necessity, but for self-defense. In that situation, any state bases its armed action taken in an emergency on self-defense rather than necessity. This is all the more so in the case of the United Nations since the Charter has an express clause providing for self-defense.

Self-defense under traditional international law is quite different from that under the system of collective security with respect to the circumstances of invocation. The conditions of the former cannot be that of the latter, in theory or practice, since the latter developed in the state of non-belligerency existing before the organization was created.

---

[11] A religious norm may be enforced in a society under the rule of a religious government, but has only spiritual influence in another society ruled by a secular government. The norm is the same in terms and content, but operates differently in each society.

However, as far as collective action is politically handicapped, self-defense is invoked on the same conditions of traditional international law, even in the collective organization. The Cold War continued too long for self-defense to be established on conditions specific to collective security. The situation is that self-defense is argued both before a collective organization and an international court by the analogy of legitimate defense in municipal law.

(2) The intermediate function of self-defense between individual and public acts

a) As international organization has developed in international society since the middle of the nineteenth century, the importance of states has diminished in that they have lost their status as the only subjects of international law. This has involved a decline in the principle of sovereign equality in international society, which originated in civil law principles of European society.

The development of the Western legal order differed from the Oriental in making a distinction between civil and public law. Civil law is the regulation of parties equal in legal capacity. In relation to civil law, no party has an obligation imposed upon it against its will. International and civil law both have sovereign equality as a fundamental principle insofar as a state is analogized to an individual person in municipal society.

In disputes between individual persons, the victim is satisfied with the balance of loss with the wrongdoer. To bring such disputes to a peaceful resolution, a judicial procedure is provided in municipal society. By contrast, in international society, the victim seeks to recover the injured right by means of reprisal. There is no judicial procedure according to which disputes between states are generally settled.

Public law is applied to relations between persons unequal in capacity, such as those between governments and civilians. It develops in a society in which the members have unequal power in their relations. In such a society, one person is powerful enough to impose a disadvantage upon the other unilaterally, such as a charge, compensation or punishment.

The main part of Oriental law is public law, including criminal and administrative law. It was codified by dynasties such as the Tang in China and Ohmi in Japan in the seventh century as a means of ruling a unified country. There was nothing in their societies motivating them to develop civil law doctrine. The Oriental tradition has made them familiar with public regulation, even after their adoption of the Western legal system.

It is characteristic of legal systems in the twentieth century that, regardless of their cultural traditions, the element of public law has increased. The Communist and Fascist states placed the economy under the control of the government in order to carry out the domestic and foreign policies leading to war. Other states also adopted a similar policy in relation to economic crisis and social disorder as a result of their influence. These circumstances drove legal systems to incorporate public law to a greater extent than ever before.

The European nations have been caught up in this trend of international society, with an ever-increasing element of public law in their legal systems. A majority of the members of international society are now non-European nations with a tradition of familiarity with public regulation.[12]

For as long as international society consisted of states equal in legal capacity, it was believed that international law was inconsistent with public law in nature and principle. In the early twentieth century, however, international organization came to be recognized as "international government" or "public international union," through which individuals in each state are coordinated in their international activities.[13] The development of international organization is seen to have increased the public law element in the international legal order in tandem with municipal law.

As the principle of no use of force is realized through the activities of international organizations for collective security, including the League of Nations and United Nations, there will be a further increase in the public law element in the international legal order. No concept, including self-defense, can be discussed without mentioning the fact that traditional principles of civil law have come to be obsolete.

It is no coincidence that the public law element has developed in tandem with the increase in the number of non-European states in international society. The present international order cannot proceed without greater conciliation with Oriental society through the giving of serious consideration to the public law element. Under the circumstances, a state has the obligation imposed upon it not to use force, even if reprisal is handicapped by the incomplete nature of collective security.

b) War is a concept inclusive of every function of force in international society. It is characteristic of such a society that all legal relations are reduced to being "civil" in nature. In international society, it finds expression in the principle of the sovereign equality of nations.

As public law plays a part in the international normative order, the unified function of war is divided according to each function of society. International society has no governmental organization to execute the "public" part of the legal order, so states are burdened with the execution, over and above reprisal, necessary to defend their own rights. For example, members of the North Atlantic Treaty Organization took part in the bombardment of Kosovo to carry out "humanitarian law" in 1999, without regard to each individual right and interest.

The North Atlantic Treaty has no express provision requiring its members to participate in public action. In contrast, the United Nations Charter requires members to give "every assistance" to the United Nations (art 2-5). The League of Nations had a procedure to realize the objective of "promoting international co-operation and to achieve international peace and security" (Preamble to the Covenant) by deeming an act to be "a legitimate war." What was distinctive of the League system was that it took any organizational action on the assumption of the legality of war.

---

[12] Needless to say, the author has no universal knowledge of the legal systems and traditions of non-European nations, including Islam and Hindi. However, the general trend of public law prevailing over civil in the legal traditions of non-European nations, as distinct from European ones, is clear.

[13] N.L. Hill, *International Administration*, 1931 and C. Eagleton, *International Government*, 1932.

Under the circumstance that use of force is illegal, any such action is presumed illegal unless it is declared "public" or based on any concept exempted from the illegal use of force. This depends on the persuasiveness of the organizational decision of which system is more effective to realize the public purposes, the League of Nations or the United Nations. The League could not mobilize members to engage in armed activity against the declared aggressor, but censured the Japanese invasion of Manchuria, the Soviets' attack on Finland, and the Italian invasion of Ethiopia in the form of recommendations. Bearing in mind the duration of its activities, the League of Nations was not necessarily any less effective than the United Nations in distinguishing anti-social actions.

The Allied Nations in the Second World War carried out full-scale counteractions against aggressors, the central power of the Allied Nations being the United States. The United Nations was established in line with this practice at the end of the War. An international legal order integrating the United Nations is necessarily "public," having means of actualization, unlike the case of the League of Nations.

A state's act to realize the public purpose cannot be an act of war, in any case, after invalidation of the concept of war. The right of self-defense is only an individual act exempted from the prohibition on no use of force, so an individual act to realize the public purpose cannot be unrelated to self-defense.

In this situation, any act of self-defense can connote a public act as the only practical means of realizing the "public" purpose, or the principle of war renunciation or no use of force. Nevertheless, it is not as persuasive as an act on a collective decision joined by other states. That is because the injured interest, rather than the function, is believed to be personal or "private."

c) Apart from the provision in the UN Charter that self-defense is "inherent" to all member states, self-defense in the postwar situation is distinctive in having in its function an intermediary character between individual and collective, public and individual, civil and criminal, average and distributive. In contrast to war, necessity and reprisal, there was no rich practice in self-defense before the principle of war renunciation was established. There were few cases of self-defense being invoked instead of other concepts to persuade the disputants. It is not disadvantageous, but rather advantageous, for self-defense to be reorganized under collective security.

Faced with the need to have her attack on a ship in American territorial waters in 1837 excused, Britain would not invoke war and reprisal to justify the action, but sought to use other concepts, including self-defense. Following municipal legal theory, they would find "necessity" more persuasive to excuse such violation. Indeed, one writer has cited this case as a precedent for "necessity."[14] Another discussed this incident as a case of "self-preservation."[15] British commentators would not insist on the justification of self-defense either.[16]

---

[14] Self-defense and necessity have been proved on common cases and materials: see B.C. Rodick, *The Doctrine of Necessity in International Law*, 1928.

[15] W.E.A. Hall, *Treatise on International* Law, 1909, ch. 7.

[16] With respect to the Caroline case, see Moore, *Digest of International Law*, vol. 2 and R.Y. Jennings, "The Caroline and McLeod Cases," 32*AJ*, 1938, p. 82.

The circumstances in which self-defense was made an exception to the principle of war renunciation were quite different from this incident. In the Caroline Incident, Britain had no intention of making war with the United States. Indeed, the incident was not so serious as to lead to a war between the two countries. On the contrary, in concluding the War Renunciation Pact, they discussed self-defense as a reason for exempting an act, the continuance of which would develop into war. This is also the case with the provision on self-defense in the UN Charter.

From a theoretical standpoint, necessity and self-preservation, rather than self-defense, can be adapted to an act taken to excuse a violation of the prohibition on the use of force. Among other things, necessity is an acceptable excuse for a minor violation of the rights and interests of another state, such as the sinking of a wrecked ship to prevent an oil spill from contaminating a shore.[17] On the other hand, necessity is hardly an acceptable excuse for a major violation of the rights of another state, such as threatening the existence of the state itself.

In municipal law, an act is excused on the basis of necessity when it is taken to defend an individual or private interest. In contrast, an act against a social wrong or criminal offense is excused on the basis of legitimate defense because public organs should ordinarily take it. Legitimate defense has social characteristics as it is taken on behalf of the government in the face of an emergency.

According to article 51 of the UN Charter, all members are free to seek recourse to the right of self-defense "inherent" to them. This implies that the right had already been established in international society by then. Indeed, necessity is found in concept at every stage of development in international society. However, no excuse based on emergency other than necessity is found at any stage in the development of international society without that public element.[18]

According to Professor Bowett, the practice of self-defense includes such acts as powerful states sending armies overseas to protect the nationals and their property.[19] Most of the practices cited by him would be criticized as violations of the principle of no use of force if discussed before organs of the United Nations.

What is certain is that the United Nations needs to reserve a kind of forcible act for its members, while acting in the capacity of a public organization. The reserved act is termed "*légitime défense*" by the Locarno Pact[20] and "self-defense" by the War Renunciation Pact and United Nations Charter.

d) Unlike other relevant treaties, the United Nations Charter places no conditions on the concept of self-defense. In postwar international society, no state fails to invoke self-defense in an attempt to avoid censure for breach of the principle of no use of force, whether it is a member of the United Nations or not. Out of the practice

---

17 The Tory Canyon Affair, 1967.

18 In this sense, it is rightly observed that every practice of self-defense is paraphrased to be an act of necessity: R. Taoka, *Self-defense in International Law*, 1978.

19 See D.W. Bowett, *Self-defense in International Law*, 1958.

20 Article 2 of the Locarno Pact, 16 October 1925, 54 *League of Nations Treaty Series*, p. 305.

adopted after the Charter came into effect, there is no difficulty in finding the condition upon which self-defense has been claimed legal.

As is the case with individual persons, a state will take action necessary to defend its vital interest, whether the right to act is established or not. Law in any society allows members to take such action provided the defended right is balanced with the right of the party counteracted against. "Necessity" is the most natural concept for excusing a contravention of the laws of society.[21]

However, necessity has not been persuasive in defending major interests of the actor in light of practices including the Danish Fleet case, the German violation of Belgian neutrality, and the Israeli attack on the Iraqi nuclear reactor. In cases where the legitimacy of self-defense is affirmed, no state would invoke necessity in seeking to be excused from its obligation not to resort to armed force.

If it is taken over by a "public authority," an individual act is certified to be public, beyond the defense of a private interest of the acting state. In municipal society, such acts do not fail to be taken over by public authorities. In contrast, international society has no definite authority to take over such individual acts, although it is a counteraction against aggression.

Even in municipal society, an individual act can be public as it substitutes a police act. The police system is not necessarily complete in every state. Where a state is divided into political and military factions, no public authority is specified to take over individual acts.

The individual act corresponding to legitimate defense is called self-defense in international society, not because the term is theoretically relevant, but because it follows the terminology in international instruments such as the UN Charter. They were concluded amid the process of increasing the public element in international society or the development of international organization. The fact was that an individual concept distinct from necessity needed to be established. Viewed in this light, the condition of self-defense can neither be deduced from the preceding practices nor analogized by legitimate defense in municipal society.

(3) The positive conditions of self-defense

a) According to article 51 of the United Nations Charter, the right of self-defense is "inherent" to all the member states. However, the evidence indicates that the right is not inherent, but vested in member states to compensate for their renunciation of the right to war and warlike action.

The UN Charter follows the precedents of the Locarno Pact in 1925 and the Renunciation of War Pact in 1928, which exempt an individual act of counter-aggression from the obligation of no recourse to war in the name of self-defense. However, the conditions on the right of self-defense could not necessarily be found from the practice taken on those treaties.

---

[21] In the draft Convention on State Responsibility by the UN International Law Commission, prime position is given to state of necessity among "circumstances precluding wrongfulness" entailing international responsibility: Part I, art 33, *YBILC*, 1980.

The practice before those treaties shows that self-defense coincides with an act of necessity, which has been based on the municipal legal system's condition of "imminent danger." When a ship was attacked by Britain in American waters in 1837, it was contended on the part of the United States that the concept of self-defense was conditional upon the fact situation being "instant, overwhelming, leaving no choice of means, and no moment of deliberation."[22]

In the Case concerning Military and Paramilitary Activities in and against Nicaragua, the International Court of Justice did not express an opinion on the criteria of necessity and proportionality because they were not disputed by the parties.[23] Every legal system excuses violations by reason of necessity, so any anti-aggression treaties are duly interpreted to excuse violations on the condition of "imminence." However, no such treaties have express provisions recognizing the exception on the grounds of emergency or necessity.

The condition of self-defense, which the UN Charter expressly provides in article 51, is the occurrence of "an armed attack." This follows the practice since the late 1920s of self-defense being sought to exempt a state from the obligation of no recourse to war.

As it is invoked to prove the response to "an armed attack" or aggression, self-defense is naturally accepted as a political concept rather than a legal one. In fact, the United States, the respondent in the Nicaraguan Case, withdrew from the jurisdiction of the International Court of Justice in opposition to the "justiciability" of the subject, which was discussed in relation to self-defense.[24]

Another condition of the Charter is "until the Security Council has taken the measures necessary." The Charter is silent as to whether self-defense is taken in the process of taking enforcement measures against an armed attack or aggression. If the answer is in the affirmative, then the act of self-defense is synonymous with enforcement measures in substance. In that case, "the measures necessary" may be taken by recognizing the act of self-defense as conforming to the United Nations.

In municipal society, the "public" and the "private" are distinguished according to the actor of the forcible action. There is a power-monopolizing organ that does not fail to take enforcement itself. In international society, "public" action is, in any event, taken by the forces of individual states. In such a society, the difference between collective and individual in the nature of the action depends not on the actor, but rather on the procedure declaring the action to be public.

If the procedure is completed, then the employment of force without fulfillment of the prerequisite condition will not have any legal connotation. At this stage in the development of international organization, an individual act may be left undeclared to be collective or individual. It could not be declared legal or illegal, in any case, as

---

[22] Moore, op. cit., vol. 2, p. 412.

[23] ICJ Case concerning Military and Paramilitary Activities in and against Nicaragua, Merits, 27 June 1986, para 194.

[24] See Statement of U.S.A. at the case concerning Military and Paramilitary Activities in and against Nicaragua (Nicaragua v. U.S.A.), I.C.J. 1984, *International Legal Materials* (hereafter cited as "ILM") 1985, p. 246.

the Security Council is not bound by legal practices, but takes action from the standpoint of the restoration of peace.

What has been improved in international society since the 1920s is not the act, but the procedure through which an individual state's act is ascertained to conform to the public interest. At the present stage of international society, there is still no organ ready to discharge the duty of "the police" all the time. On the other hand, there are organs, including the Security Council of the United Nations, having the capacity to recognize acts as being in accordance with the collective purpose.

The response to aggression or international crime should be certain and efficacious, whether it is public or individual. Self-defense must comprehend every individual act in concept, one part of which accords with the collective purpose and the other part of which may be done in pursuance of an individual interest. Under the circumstances, the victim state and states collaborating with the victim on a voluntary basis must have a common interest in responding to the danger. Such common interests include irrevocable anti-social actions, such as aggression, to be responded against by all members of international society.

The Charter is reasonable in specifying the conditions of self-defense as "if an armed attack occurs" and "until the Security Council has taken the measures necessary" to make it apparent that self-defense has a social function as distinct from other individual concepts. The other conditions of self-defense are not specified, but left to formulation of the practice by the United Nations in a manner consistent with its essential character.

b) In the United Nations system, the Security Council is not bound by legal practices, but acts from the standpoint of the restoration of peace in taking enforcement measures against armed attacks or aggression. In light of the practices during the Second World War, which were responses to violations of the War Renunciation Pact or action against aggression, the legitimate act is not balanced against the injury done to the victim. If it were based on any existing concepts, including war and reprisal, it might end in compromise, without involving an "unconditional surrender" on the part of the aggressor.

The Allied Nations departed in action from traditional international law, under which there had to be a balance between the injury suffered and the remedy, as is the case with relations in civil law. If self-defense were discussed under traditional international law or deduced from the law and practice of municipal society, it would be conditional upon a balance being struck between the injuries sustained by the assaulting state and the assaulted.

However, self-defense conditional upon proportionality is not the same as necessity. There must be a distinction between self-defense and necessity because the War Renunciation Pact and the UN Charter reserved not necessity, but rather self-defense, for states to be exempted from the prohibition on war and the use of force. They must have selected a concept under which every act would be excused as the occasion demanded. If they selected necessity, they would be limited to actions proportionate to the injury sustained in taking counteraction against the aggressor.

As the United Nations is a creation based on the practices of the Second World

War, a forcible act permissible under the system need not be balanced with the injury suffered by the counteracted. Self-defense is the only forcible act expressly recognized as being consistent with the collective purposes, so is not taken in balance with the injury to the victim or, in other words, is free from the principle of proportionality.

In the absence of forces proper to the "enforcement," an act of counter-aggression commenced as an act of individual and collective self-defense could hardly be proportionate between the armed attack and the response. Contrary to being proportional, an act against a social evil or an aggressor in violation of the principle of no use of force should be assisted by every member of society. Thus, violations of the War Renunciation Pact were responded against by acts of international society, which developed into the organized operations of the Allied Nations.

However, not every forcible act is free from the principle of proportionality. An act to redress damage inflicted upon nationals in violation of a commercial treaty, for example, need not be taken over by an act of a "public authority." A necessary act in relation to an injury innocent of illegality, such as the sinking of a wrecked ship to prevent an oil spillage, must be proportional to the injury. In this context, it is no coincidence that self-defense is conditional upon "an armed attack" under the system of the United Nations, which is an institutionalization of the acts of the Allied Nations. Any term other than self-defense, such as necessity, is preferable in allowing a counteraction in relation to an injury not involving "an armed attack."

When we consider the aspect of collective self-defense, it becomes even more difficult to make proportionality a condition of self-defense. Collective self-defense taken on behalf of another state corresponds to legitimate defense on behalf of another person in municipal society. However, the situation is different between the two societies. Collective self-defense is taken by a third state that has no exact knowledge of the initial armed attack. The state could not cease the act of assistance at the instant it became perfectly balanced with the initial attack.

Conceived on the basis of the theory and practice of legitimate defense in municipal law, self-defense would have proportionality as one of its conditions. Other concepts of traditional international law, including reprisal and necessity, were established through practices made on the basis of conditions derived from municipal law. The history of the UN Charter is too short for collective self-defense to be consolidated as a concept corresponding to legitimate defense in municipal law.[25]

That does not mean, however, that self-defense is free of any conditions in ending. There may be excessive self-defense when more action is taken than is necessary for the defense. It has been recognized since the signing of the War Renunciation Pact

[25] In the Nicaragua Case, the International Court of Justice was unable to argue collective self-defense without reference to the UN Charter and the practice thereon, nor could it invoke any international agreements, including the Charter, in its own defense against the argument that it had no jurisdiction over the international agreements on account of the Declaration of the United States. See Judgment of 27 June 1986, paragraph 42 and thereafter.

that self-defense is conditional upon the occurrence of an armed attack or armed aggression from the start. The Charter of the United Nations expressly confirms this condition. No further act is acceptable in the name of self-defense once an armed attack is over.

c) Under the present power structure in international society, there could not be any collective activities independent of acts taken by member states making use of the armed forces maintained by each. The League of Nations did not hesitate to state that the task of sanctions was assigned to national forces offered by each member state (Covenant, art 16 para 2).

The principal purpose of the United Nations is the maintenance of international peace and security (Charter, art 1-1). The primary responsibility for the maintenance of international peace and security is conferred on the Security Council (art 24). It discharges the responsibility according to the procedure provided in the Charter, particularly in Chapter VII.

"If an armed attack occurs," an individual state may react to it by exercising its right of self-defense (art 51). The French text of article 51 states, "dans le cas où un Membre des Nations Unies est l'objet d'un aggression armée." Responding to an "armed aggression" is the responsibility of the United Nations. An attacked state will inevitably react to an attack or armed aggression earlier than the Security Council, however quickly the latter brings it up for discussion. Accordingly, the occurrence of an armed attack must be defined beforehand in relation to the responding act of an individual state.

Aggression is defined through the works of the Special Committee of the General Assembly of the United Nations. A crucial point in the definition was on "the indirect aggression." The resolution of the General Assembly adopted on 14 December 1974 solved this problem by including "the indirect aggression" in "aggression" (art 3 g). Provided the aggression takes the form of latent threats (such as preparation for war) or other type of aggression (such as "indirect aggression"), "if an armed attack occurs" is identified with "if an armed attack is impending."

The "indirect aggression" defined as a kind of aggression by the resolution of the General Assembly includes "the sending by or on behalf of a State of armed bands, groups, irregulars or mercenaries (art 3 g)." The sending of terrorists to destroy a state is not an "aggression," as defined in the resolution, unless it is done on behalf of a state. Terrorism is, nonetheless, an international crime requiring some response by international society. The procedure for such response has only been established in certain fields, such as piracy, the slave trade, and aerial hijacks. Under these circumstances, the victim state could respond to it by the right of self-defense, deeming the terrorists' attack an "armed attack," as provided by the UN Charter.

A state's ability to exercise its right of self-defense to deal with the occurrence of an "armed attack" or armed aggression is not impaired by the attitude of the Security Council toward it. The interpretation of "an armed attack occurs" to mean that "an armed attack is present" is too restrictive to remove the contradiction that member states are forced to be inactive while the Security Council allows the situation to deteriorate.

The War Renunciation Pact requires the contracting parties to settle their dispute by pacific means instead of war (art 2). Under the system of the League of Nations, members are required to submit any dispute likely to lead to a rupture to arbitration, judicial settlement or inquiry by the Council (Covenant, art 12). The members of the United Nations are not exempted from the obligation to seek to settle their disputes by any peaceful means which they choose freely out of negotiation, conciliation, arbitration and so on (Charter, art 2 para 3 and art 33).

Where peace still remains in a dispute, the parties are obliged to refer it to the Security Council as a last resort, but the Council is not responsible for the final solution. Even if the Council makes a decision, it is recommendatory in effect insofar as it is taken under Chapter VI of the Charter.

This situation is contradictory in that the members are prohibited from taking further action – that is, armed action to resolve the dispute – while the Security Council takes no responsibility for the solution. The only change occurs when the Security Council makes a binding decision under Chapter VII of the Charter in relation to a situation developing into a "threat to the peace" in time. However, the Council is not bound to make such decisions either legally or politically. In this situation, it would be illogical for member states not to be able to deal with a "threat to the peace," not to mention the more serious situation of a "breach of the peace" or an "act of aggression" by armed means.

Interpretation of the phrase "to an armed attack in presence" would leave "threats to the peace" short of "breaches of the peace" unable to be responded against by self-defense. It would leave the situation unchanged that neither the Security Council nor individual states would take any action against "threats to the peace."

"Restrictive interpretation," or interpretation of the phrase "to an armed attack in presence," would be impractical at this stage in the development of military technology as it reduces the right of self-defense to the right of "the second blow."[26]

On the other hand, it is feared that a wider interpretation of self-defense encourages the misuse of force in the name of "preventive self-defense." In fact, Japan defended herself against censure for violation of the agreement on war renunciation by invoking the right of self-defense.[27] Similarly, Israel invoked the right of self-defense before the Security Council in order to legalize her attack against Arab states on 4 June 1967.[28] In spite of these cases, the drafters of the Charter of the

---

[26] The contrary view is prevalent among writers. With respect to the alternative view of restricting self-defense to a reaction to "an armed attack in presence," see P.C. Jessup, *A Modern Law of Nations*, 1950, p. 116. As a matter of fact, no states have been condemned for "anticipatory defense" before any United Nations organs: see I. Brownlie, "The Use of Force in Self-defense," *British Yearbook of International Law* (hereafter cited as "BY"), 1961, p. 165.

[27] Past Japanese military authorities sought to excuse their actions in Manchuria by reason of self-defense. Their contention was not accepted by the report of the League of Nations investigating the circumstances in Manchuria in 1932. The "restrictive theory" on self-defense adopted by most Japanese writers may come from their historical experience. It is, at the same time, undeniable that their inclination to place hope in the activities of the United Nations leads them to take a "restrictive interpretation" of self-defense, as less individual action encourages the activities of collective security.

[28] *Security Council Official Records*, 1347 mtg.

United Nations could not be criticized for the provision made by them in the article. As far as the members of the United Nations act in accordance with the Charter, self-defense would develop as the article provided, although the conditions were found to be different from those invoked under traditional international law.

d) Although the terms of the United Nations may be different from those invoked under traditional international law and practice, we cannot say that two concepts of self-defense with different conditions coexist in the present international society. What exists is one concept of self-defense, according to which either the UN Charter or international law may be invoked.[29]

The self-defense in existence is conditional upon the occurrence of an armed attack, which is interpreted to include threats of such an attack. This has been consolidated not by the practices taken throughout history, including those taken before the establishment of collective security, but through invocation of article 51 of the Charter of the United Nations.

On the other hand, there is a possibility that self-defense will be discussed by reference to the doctrine of municipal law, especially when it is brought for deliberation by a judicial court. In the Nicaragua Case, the International Court of Justice did not discuss the conditions of self-defense, simply because the parties would not take up the issue as a moot point. It is foreseeable, however, that a court would adjudicate a suit on the conditions of necessity and the proportionality of self-defense, which are established in both the theory and practice of municipal courts.

Against the background of municipal law, national governments may adhere to the conditions of legitimate defense of municipal law and practice in proving their acts of self-defense.[30] Nevertheless, they would not in fact act in accordance with the conditions of self-defense thus proved when responding to an armed attack. Among other things, they would not adhere to the condition of proportionality in ceasing their action.

In contrast to legitimate defense in municipal society, self-defense in international society has taken on positive characteristics through the practice of collective self-defense or defense of another state. Any state would have trouble identifying the exact conditions on self-defense for acting in defense of another state, which leads it to behave in a looser way than in action for itself.

Self-defense would be wrongly conceived if it were discussed from a purely theoretical standpoint, confused with legitimate defense in municipal society. This would be the case when an international court discusses an act in relation to the

[29] In the Report on State Responsibility by the UN International Law Commission, the notion of a contrary existing concept of self-defense is categorically denied: The 8th Report of R. Ago, *YBILC*, 1980. A full understanding of the concept of self-defense is not possible without reference to the Charter.

[30] The Japanese Government declared that self-defense is conditional upon (1) the presence of imminent and illicit injury, (2) being the only means of excluding the injury, and (3) the minimum use of force not beyond what is necessary to exclude the injury: Reply to a Member of the Diet by the Government, 27 September 1985.

conditions of self-defense.[31] The United States was right in developing the argument on the "justiciability" of the International Court of Justice on the occasion of the reference of a political dispute to it under the system of compulsory jurisdiction.[32] Adjudication may be useful where it applies effective theory based on the practices of that society.

2. The Social Functions of Self-defense

(1) Enforcement in succession to self-defense

a) According to the UN Charter, enforcement measures by military means are taken by members' forces offered by "special agreements" under the command of the Military Staff Committee (arts 43, 46 and 47). They have not materialized since the permanent members of the Security Council composing the Committee failed to reach agreement on the basic structure of the "the United Nations Force."[33]

The Charter recognizes joint action by the main members of the Allied Nations to be an enforcement action pending the coming forth of special agreements under article 43 of the Charter (art 106). The United Nations follows wartime cooperation among the Allied Nations to resist the common enemies. As the joint action is equivalent to an act of the Allied Nations in the Second World War, there is no difficulty in deeming it to be an enforcement action taken by the United Nations.

If the United Nations intends to be the world government, it should maintain an "international force" to attain its purposes through enforcement action. The United Nations has no means of enforcement other than individual states' forces voluntarily offered to it. Their organization is dependent on each nation in terms of personnel, equipment and command. As a result, such forces are invariably subject to the direction of their home governments.

In the hostilities between the two Korean regimes beginning on 25 June 1950, the American forces in Japan were sent to defend the southern regime. Encouraged by the resolutions of the Security Council, fifteen nations joined the United States. The name of the United Nations Forces in Korea is based on the resolution of 7 July 1950 authorizing the unified command to use the United Nations flag in the course of operations against the North.

---

[31] Indeed, the International Court of Justice did not discuss the conditions of self-defense in the Nicaragua Case, but determined that proportionality and necessity to respond to the armed attack are established conditions of the customary international law on self-defense: The Case concerning Military and Paramilitary Activities in and against Nicaragua, ICJ, 27 June 1986, Merits, para 176.

[32] "I believe that the Nicaraguan Application should be declared non-justiciable, since in my view the dispute at issue is one which does not fall into the category of 'legal' disputes within the meaning and intention of article 36, paragraph 2, of the Statute. [T]he question as to whether this dispute should be considered as justiciable in terms of the concept of 'legal disputes' within the meaning of the Statute is related to the merits of the dispute: Dissenting opinion of Judge Oda, para 17. See also E. McWhinney, *Judge Shigeru Oda and the Progressive Development of International Law*, 1993.

[33] Report of the Military Staff Committee, 30 April 1947; L. Sohn, *Cases and Materials on World Law*, 1950, p. 834.

The United States and allied forces assisting South Korea acted in the capacity of United Nations forces based on the resolutions of the Security Council. The resolution of 25 June 1950 determines that the attack on the Republic of Korea by forces from the North constitutes a breach of the peace and calls for the immediate cessation of hostilities. It is not based on any particular provision of the Charter, but uses the expression in article 39 of Chapter VII.

All of the resolutions were adopted, thanks to the fortuitous absence of the Soviet Union from the Council at the beginning on account of her discontent with the presence of representatives of the Nationalist Government of China. If the War had been discussed by the Security Council under normal circumstances, any decision recommending assistance to the South Korean regime would not have been adopted. This was certainly the case in the Council after the return of the Soviet representatives.

In autumn of the same year, Chinese "volunteer corps" joined the North. The hostile actions between the North assisted by Communist China and the South assisted by UN Forces came to a standstill around the 38th parallel of latitude, which had demarcated the two regimes. They ceased fire not because the aim of the resolutions had been attained, but because the belligerents came to conclude armistice agreements. This process was inevitable under the present circumstances of international society, where the United Nations took action not with forces of its own, but rather by confirming acts of individual states' forces taken in accordance with the collective purpose.

Amid tensions like the Cold War, a forcible action would worsen rather than improve the situation in international society, whether based on UN resolutions or not. In fact, the activities of the United Nations Forces in Korea brought the world to the brink of a Third World War.

The Security Council is wise to refrain from authorizing states to act according to Chapter VII of the Charter when it foresees the situation becoming serious. In such a case, it will ask the states to cease the action, even though they are duly responding to the initial armed attack. On the other hand, the Security Council will encourage them if it foresees the situation differently. In either case, an individual act should cease when the Security Council takes "the measures necessary."

In the history of the United Nations, no action in self-defense has been replaced by necessary measures of the Security Council in a way different from the actions of states taken in self-defense.[34] The Gulf War in 1990 proved that the Security Council will authorize the taking of forcible action before it is taken rather than recognize it afterwards. In the War, the Security Council authorized "the multinational forces," comprising the United States and its allies, to realize the preceding resolutions.[35] On that occasion, "the measures necessary" were taken before the acts in self-defense were performed, rather than afterwards as provided under the Charter.

---

[34] This is a natural consequence of "measures necessary" being construed as "effective measures": R. Lavalle, "The Law of the United Nations and the Use of Force, under the Relevant Resolutions of 1990 and 1991, to Resolve the Persian Gulf Crisis," *Netherlands Yearbook of International Law*, 1992, p. 11.

[35] See Resolutions 665 on 25 August 1990 and 678 on 29 November 1990.

The Security Council of the United Nations does not have exclusive power to authorize individual actions in accordance with collective purposes. After Soviet attendance at the deliberations of the Security Council, the General Assembly of the United Nations adopted the Uniting for Peace Resolution on 3 November 1950, affirming the capacity of the General Assembly to consider matters on peace and security, including the Korean situation.[36]

A phenomenon similar to the Uniting for Peace Resolution is found in the League of Nations practice. The Protocol for the Pacific Settlement of International Disputes, the so-called Protocol of Geneva, adopted by the Assembly on 2 October 1924, presented the following idea: If the Council failed to determine the aggressor, the Assembly should enjoin an armistice upon the belligerents by a two-thirds majority. Any party refusing the armistice should be deemed an aggressor and have sanctions imposed against it.[37]

From a practical standpoint, the collective decision is a statement clarifying that an individual act may be deemed to be a collective act. The Allied Nations in the Second World War decided themselves that their acts were a sanction against anti-social actions, as the Atlantic Charter on 14 August 1941 and the Joint Declaration on 1 January 1942 declared. The United Nations is a creation of the Allied Nations based on the principles of those instruments. It is an international organization recognizing, through its procedures, the legitimacy of actions in international society thereafter.

In postwar international society, any act may claim to be collective or public on the procedural ground of the United Nations. The difficulties of decision-making in the UN organs since immediately after the Second World War have lessened since the end of the Cold War in 1989. In the Gulf War of 1990-1991, the decisions of the Security Council – especially Resolution 678 on 29 November 1990 – gave the "multi-national forces" collective authority. Insofar as the Security Council authorized the forces deployed in the Persian Gulf to take necessary measures to implement relevant resolutions, they had a basis for calling themselves the United Nations Forces.

If the multi-national forces were not deployed in the Gulf region on the ground of individual and collective self-defense, the Security Council would not have been so closely involved in the War by adopting resolutions. In fact, the Security Council remained aloof from the Iran-Iraq War in 1980-1990, to which the United States and her allies had declared themselves neutral.[38] The Security Council did not fail, in response to the armed attack on Kuwait by Iraq, to affirm the inherent right of self-defense of each

---

[36] This is a problem in interpreting the Charter. The General Assembly has competence to deal with any situation within the scope of the Charter (art 10) and may decide on enforcement actions when the Security Council is not exercising its function assigned in the Charter (art 12–1). After China's participation in the Northern Force, it recommended that the Member repel the armed attacks (Resolution, 7 October 1950) and requested that the parties reach a satisfactory ceasefire (14 December 1950), while the Council kept silent throughout the development of the hostilities.

[37] Protocol, art 10(2); Watkins and Robinson, *General International Organization: A Source Book*, 1956, p. 94.

[38] Press release of President Carter, 24 September 1980; Declaration of the Japanese Ministry of Foreign Affairs, November 1980.

member state by adopting the resolution under Chapter VII of the Charter (Resolution 661, 6 August 1990). Nevertheless, it would not proceed with collective action by any means, including authorizing a specific nation's forces to act in accordance with the collective purposes, unless self-defense was rightly taken beforehand.

b) In both the Korean and Gulf Wars, the forces were organized ad hoc in response to the aggressors. Originally, they were organized to restore order to the region independently of the UN resolutions. It was by a series of resolutions adopted after the incidents occurred that they were recognized as according with the purposes of general collective security.[39]

The Korean War originated in the division of the Korean Peninsula into two regimes, unification of which was sought by a commission of the United Nations. If a peace treaty had been concluded between all the Allied Nations and Japan shortly after the Second World War, then the Korean War may never have broken out. The fact was that no peace conference was held with Japan on account of the ongoing Cold War, and American forces remained stationed in Japanese territory at the time of the outbreak of hostilities. They were determined to fight on the Peninsula to recover the power balance of the region even if the Security Council failed to adopt a resolution authorizing them to act in the capacity of United Nations Forces.

Japan was not in a position to collaborate with the American forces in action on the Peninsula, as she was still in a state of war with the Allied Nations, including the United States. To resolve this problem, the Government of the United States moved to make peace with Japan as soon as possible. The Peace Treaty concluded in September 1951 restored peace between the Allied Nations and Japan. Japan backed up the United States forces thereafter in accordance with the US-Japan Security Treaty, which took effect simultaneously with the Peace Treaty.

According to the US-Japan Security Treaty, the American armed forces were kept "to contribute to the maintenance of international peace and security in the Far East" and "to the security of Japan against armed attack from without, caused through instigation or intervention by an outside power or powers." The garrison forces can meet "large-scale internal riots and disturbances in Japan" at the express request of the Japanese Government (art 1).

If an action against aggression is public in nature, any state, including Japan, will be obliged to cooperate with the forces engaging in it. As members of the United Nations met the aggression in Korea according to the Charter, so Japan, then a non-member of the United Nations, granted foreign forces the right to use its territory by bilateral treaty. Under the concept of *bellum justum*, whether conceived naturally or positively, a just war is never lost because the just party is joined by other members

[39] The Security Council recommended that the members place their forces under the unified command of a commander-in-chief named by the United States at its request: Resolution, 7 July 1950. There may be another cause for doubt as to its legitimacy, including the fact that no UN authority participated in the truce negotiations. No states or organizations other than the United States participated in the truce negotiations between the states offering military assistance to the UN Forces. The truce agreement concluded was thus not registered in accordance with article 102 of the Charter: R. Higgins, *United Nations Peacekeeping 1946–1967: Documents and Commentary*, vol. 2: Asia, 1970, pp. 183–184.

of society. The legitimacy of the United Nations Forces in Korea may be doubted not because of a problem in the decision-making process, but rather because of the failure to be proven "just" on the defeat of "the aggressors."

In adopting resolutions on the war in Korea, the Security Council was not joined by Soviet representatives, who were absent due to disagreement regarding the representation of China. The Council may have not been legitimate as it failed to accord with the Charter provision requiring an affirmative vote including the concurring votes of the five permanent members of it. In light of the observations above, however, the legitimacy of the action in Korea was based not so much on resolutions of the Security Council as on public purposes found by every means, including decisions of collective organization.

The position of Japan cooperating with foreign forces within her territory may be better grounded on individual and collective self-defense than any other conventions, including the United Nations Charter. Continuing the garrison of American forces in Japanese territory after peace was attained would be less doubtful on the ground of self-defense than the decisions of the Security Council. Notwithstanding the non-membership of Japan, the decisions of the Security Council made during the Korean War were fortuitous and would be improbable under normal circumstances. It was natural that the object of utmost importance in the revision of the US-Japan Security Treaty in 1960 was the provision of self-defense as the basis of action in it, which was not provided in the original Treaty of 1951.

There was no further act of armed sanction during the Cold War because the United Nations was not prepared to risk a failure in enforcement as had happened in the Korean War. Even after the conclusion of the Cold War, few aggressive acts have been counteracted by the Security Council on account of the difficulty in reaching consensus due to the veto power of the permanent members.

Under the circumstances, there is no means of giving effect to the principle of no use of force other than activating the social function of self-defense. The only other means would be to place an international organization on an equal footing with the United Nations in acting as a collective organization. Bombardment of Kosovo in Yugoslavia in 1999 could not be legitimated in light of the principle of no use of force unless NATO was a collective organization in parallel with the United Nations.

Even after the Cold War, enforcement by the United Nations cannot be the only assurance of achieving an effective international order due to the structural impediments to decision-making. One solution is found in the function of self-defense, through which an individual or private act may be converted into a collective or public one. Another is in the activation of regional organizations. Some would hesitate to recognize a regional organization as being collective in parallel with the United Nations, but an organization and arrangement based on regional solidarity are efficient enough to be entrusted with collective activities.

(2) Peacekeeping practiced as self-defense

After the conclusion of the War Renunciation Pact, no state would acknowledge that it was engaging in war, for fear of being censured for violating the Pact. An armed conflict short of war ends without a conference leading to the conclusion of a peace treaty as it has not converted the legal status between the belligerents from peace into war. An armed act developed in the state of "intermediacy" ceases not through a peace agreement, but rather by an armistice.

The League of Nations presupposed war in handling conflicts through the Covenant system. Any war or threat of war was a matter of concern to the whole League of Nations (art 11). If the conflict developed into war in disregard of the Covenant provisions, the League of Nations would address the situation with the functions provided in article 16 of the Covenant. However, if the conflict fell short of war, or insisted that it was so, the League did not find any means to deal with it in the provisions of the Covenant.

The League dealt with situations falling short of war, which often occurred during the period of its activity, in a practical way.[40]

In the Suez Crisis in 1956, the United Kingdom and France intervened in the armed clash between Egypt and Israel in order to preserve the safety of navigation on the Canal. If the practice in the Korean War had been followed in this crisis, the United Nations flag would have been bestowed on the United Kingdom and France, who were in the most powerful position to pacify the region.[41]

The Suez Crisis was discussed in the Security Council in circumstances where any resolutions disadvantageous to the United Kingdom and France were vetoed, while any measures benefiting them were opposed by the other veto-holding powers, including the Soviet Union and United States. The situation was more normal than in the Korean War in that all members of the Security Council, including the five permanent members, discussed it.

It was the General Assembly convened according to the Uniting for Peace Resolution that sent the United Nations Forces, named the United Nations Emergency Forces (UNEF) to the region of the dispute (Resolutions on 4 and 5 November 1956).[42] In the ordinary sense of the word, "the Forces" are corps with the ability to fight the peace-breakers. UNEF did not need such ability because it was sent after the ceasefire had been agreed between the disputing parties.

The League of Nations involved itself in conflicts by sending investigatory committees and observation forces, as was the case in the Saar plebiscite in 1934. The planners of the United Nations did not take notice of the conciliatory activities practiced by the League of Nations to supplement enforcement activities, so adopted no provisions on "peacekeeping" in the Charter.[43]

---

40 The cases dealt with in a practical way by the League included the Corfu Incident in 1923, the Affair between Greece and Bulgaria in 1925, the Manchurian Incident in 1931–1933, the Chaco Conflict in 1932–1935, and the Crisis between Hungary and Yugoslavia in 1934. The Ethiopian War in 1934–1936 may have been the only case in which the machinery of the Covenant worked as intended in dealing with a war fought by a significant power: see Walters, *op. cit.*

41 D.W. Bowett, *United Nations Forces*, 1964, p. 91.

42 The Uniting for Peace Resolution on 3 November 1950 requested every member state to maintain within its national armed forces elements so trained, organized and equipped that they could promptly be made available for service as a United Nations unit (C8).

43 Shigeru Kozai, *Kokuren no Heiwaijikatsudo* (United Nations Peacekeeping Operations), 1991, ch. 2.

However, the observations of ceasefire under the auspices of the United Nations had been practiced before UNEF engaged in such activity in the Suez Crisis. The Special Committee on the Greek Border Case in 1946, the Consular Commission on the Independence of Indonesia in 1947, the Truce Supervision Organization on the Palestine situation in 1949, and the United Nations Military Observer Group (UNMOGIP) in Kashmir in 1965 had similar observation functions to UNEF.[44]

UNEF was a corps better defined as an observer mission than a UN Force. In that respect, it was novel in the practice of the United Nations. It was based on an interpretation of the Charter that enforcement measures under article 42 were not limited to those taken by the armed forces offered under article 43 and placed at the disposal of the Military Staff Committee.[45]

The practices of UNEF have been followed in a series of observation activities by the United Nations, including the United Nations Force in Cyprus (FICYP) in 1964, UNEF II in 1973-1979, and the Disengagement Observer Force (UNDOF) in the dispute between Syria and Israel from 1974. They consisted of national contingents voluntarily provided by the member states for the purpose of supervising ceasefires, assisting in the withdrawal of the opposing forces, and other activities designated by the particular resolutions.

The United Nations Transition Assistance Group (UNTAG) in Namibia in 1978 and in Cambodia in 1992 extended the tasks from the observation of ceasefires to the supervision of planned elections by civilian staff. These undertakings were carried out through the interrelated activities of various military, technical and civil components in the Forces.[46]

These activities were not enforcements as such since they were mostly carried out voluntarily by technical and civil components of the Forces concerned about the conflict rather than military ones. They were related to the maintenance of international peace and security, which is the primary purpose of the United Nations (Charter, art 1 para 1). There may be some reason for their generally being regarded as "peacekeeping," though this does not coincide with "peace-maintaining."

In view of the confrontations between East and West, it was impracticable for the United Nations Forces to be organized on the basis of article 43 of the Charter. "Peacekeeping" has attracted attention as a realistic approach to maintaining

---

[44] See D.W. Bowett, *United Nations Forces*, p. 61. The Special Committee on the Greek Border Case and the Committee of Good Office in the Independence of Indonesia are not officially counted as peacekeeping: see Higgins, *United Nations Peacekeeping 1946–1967*, Preface and Acknowledgements. This indicates that peacekeeping is not a definite concept. "There was not, and still is not, any particular theory and doctrine behind peacekeeping": UN Department of Public Information, *The Blue Helmets* (2nd ed.), 1990, p. 4.

[45] A "Force" not engaging in an "enforcement" under Article 42 of the Charter and not offered to be placed at the disposal of the Military Staff Committee under Article 43 is recognized as a "UN Force": *Repertoire*, Supplement 1956–1958, p. 172.

[46] These undertakings began the military observer mission at the Special Committee on Peacekeeping Operations set up in 1965 by the General Assembly and came to be an extensive concept including military and civil activities: R. Siekmann, *Basic Documents on UN and Related Peacekeeping Forces*, 1984.

international peace and security. It means that the success of an international peace organization depends on the structure employed to manage an armed conflict until its conclusion by armistice.

The increasing importance of "peacekeeping" signifies the adaptation of the United Nations to the realities of an international society that has adopted the renunciation of war as its guiding principle. It is not conditional upon the existence of a "threat to the peace," "breach of the peace" or "act of aggression" decided in accordance with article 39 of the Charter. Such forces are sent to prevent the situation from developing into a "threat to the peace" or one of the others. That has proven practicable when a decision under article 39 is hardly possible.

The practicability of peacekeeping does not mean that the United Nations has come to dispense with enforcement in acting as a collective organization. When the situation changes, "peacekeeping" will be compelled to use force to deal with it, notwithstanding the original intention that it be confined to observation.

The United Nations Force in Congo (UNUC), sent to provide the Government of Congo with military assistance to contain internal conflict after it gained independence on 14 July 1960, engaged in military activities under the changed situation. They were authorized by the Security Council, which declared that the conflict seriously imperiled peace and order and threatened international peace and security. On 21 February 1961, the Council urged the UNUC to take all appropriate measures, including, if necessary, the use of force as a last resort.

The International Court of Justice contrasts a coercive or enforcement action with peacekeeping operations organized at the request, or with the consent, of the states concerned.[47] The Soviets were not justified in opposing UNUC's involvement in combating civil strife on the ground that the Security Council monopolized enforcement actions.[48]

After the experience in Congo, the Secretary-General of the United Nations ruled in 1964 that the United Nations Peacekeeping Force in Cyprus could use armed force only as a counteraction to an armed attack against its personnel.[49] It is natural that a national unit of a peacekeeping force should have recourse to the right of self-defense without authorization by the Security Council when attacked during the performance of its duties. This ruling by the Secretary-General is recognition of the fact that UN Peacekeeping Forces act on resolutions made under Chapter VII of the Charter, conditional upon the right of self-defense. In other words, self-defense may be converted into collective action through the relevant procedure of international society.

According to recommendations made in the Report of the Secretary-General Boutros-Ghali on 17 June 1992, peace-enforcement units, armed heavily enough to

---

47 Certain Expenses on the United Nations, opinion of 20 July 1962, *ICJ Reports*, 1962, pp. 164 and 166.

48 The Soviets moved to oppose the UNUC and refused to fund its activities, thus threatening its continued existence as a military force: see The Case concerning Certain Expenses on the United Nations.

49 Aide-memoires of the Secretary General concerning questions relating to the function and operation of the United Nations Peacekeeping Force in Cyprus, 10 April 1964.

deter breaches of the peace, should be created to cope with situations beyond the capacity of peacekeeping. They would consist of troops from member states who undertake to make them available to the Security Council for the purpose of article 42 of the Charter.[50] They are similar to a United Nations unit organized and equipped by every member state under the Uniting for Peace Resolution of 3 November 1950.

There is little difficulty in converting peacekeeping forces into peace-enforcement units. The Japanese Diet has enacted a law to facilitate cooperation with UN peacekeeping activities. However, it excludes activities like the UN Forces in Congo from the subjects of cooperation, as they are "peacekeeping forces" rather than "peacekeeping operations."[51] In fact, the capacity and scale of the United Nations Operations in Somalia (UNOSOM) were widened to such an extent that they operated as "peace-enforcement units" in situations of civil strife there.[52]

UNOSOM failed to restore peace in Somalia, just as the UN Forces had failed to unify the Korean Peninsula and could not appease the civil strife in Congo.[53] As can be seen from the practice in the Gulf War in 1990, action commenced as self-defense and later recognized to be collective is more object-oriented than that which is started as peacekeeping. The origins of the United Nations were in the collaboration of the Allied Nations to oppose the aggressors together. An action on the right of collective self-defense has more in common with the collaboration of the Allied Nations than an action of the United Nations in the Cold War. They cooperate with each other in assisting the attacked states, even though the assisting states are completely safe from attack.

What is supplementary to action under Chapter VII of the Charter is the practice of self-defense rather than that of peacekeeping. Peacekeeping has been practiced from the outset of the operations of the United Nations, but there is no express provision for it in the Charter. Self-defense has also been practiced from the outset, but is expressly provided for in the Charter. It is distinguished from enforcement, but supplements it through the interchangeable function of enforcement in accordance with the mandate of the particular collective organ. Self-defense is thus carried out in a manner more consistent with collective security than peacekeeping.

---

50 Boutros Boutros-Ghali, *An Agenda for Peace*, 1955, paras 43–44.

51 The Government explains the stipulation on the basis that recourse to the right of collective self-defense is prohibited by the Constitution of Japan. It assumes that UN enforcement actions depend on the use of the right of self-defense by each state. The law was amended in 2001 to enable the Self-Defense Forces to operate in the same way as foreign forces, without any change in interpretation of the Constitution: see Chapter 3.

52 In a letter dated 29 November 1992, concerning the deteriorating situation in Somalia, the Secretary-General concluded that the Security Council had no alternative other than to adopt more forcible measures to secure humanitarian operations in Somalia, as recommended in the Ghali Report.

53 Italy ceased to operate there on account of criticism of the "excessive" actions that had been taken by the United States and resulted in many casualties on the Somali side. However, it was the breakdown of the United States' operations that forced UNOSOM to cease activities in 1995 without notable results.

3. Regional Principles Achieved through Self-defense

(1) General principles yielding to regional realities

The Charter of the United Nations finds its origins in instruments in which the Allied Nations declared the legitimacy of their actions against the enemy. The Atlantic Charter, issued by the heads of the United Kingdom and United States in August 1941 and joined by the other Allied Nations on 1 January 1942, mentioned "the establishment of a wider and permanent system of general security." The Four Powers Agreement in Moscow endorsed the creation of a "system of general security" (Moscow Declaration, 1 November 1943, para 5). In spite of these provisions, only the United States was qualified as a global power to deal with international affairs from a general perspective.

In view of the fact that most of the members were region-oriented, no organization intending to be a positive international one could preclude regional arrangements or agencies. In fact, "the system" does not preclude "the existence of regional arrangements or agencies for dealing with such matters relating to the maintenance of international peace and security as are appropriate for regional action (Dumbarton Oaks Proposal, Chapter VIII, section C 1)."

The League of Nations was intended to be a general international security system, but failed to be so on account of the main states in the world having greater interest in the particular region to which they belonged.[54] Most Latin American states participated in the League, but the United States never did. The Soviet Union, a power across Europe and Asia, only participated for a short period in the middle. Japan and Germany, who aspired to rise to great power in their respective regions, regarded it as a hindrance to their policies. Britain and France took the lead throughout its activities, but were more interested in their domestic and colonial matters than global affairs dealt with by the League.

Economic conflicts between regional blocs were the main cause of the Second World War. The League failed to solve them because it had no jurisdiction over economic matters. Indeed, it conducted studies on the cause of the economic crisis and produced an excellent work in this field through comprehensive research.[55] However, these results did not compensate for the political loss resulting from the withdrawal or purge of great powers other than Britain and France. Among other things, the League of Nations failed properly to address the grave situation of

---

[54] In discussing the postwar international regime, British Prime Minister Churchill attached great importance to the regional principle, saying, "It was only the countries whose interests were directly affected by a dispute who could be expected to apply themselves with sufficient vigor to secure a settlement. If countries remote from a dispute were among those called upon in the first instance to achieve a settlement the result was likely to be merely vapid and academic discussion": W.S. Churchill, *The Second World War*, vol. 4; *The Hinge of Fate*, 1951, pp. 718–719.

[55] The Economic and Social Council of the United Nations, an organ executing another function of the Security Council, is the realization of a proposal made on the basis of research made in the final stage of the League's activities: see "Bruce Report," 22 August 1939 (Report on the Development of International Cooperation in Economic and Social Affairs, LN Document A.33, 1939).

Germany clashing with the French-British alliance formed to oppose the German invasion of Poland.[56]

In the history of the League of Nations, there were some cases where disputes were discussed from a regional perspective rather a global one. Ethiopia received sympathy from the League of Nations for its invasion by Italy. China brought world attention to East Asia by introducing an act of provocation by the Japanese military authorities in Manchuria as an item for discussion by the League. Finland brought the issue of its war with the Soviets to the Assembly in the hope that the Soviets would be persuaded to stop. Not all of these were resolved in the victims' favor as the invaders chose not to remain members of the League.

Under the Covenant, regional understandings were not taken into consideration in discussions on regional issues as the League had no competence over "regional understandings like the Monroe doctrine" (art 21). On the other hand, there was a practice of taking regional solutions out of the jurisdiction of the Covenant. Germany's European neighbors reached "regional understandings," the Locarno Pacts in 1925, before German membership became an issue at the League of Nations.[57]

The United States is a region-oriented state, as evidenced by her remaining a non-member of the League despite the President having proposed membership. At the same time, she is a global power, having fought a great war against the Axis nations globally.

In conceiving a postwar international order, there could not be a revival of the League of Nations as the United States was not in favor of it.[58] However, there may have been the option of formulating a postwar international order on a regional basis, recognizing that collective security was effective in achieving regional solidarity.[59] If an international regime had been formulated on a regional basis after the War, it would have been the union of several organizations created for each region, in the center of which the main Allies were situated.

According to the draft of the U.S. Department of State for a general international organization, the United States, Great Britain, Soviet Union, and China were appointed as "policemen" out of the 26 Allied Nations who joined the Declaration of 1 January 1942. They were named not for their ability of maintaining the global order, but because they were ideologically appropriate to be the centers of their respective regions. Great Britain and the Soviet Union had reservations about Nationalist China's suitability to be "police," while Great Britain supported

---

[56] Walters, *op. cit.*, especially pp. 490, 608 and 802.

[57] The Pacts came into effect on the same date as German membership of the League of Nations, 8 September 1926.

[58] President Roosevelt placed revival of the League of Nations out of consideration: W. Range, *Franklin D. Roosevelt's World Order*, 1959, p. 164.

[59] The British Prime Minister, Winston Churchill, and American President, Franklin Roosevelt, were, until the spring of 1943, reportedly strongly in favor of organizing the postwar international system on a regional basis: R.A. Akindele, "From the Covenant to the Charter: Constitutional Relations between Universal and Regional Organizations in the Promotion of Peace and Security," *Israel Law Review*, 1973, p. 102.

France's addition to the "police" on the condition that she be strengthened to enable her to discharge that task.[60]

This allocation may be reasonable because no state other than China could be deemed "the center" of East Asia, and France had to represent Continental Europe, since the Second World War ended with the virtual disappearance of Japan and Germany.[61]

In less than half a century, enemy states have recovered their prewar positions, except in military power. At this stage in history, there is no reason for restricting permanent membership of the Security Council to the original five unless that privilege is based on ideological appropriateness.

If the international regime continues to be positive, independently of the circumstances in which the Allied Nations created it, ideological rigidity should be eased in the interest of regional realities. At the time when international organization was conceived, there were mutual defense treaties concluded bilaterally, such as those between the Soviets and East European states from 1943 to 1948 (including the treaty between the Soviets and Czechoslovakia on 12 December 1943), the United Kingdom-Soviet Pact of 26 May 1942, the French-Soviet Pact of 10 December 1944, and the Chino-Soviet Pact of 14 August 1945. China had been assisted by the British and Americans, whether based on express agreements or not, throughout her defense against Japanese invasion. The agreements among the American States would have taken effect to defend them in the event that they were threatened by the Axis powers.

What combined each bilateral undertaking into common belligerent actions was the doctrine of the Allied Nations. The postwar international organization came to be created, so to speak, on the basis of the practices of the bilateral undertakings, but was founded ideologically in the doctrine of the Allied Nations.

As the enemies were destroyed materially as well as ideologically, there would be no further need for such arrangements to be directed against a renewal of their aggressive policy. The exclusion of enemy matters from the jurisdiction of such international organization might be reasonable from the standpoint of ideological consistency.

Adherence to such treaties until the enemy's threat had past suggested that states consistently sought regional solidarity as the basis of collective security. It was also an indication that no states other than the United States could afford to assist the Allies on a global basis.

The original idea of the War Renunciation Pact was a bilateral agreement between France and the United States.[62] If any states other than the United States

---

60 R.B. Russell, *op. cit.*, pp. 96 and 103–106.

61 If the allocation of such posts had been discussed during peacetime, the resulting controversy would have been so fiery as to dissolve the alliance. As a matter of fact, a special session of the LN Assembly to be called to accept Germany as a permanent member of the Council was cancelled, and Brazil and Spain withdrew from the LN when Germany acceded to it in August 1926: Walters, *op. cit.*; Royal Institute of International Affairs, *Survey of International Affairs*, 1926.

62 J.W. Wheeler-Bennett, *Information on the Renunciation of War: 1927–1928* (reissued in 1973), p. 1.

had taken the initiative in concluding such a pact, there would have been no general agreement concluded by almost every state in the world.

When the draft Pact was circulated by the United States, Great Britain sought to have conduct in an area where she had special interests exempted from the obligation. In response to this, the Secretary of State of the United States confirmed free recourse to the right of self-defense by every party.[63] This exchange between Britain and the United States removed the apprehensions of Japan, who needed a free hand to act in mainland China. The United States herself had special interests in the Americas in parallel to those of Britain in the Middle East and Japan in China.

They reached agreement regarding the Pact in the belief that they would be free to take action in their respective areas with recourse to the right of self-defense. The negative aspect of self-defense is in the disintegrating function found by the parties at the time of signing the Pact. The positive one is in giving effect to the Pact by mobilizing each region towards closer defense cooperation. If the contracting parties had recourse to the right in the correct way, then the purport of the treaty could be attained more practicably than in the case where the treaty had no reservation for self-defense.

The Dumbarton Oaks Proposal for the postwar international organization provided that the Security Council should utilize regional arrangements or agencies for enforcement action. The problem was that no enforcement would be taken under regional arrangements without authorization by the Security Council (Chap VIII sec C 2).

At the conference at Dumbarton Oaks, the Soviet delegate insisted that the treaties directed against the renewal of a policy of aggression on the part of aggressor states, which had been concluded already, should be exempted from the requirement of authorization by the Security Council in enforcement actions taken thereon. The delegate from the United Kingdom agreed with the Soviet one, as she intended to seek exemption of the agreements between the United Kingdom and the Soviet Union and France to be concluded after ratification of the UN Charter.[64]

The Dumbarton Oaks Proposal had an "enemy clause" corresponding to article 107 of the adopted Charter, which exempted members from the obligations.

At the San Francisco Conference, another "enemy clause" was inserted in article 53 to exempt members from the requirement of authorization by the Security Council in taking action against a "renewal of the aggressive policy of the enemies." The initiative to insert the phrase was taken by the Soviets and France, who were particularly sensitive about the resurrection of Germany.[65] The right of self-defense was provided in article 51 as a balance against the "enemy clause" in article 53, which could not be invoked by the majority of member states.

---

[63] Reply to the U.S., 19 May 1928. The region she sought to have exempted was assumed to be the Near East: J.W. Wheeler-Bennett, *op. cit.*, p. 37.

[64] U.S. Department of States, *Foreign Relations of the United States* (hereafter cited as "FRUS"), 1945, vol. 1, p. 568.

[65] UN Information Organization, *Documents of the United Nations Conference on International Organization* (hereafter cited as "UNCIO"), vol. 12, p. 721.

On the other hand, states in other regions, including the Latin American states, were not exempted from such authorization. In order that their interests be balanced with those of the European states, the American States sought to make their regional organization immune from the requirement of authorization by the Security Council in actions taken on their regional arrangements.[66] To place the American States on a footing parallel to the European, which were exempted from the requirement for authorization in taking an enforcement action, an article was provided in another Chapter, namely, article 51, the last article in Chapter VII.

Article 51 does not specify any region, including the Americas, but stipulates in a general way that "nothing in the present Charter shall impair the inherent right of collective self-defense." In light of the circumstances in San Francisco, the article is provided for the purpose of confirming the right of collective self-defense or mutual assistance of all members to prevent some members from withdrawing from the Conference.[67]

This suggests that the right of individual self-defense is inherent. However, in view of the circumstances of the provision, the real intent of the article is to indicate a general ground of exception from the principle of no use of force by stressing the collective aspect of self-defense. This was possible partly because self-defense had been accepted as such an exception since the War Renunciation Pact and partly because self-defense was less conceptualized than other individual concepts such as war, necessity and reprisal.

The realization of the postwar international regime depends upon regional actions based on the collective aspect of self-defense. Under the circumstances, what is necessary is not an ascertainment of the concept, but growth in the practice of it through which general collective security will be achieved.

Since the United Nations commenced its activities, any arrangements for mutual security have tended to choose self-defense as the basis of the action in preference to the "enemy clause."

The Organization of American States asks members to act on the right of self-defense to assist each other when an armed attack occurs, while recognizing itself to be a regional agency within the United Nations system (Inter-American Treaty of Reciprocal Assistance, the Rio Pact, 2 September 1947, art 3; Charter, 3 April 1948, art 1). The North Atlantic Treaty contains no provision recognizing that it is a regional agency of the United Nations, but does contain a provision basing mutual defense on the right of self-defense (art 5). The Warsaw Pact, signed on 14 May 1955 and then invalidated in 1991, and the US-Japan Security Treaty of 1960 both presume that each contracting party will act on the basis of the right of self-defense.

---

66 In the course of the San Francisco Conference in 1945, there were repeated proposals to specify the Regional Arrangements on American States to be exempted from authorization by the Security Council: *UNCIO*, vol. 12, 1945, p. 771.

67 To be balanced with the Soviets' advantage in being exempted from the requirement of approval by the Security Council by virtue of article 53 of the Charter, and prevent the Latin American countries from walking out of the San Francisco Conference, article 51, including the term of "collective self-defense," was adopted from among many proposals: J.F. Dulles, *War or Peace*, 1950, p. 88.

If the postwar international order were founded on security arrangements concluded to promote regional interests and security, it would be less doctrine-oriented than the United Nations. There are regional international organizations that are more practical than doctrine-oriented with respect to regional security. If we only take those into account, we could call the postwar international order a league of regional international organizations.[68] It was no coincidence that the provision of self-defense was advocated by the Latin American nations, who were almost neutral in substance during the Second World War and thus freer from ideological insistence than other members, including the five permanent members of the Security Council.

(2) Collective self-defense distinguished from individual self-defense

From the standpoint of traditional international law, the collective aspect of self-defense corresponds to "lawful intervention" or "reprisal by third states."[69] Although intervention has been discussed since the classical era of international law, it ultimately contravenes the principle of the sovereign equality of states.

Collective self-defense has appeared in circumstances where forces should be used orderly, although maintained separately by each state. According to this concept, a third state responds to the attacking state by right of collective self-defense, while the attacked state responds by its right of individual self-defense. The right of individual self-defense is exercised in the interest of the exercising state, whereas the right of collective self-defense is exercised on behalf of both international society and the attacked state. In the United Nations, these rights are exercised pending the taking of effective measures by the Security Council. In this situation, collective self-defense is not so much an individual act as a quasi-collective action.

Without the principle of no recourse to force or the renunciation of war, on which collective security develops, self-defense would not be as noteworthy as it is in either its individual or collective aspects. Without the establishment of collective security, self-defense would not have such an intrinsic function in international society as it does.[70]

In municipal society, where the public authority is always ready to take social actions, the authority succeeds sooner or later in an act of legitimate defense, whether it is taken for the actor's sake or for the sake of another person. In

---

[68] They are not fit for the task of collective security, and include the Arab League, Association of South-East Asian Nations, Organization of African Unity, and Economic Community of West African States: R. Higgins, "The New United Nations and former Yugoslavia," *International Affairs* 1993–3, p. 475.

[69] M. Akehurst, "Reprisals by Third States," *BY*, 1970, p. 2.

[70] In view of this fact, the International Court of Justice's proof of the right of collective self-defense established on customary or general international law, which is distinguishable from the United Nations Charter, is questionable. The Court is also contradictory in making the right conditional upon the request of the attacked state: Nicaragua Case, Merits, 27 June 1986, para 199. If the Charter is correct in characterizing the right to be "inherent," then any right conditioned on the will of the other person is not inherent in the true sense of the word. As a matter of fact, no collective self-defense has been taken to comply with a request by the attacked state: L.P. Rowles, "'Secret Wars', Self-Defense and the Charter: A Reply to Professor Moore," 80*AJ*, 1986, p. 568.

international society, self-defense is not necessarily replaced by collective action, whether it is individual or collective self-defense.

Established concepts under traditional international law, including reprisal, intervention and neutrality, are almost invalidated in the changed circumstances of postwar international society. Less established concepts such as self-defense intermediate between the public and the individual, filling the blank caused by the invalidation of traditional concepts.

As criminal punishment may be disproportionate to the injury in municipal law and practice, so damage resulting from the response to an assault may exceed the injury caused by the assaulter. It is not so much a theoretical consequence as an actual one, as evidenced by the practices of the Second World War.

In this context, neither collective nor individual self-defense is conditional upon proportionality. An analogy cannot be drawn between self-defense and legitimate defense in municipal law on account of the differences in the societies upon which each concept is practiced. It is often the case in international society that public actions, including criminal punishments, are continued by states acting on the right of self-defense without interruption by other actors, including the United Nations Forces.[71]

To make the act of defense more effective, they do not fail to seek alignment with other states on the basis of the right of collective self-defense. Enforcement by an international organization, including the United Nations, is practical when taken through the acts of individual states based on regional arrangements. The competent organs for collective action, including the Security Council of the United Nations, are free to deem an act collective, among acts taken individually or by regional organizations and arrangements.

This situation is possible when a concept is available for authorization that differs from reprisal, necessity, intervention and war in being less established under traditional international law. It is also true that no international forces have appeared in place of the individual states', even after the practice of effective collaboration between the Allied Nations during the War.

The effect of the function depends, in any case, on the power of the United States. She is a global power as well as a power in more than one region, including the Americas, Western Europe, East Asia, and the Pacific. It is natural that an international regime conceived by her initiative is not necessarily general in principle or structure. No international regime could be conceived without taking closer regional cooperation, which was practical throughout the Second World War, into consideration. The postwar international regime would not be as clear in legal character or concept if collective self-defense were not specifically provided for in article 51 of the UN Charter.

---

[71] China insisted that the action against Vietnam was a "punishment" or sanction. She did not expect the action to be recognized by the United Nations, much less replaced by UN Forces. If she excused the action before the UN organs, she would do so on the basis of self-defense.

(3) Practice and development

a) International agreements concluded to protect regions provide self-defense as a ground for action, with the intention of freeing member states from the conditions required by Chapter VIII of the United Nations Charter.

The Inter-American Conference, held in Mexico City in 1945, reconciled the Inter-American system with the United Nations one by recognizing itself as a regional agency presupposed by Chapter VIII of the UN Charter. However, the Inter-American Treaty of Reciprocal Assistance (the Rio Pact) of 2 September 1947 asks members to act on the right of self-defense to assist each other when an armed attack occurs (art 3). In the former capacity, it acts as a sanctioning organ from the standpoint of the public interest, while in the latter, it acts to help member victims who are facing an "armed attack." In whichever capacity it acts, it responds to armed attacks against any member of the organization.

The North Atlantic Treaty contains no provision as to it being a regional agency of the United Nations, but expressly provides for a right of self-defense, on the basis of which the parties mutually defend each other (art 5). Other regional treaties, including the Warsaw Pact signed on 14 May 1955 and the US-Japan Security Treaty revised in 1960, also provide it as the basis of mutual defense.

In municipal society, an individual person need not take any action by him or herself, except in an emergency. In international society, there is no authority comparable to national government, so an individual state acts in the capacity of a social organ even under normal conditions. Mutual defense against aggression accomplishes the states' function in actions in the public capacity.

In the Gulf War in 1990, the multi-national forces took action in the Gulf region at the request of the Government of Kuwait in exile. They had no agreement on mutual assistance in the event of an armed attack, but experienced no difficulty in complying with the request of the victim to be freed from the invader.

The United Nations observed that the action of Iraq was an aggression to be responded against by enforcement measures. They were put into practice by authorizing the multi-national forces to take "all necessary means" to realize the preceding resolutions (Security Council Resolution 678, 29 November 1990).

The Security Council took such means under Chapter VII of the Charter. In taking such action, it did not fail to affirm the right of self-defense of all members, including members participating in the multi-national forces (Resolution 661, 6 August 1990).

The Charter has provisions on the use of regional arrangements and agencies (Chapter VIII), but is silent on the use of individual states' forces for enforcement action. The multi-national forces acted, in practice, as forces on regional arrangements in enforcement actions under the authority of the United Nations (art 53). The United Nations enforced its will by authorizing individual acts taken on the right of self-defense to be in accordance with the collective purposes.

Under present circumstances, an act on the basis of regional arrangements and by regional agencies is the same as an act by an individual state in that it is taken by forces organized exclusively by national governments. An act is collective not because it is taken by forces organized through collective procedure, but because it is taken by forces authorized to be collective.

In contrast, peacekeeping is a collective act as it is organized on the initiative of an international organization. The force may engage in enforcement, but is less powerful than multi-national forces based on the right of self-defense. It may act on the basis of the same right when faced with an armed attack.[72]

In view of the theory of collective security, it is irrelevant that the forces organized through collective procedure act on the right of self-defense instead of collective decisions. However, peacekeeping has not been so consolidated as a concept as to be classified as a collective activity. There is peacekeeping based on the right of self-defense on the one hand, and peacekeeping forces mobilized without reorganization for enforcement purposes on the other.

The United Nations Operations in Somalia expanded the original mandate of peacekeeping in order to bring its activities under Chapters VII and VIII of the Charter. It proved unsuccessful in achieving its original mandate of humanitarian relief operations even with the additional mandate, and eventually dissolved itself.[73]

To implement a collective decision, the most important thing is that forces of one or more powerful states are mobilized in compliance with the decision. Regional arrangements may be useful as they provide an impetus to such states to mobilize their forces. In spite of the Charter provision, the basis of the action of regional arrangements is self-defense rather than measures against the renewal of aggressive policy by enemy states. This is because regional arrangements place more importance upon regional interests than the general benefit of the suppression of aggressive policy. Amid these circumstances, no enforcement is practicable, except for self-defense action already taken, or yet to be taken, against a foreseeable armed attack.[74]

In the crisis of Bosnia-Herzegoniva in the former Yugoslavia, the United Nations Protection Force (UNPROFOR) was established in accordance with the United Nations' peacekeeping plan of 21 February 1992. The Security Cuoncil demanded that all conflicting parties cooperate with UNPROFOR, and decided to make all states suspend economic relations with the Federal Republic of Yugoslavia (Resolutions 752 on 15 May 1992 and 757 on 30 May 1992). These decisions were

---

[72] The Secretary-General asked the peacekeeping forces in Cyprus to act on the condition of self-defense when faced with danger in the discharge of their duty: see note 49.

[73] Recognizing the unique character of the situation in Somalia, the Security Council endorsed the recommendation of the Secretary-General that United Nations Operations should be enlarged in the original mandate of peacekeeping so their activities would come under Chapter VII of the Charter. It authorized the Secretary-General and member states to use all necessary means in order to establish a secure environment for humanitarian relief operations. Moreover, it called upon states to use such means under Chapter VIII of the Charter (Resolution 794, 3 December 1992). UNOSOM II, commencing in May 1993, failed to appease the situation in Somalia and ended in March 1995.

[74] In the Korean War, the United States was, in any case, prepared to send armies from Japan to defend South Korea. If the Security Council adopted no resolutions, she would insist on the right of collective self-defense to legalize the action before the United Nations. On the other hand, resolutions on the forcible exclusion of North Korea would not be effective if the United States were not engaging in armed activity, whatever the ground might be.

taken under Chapters VII and VIII of the Charter, with the intention of reinforcing UNPROFOR by making regional organizations, including NATO and individual states, join in the action.[75]

In authorizing all necessary means under Chapter VII of the Charter, the Security Council determined that the existence of "human tragedy [constituted] a threat to international peace and security" (Resolution 794, 3 December 1992). The humanitarian treatment of people may be too important to be left to the mercy of national governments, but is not provided in article 39 as a condition of enforcement in Chapter VII of the Charter.

In such cases as Nicaragua, Liberia and Yugoslavia, the Security Council did not censure forcible actions taken already on regional arrangements in the interest of regional stability in the absence of prior authorization. They did not adhere to the conditions of self-defense in taking coercive activities. This situation indicates that centralization of coercion in the hands of the Security Council is purely formal in international society.[76] It also demonstrates that the power situation in postwar international society has not been so simplified as to be legalized as either enforcement action under the authority of the Security Council or self-defense taken individually by states.

The North Atlantic Treaty Organization (NATO) acts to defend member states against armed attacks in exercise of the right of self-defense (art 5). In spite of this, NATO bombed Kosovo in the former Yugoslavia from 24 March to 10 June 1999, without the occurrence of an "armed attack" against any member state. It did not seek authorization by the Security Council, which would provide the basis for the bombardment in the absence of satisfaction of the conditions of self-defense.

In the view of the Charter provision, the hierarchical relationship between the Security Council and regional organizations in addressing disputes is not necessarily clear.[77] The case of the bombardment by NATO forces is not necessarily so much a violation of the Charter as a regional arrangement wrongly related to authorization by the Security Council. The problem is how strict an interpretation of provisions of the UN Charter is required for general and regional organizations acting for the prevention and removal of threats to peace.

The Security Council acted before and after the bombardment of NATO air forces in 1999 to force the people in Kosovo to desist from ethnic cleansing and other inhumane acts. The forcible acts of NATO may be acquiesced by the resolution of

---

[75] Some of the resolutions of the Security Council have provisions enabling members to take either Chapter VII or Chapter VIII as the basis of their actions. For example, the provisions of both Chapters VII and VIII are recalled in the preamble of the resolution authorizing member states acting through regional organizations or arrangements to take all necessary means. Resolution 816 on 31 March 1993 and Resolution 820 on 17 April 1993 have separate parts, A and B, corresponding to Chapters VIII and VII of the Charter.

[76] N.D. White, *Keeping the Peace*, 1997, p. 232.

[77] In taking a forcible action, regional organizations may construe article 53 of the Charter so liberally that it provides implied authorization by the Security Council: S.D. Murphy, *Humanitarian Intervention*, 1996, ch. 7, p. 335.

the Security Council adopted the very day it ceased (Resolution 1244), although it was not authorized beforehand.[78]

Ever since the restoration of peace through the defeat of challengers to the prewar international regime, the postwar international society has sought a system of response to breaches of the peace. Under this system, states have based individual and joint actions taken independently of the Security Council on self-defense, as the UN Charter recognizes that right as inherent. In any case, the basis of their argument in justifying their forcible actions is different from that in traditional international law.

It is often the case that NATO's air attack in 1999 is described as a lawful intervention to exclude inhumane acts in the interests of human society, taken aside from the conditions of the UN Charter.[79] It is a description based not on the postwar international legal regime as understood by the terms of the UN Charter, but on the concepts of traditional international law.

According to the announcement of the NATO authorities, the aerial attacks on Kosovo were exceptional and will never be used as a precedent.[80] In spite of this, the acts demonstrate the substance of collective security in an international legal regime under the predominance of the United Nations. According to the policy approved at the Summit meeting in April 1999, NATO may operate to respond to "some non-Article 5 crisis ... whether within or beyond Alliance territory."[81] As the policy indicates, NATO does not adhere to the inherency of the right to self-defense recognized by the UN Charter in taking a joint action independently of the Security Council.

b) Enforcement measures of the United Nations are institutionalized on the basis of the anti-enemy actions taken by the wartime alliance. They were taken on each regional arrangement under the general principle of anti-aggression. To balance the reality of regional measures with the general principle, self-defense is taken on condition of the occurrence of an "armed attack." That is to say, the expression "self-defense" connotes that the international order is dependent upon the efficacy of regional conduct.

Among the main enemies, West Germany became independent conditional upon its membership of NATO, a regional defense organization established in 1949 and

---

78 The use of force is regarded as having been implicitly authorized in six international incidents to date, namely, India's seizure of Goa from Portugal in 1961, America's prohibition on Soviet ships in 1962, Israel's air strike on the Iraqi nuclear reactor in 1981, the use of force in Liberia in 1990, the joint action of the United States, Britain and France in providing safe havens to refugees and enforcing no-fly zones in Iraq in 1991, and the American demands for a mandatory inspection regime in Iraq in 1998. As a matter of course, NATO's air attack in 1999 is not counted: J. Lobel and M. Ratner, "Bypassing the Security Council: Ambiguous Authorizations to Use of Force, Cease-fires and the Iraq Inspection Regime," 93*AJ* 1999, p. 131.

79 Regarding the series of arguments for and against humanitarian intervention, see 93 *AJ*, 1999, pp. 825–860.

80 The Secretary-General of NATO stated that the action taken without any basis in the UN Charter was an exception and made no precedent in international law: Solana, J.,"NATO's success in Kosovo," *Foreign Affairs*, November/December 1999, p. 114.

81 The Alliance's Strategic Concept, approved in Washington on 23–24 April 1999.

comprising West European states, the United States and Canada. In order to deal with this situation, the Warsaw Pact was concluded in 1955, bringing the former East European Axis, Hungary, Bulgaria and Romania into affiliation with the Soviet Bloc.

The Korean War from 25 June 1950 to 27 July 1953 led to the conclusion of the US-Japan Security Treaty, agreed in San Francisco on 8 September 1951.

Membership of the United Nations was closed to "enemy" states, including Germany and Japan, so there was no common basis other than self-defense among the parties to those treaties. The central powers of each arrangement were the main Allied Nations. They would defend the former enemies not through the system of general international organization, but through exercise of the agreed arrangements on the right of self-defense. Under those circumstances, what threatened international society was not a renewal of aggressive policy by the former enemies, but conflicts between newly created regions of the East and West, the centers of which were Moscow and Washington.

The end of the Cold War revealed a scene of international society veiled by confrontations between East and West. The Nuclear Non-Proliferation Treaty system is threatened by additional nuclear powers, including India and Pakistan. As states holding nuclear arms are not keen to disarm, the Treaty system will continue to deteriorate rather than strengthen.

Regional systems are not satisfied with being subject to the condition of self-defense in action, as was proclaimed in the "non-article 5 crisis response operations" by NATO following its action in Kosovo. Germany has been an integral member of NATO, and will participate in the event of "enforcement" overstepping self-defense against an armed attack on a member's territory.

Japan is not a member of any regional security organization, but is a partner to the United States on the basis of the US-Japan Security Treaty. Aside from the difference of arrangements, in accordance with which they defend themselves in cooperation with foreign countries, Japan will be in the same position as Germany in engaging in "enforcements" overstepping self-defense.

The United Nations is a general international organization, but has no exclusive competence for the security of all its members. Japan places more importance on the US-Japan Security Treaty than the United Nations, just as Germany does with NATO. On the other hand, Japan is consistent in seeking reform of the United Nations in order to assume impartial responsibility matched by financial burdens.[82]

To continue to be the only general international organization from now on, the United Nations cannot avoid reforms in its structure to meet the changed and changing circumstances in international society. The reforms must be made recognizing that "enemy states" have been an integral part of the institution as well as the fact that regional activities will continue to be the basis of effective operations. In this respect, the text of the UN Charter is too antiquated to guide members of international society in acting in the present situation.

---

[82] Japan's financial contribution to the United Nations had, by the 1990s, exceeded the total amount paid by the permanent members of the Security Council, excluding the United States.

In increasing activities on the initiative of each region, the international order originating in the wartime coalition of the Allied Nations will require adjustment to meet the future needs of international society. The result will be a weakening of ideological intolerance stemming from the wartime alliance and an increase in the multiplicity of values and cultures to meet the borderless intercourse of individual people and enterprises.

No one can deny, in discussing the international order for the coming age, that self-defense is no longer a concept for making it practical. This is because self-defense is a concept connected inseparably with the system brought by the Allied Nations to international society after the Second World War. In contrast, freedom of conscience, the principle on which traditional international law developed, should be resurrected on the ground that ideological confrontations would bring a new style of religious warfare. However, it is uncertain whether the United Nations will take freedom of conscience into consideration in strengthening itself this century.[83]

Enforcement measures are seen as having no limitation as to their means since the ultimate victory of the Allied Nations over their enemy was won by the use of nuclear weapons in August 1945. The American monopoly on nuclear weapons soon ended and they proliferated among the other four nuclear powers. In the late twentieth century, another two states became nuclear powers. It will not be long before the Nuclear Non-Proliferation Treaty, adopted in 1968, is almost ineffective as a result of further proliferation of the weapon among other states.

The day will also soon come when the device of placing certain states in the position of "police," in the form of positions of permanent membership of the Security Council distributed according to their ideological contributions to victory in War, is invalidated. No one can predict which will occur first: validation of the device or destruction of the globe as a result of the failure to construct an effective system to meet the existing needs of international society.

4. Ensuring Humanitarian Principles

(1) A collective system involving a decline in humanitarian principles

a) Municipal law consists of public and civil law. In contrast, international law has long been believed to be a civil law system as it is law among nations positioned on an equal footing with each other.

Civil law is characterized by the concept of self-help and is realized by retaliatory acts to injuries made in violation of it. In any society, the ultimate means of recovering rights is force, whether exercised individually or by society as a whole. In international society, power is decentralized in each state, whereas in municipal society, the government monopolizes power. International law is thus realized through individual responses to the contravention of the rights and benefits guaranteed under it.

---

83 United Nations Millennium Declaration, adopted by the General Assembly on 8 September 2000.

In municipal law, a decline in the civil element or rise in the public law is nothing more than an increase in the role of government. In international law, a decline in the civil element is the incapacitation of individual states in taking free means of recovering their rights and interests. It is an effect of the renunciation of war established by treaties after the First World War, including the War Renunciation Pact.

However, no states took the view that the Pact invalidated every aspect of the law of war, law of neutrality, and *jus in bello* in particular. Much less, they believed that the Pact made the recovery of their rights impossible by depriving them of the ultimate means of achieving it.

It was the practice of non-belligerency developed between the two great wars that convinced them of the invalidation of the law of war. The practice of the Second World War made the invalidation conclusive. Few states remained neutral throughout the War, and *jus in bello* did not prevent states from being totally destroyed or ceasing to exist.

Under the United Nations, which is a creation on the practice of non-belligerency and world war, there is no legitimate place for *jus in bello.* It was a situation that traditional international law did not foresee as its original task is *temperamenta belli,* for the purpose of which *jus in bello* has been developed.

The law of war is composed of *jus ad bellum* on the one hand and *jus in bello* on the other. It is characteristic of traditional international law that the two parts of the law of war are harmonious enough to ensure the survival of the sovereign state system under the principle of free recourse to war.

Under the strict condition of *jus ad bellum*, a state engaging in an armed action is, so to speak, either a state engaging in a sanction with the status of "the public" or a sanctioned state subject to the action with the status of "civilian" in international society. A state acting under "public" authority and the rest are not given equal legal capacity. The former might well be liberated from the obligations of *jus in bello* discriminatorily, as was practiced in the state of non-belligerency in which the law of war and neutrality was applied discriminatorily against "the aggressors."

Neither the Atlantic Charter nor the Charter of the United Nations disregards the rules of international law, the validity of which is confirmed by the Charter provisions (art 1 para 1). In spite of this, the situation in the period immediately following the War was that the international normative regime, including the law of war and neutrality, was rightly observed to be in a chaotic state.[84]

In a system where *jus ad bellum* is so intensified as to be consistent with *jus in bello,* there can be no principle of freedom of conscience or tolerance for different ideologies. Nevertheless, coexistence between *jus ad bellum* and *jus in bello* is possible in such a system because traditional international law, an integral part of such a system, is a system of conciliation of doctrines believed to be inconsistent with each other.

So long as the system of conciliation of doctrines is valid, no destruction involving

[84] J. Kunz, "The Chaotic Status of Law of War and the Urgent Necessity for Their Revision," *op. cit.*, ch. 41.

loss of national sovereignty occurs as a result of warfare. The Allies' actions may have been defensive against their enemies in some part, but they were punitive for the most part, as was declared in the Cairo Declaration in 1943, stating, "The Three Great Allies are fighting this war to restrain and punish the aggression of Japan."

The United Nations, an international organization formulated on such Allies' practice, came to incorporate elements of public law in it, unlike traditional international law, which was based solely on civil law doctrine. Under the organization, no member state may follow "civil law procedure" or procedure of traditional international law in order to give precedence to the "public" purposes in dealing with the item on the agenda.

That does not mean that the international organization holds itself responsible for recovery of the rights of all member states. On the contrary, it is for each member to realize the "public" purposes in accordance with the organizational decisions. In such a situation where each state takes collective actions, there could be no invalidation of *jus in bello*, despite the practice of invalidation in the state of non-belligerency and the state of war.

Under the League system, any forcible action taken in its name could be no more than a war of sanction or war made in *justa causa*. As long as it is fought as a "war," it is executed under regulations of the law of war or *jus in bello*, although distinguished to be a "war for sanction" or "just war" in the light of *jus ad bellum*. This forms a contrast with the Second World War, which was fought as a war for punishment as distinct from a war in the traditional sense, with little regulation by the law of war or *jus in bello*.

Collective measures under the UN Charter are taken to promote the public interest in maintenance of "international peace and security." They are beyond the function of the Covenant 16 of the League of Nations as they are taken for broader purposes than sanction, which is a response only to "threats to the peace" and "breaches of the peace" (UN Charter, art 39).[85]

The postwar international legal regime, a large part of which has been incorporated into the system of the United Nations, was deduced from the practice of excluding aggressors or challengers to the preceding international regime. The result is a system prohibiting use of force in general, reserving forcible actions for either self-defense or collaboration with enforcement actions. As far as the system is an exact reproduction of the War practice, it must be sufficiently positive to maintain international peace and security in postwar international society.

The postwar international legal regime has traditional international law as one part, though it is not as important as the system of the United Nations. The problem is how each part interacts to improve the regime, which was incomplete in its original formulation.

---

85 In contrast to the LN Covenant, the UN Charter uses the word "security" 32 times, following the terms of the Moscow Declaration in 1943: J.F. Dulles, "A First Balance Sheet of the United Nations," 420 *IC*, 1946, p. 183.

b) Theoretically speaking, aggressors are not equal in claiming rights in belligerent actions in opposition to the "just powers." The practice of the Second World War endorses this theory in denying the "enemy states" full rights to *jus in bello*. However, the postwar international regime, a substantial part of which has been incorporated into the United Nations, is open to the question of how it compensates for the invalidation of the law of war to prevent destruction and inhumanity from recurring on any pretext.

As belligerent states are divided into the just and the unjust, so they can be discriminatory in enjoying rights in taking forcible action, depending on the side to which they belong. However, a discriminatory application of *jus in bello* is impracticable because the positive basis of *jus in bello* is on mutual contract subject to common regulation. No state would unilaterally subject itself to regulation to which another state would not.

If an enforcement action were taken as the Charter intended originally, the United Nations would enforce the collective decision, with overwhelming power over the opposite party. It would bring about a complete realization of what the decision intended, with greater destruction on both sides, as was the case with the Second World War.

When the Korean War broke out in June 1950, it was generally accepted that states engaging in enforcement were not on an equal footing to the sanctioned with respect to the application of *jus in bello*.[86] As a matter of fact, however, most hostile actions were taken on the basis of *jus in bello,* such as regarding the treatment of prisoners of war. The parties to the hostilities in Korea treated each prisoner according to the Geneva Conventions signed one year before the outbreak of war.

The United Nations came to encourage members to subject themselves to *jus in bello* in the late 1960s, when it came to realize that enforcement in the precise manner envisaged by the Charter was not possible. *Jus in bello* was recognized to be consistent with the Charter, and construed to be humanitarian law in an armed conflict.[87]

Recognition of *jus in bello* is concomitant with a decrease in the importance of *jus ad bellum* in the activities of the United Nations. After the conclusion of the Cold War, enforcement came to be practical by authorizing individual states to take necessary measures in order to realize the intent of the UN Charter. In fact, there have been several cases in which an enforcement action under Chapter VII of the Charter has been taken through authorization of an individual action.[88]

In the Gulf War of 1990, the aggressor was forced to evacuate the occupied area, Kuwait, by great powers including the United States, who were authorized to take all necessary measures to realize the UN decisions. It was a case of complete success in realizing a collective purpose by the use of force. Nevertheless, it was individual states that brought the collective purpose to realization. Moreover, *jus ad bellum* embodied in

---

[86] See Chap. 1 note 48.

[87] See Report of Secretary General A/7575, 1 July 1969.

[88] See note 73.

the collective decisions was not completely realized as the action of the multinational forces did not result in resignation of the government of the aggressor state.

Peacekeeping is an operation after the conflicting parties have agreed on equal terms to a ceasefire. Peacekeeping can be reinforced so as to allow the forces to engage in enforcement action, as was the case with the peacekeeping in Somalia in 1992. According to the terms of reference of the Secretary-General issued in the instance of peacekeeping in Cyprus, peacekeeping forces may act against an armed attack in a manner not exceeding self-defense.[89] There would be no enforcement in the true sense when it was taken on the right of self-defense inherent to member states, even though it was taken by United Nations Forces.

There is also the case of collective action being taken in a different way from what is provided by the UN Charter. This is the case where an act is based on a decision that does not clearly authorize the sanction. The North Atlantic Treaty Organization took forcible action in Kosovo in the former Yugoslavia in 1999 to realize a series of resolutions by the UN Security Council requiring an improvement in the inhumane circumstances in that area.

In such a case, an act is taken without full conviction that it is enforcement. This case is highly probable under the present circumstance that it is difficult for a general international organization to make such a decision, but another international organization or regional one does it on the basis of the solidarity of that particular region. In most cases where regional organizations take an action on the basis of self-defense, there is no problem in applying *jus in bello* to it from either a theoretical or practical standpoint.

The situations in which belligerent actions start and develop with recourse to the right to self-defense on the basis of regional agreements are, in most cases, desirable rather than deplorable from the standpoint of humanity. As was practiced in the Second World War, an anti-aggressive action may end in total destruction by the use of every possible means of hostility. If the Charter had been discussed after the nuclear bombardments of Japanese cities in August 1945, it may have had more restraints on enforcement actions and more provisions on disarmament, as the Covenant of the League of Nations did.

The International Court of Justice gave an advisory opinion in 1996 that the threat or use of nuclear weapons would generally be contrary to the rules of international law applicable in armed conflicts and the principles and rules of humanitarian law. However, it did not conclude decisively as to whether the threat or use of nuclear weapons would be lawful or unlawful in an extreme circumstance of self-defense in which the very survival of a state was at stake.[90]

The opinion is incorrect in hesitating to declare the illegality of nuclear attacks in the course of actions in self-defense. A nuclear attack is practiced in the course of enforcement taken by one party with overwhelming power over the other and with the clear intention of making a sanction. However, it has not been practiced since

---

[89] See note 49.

[90] Advisory opinion of the International Court of Justice, 8 July 1996, para 105.

1945, partly because it is so hazardous and partly because it cannot be reconciled with actions in self-defense.

Self-defense may be authorized as enforcement, but is still bound by *jus in bello*, which is applied indiscriminately to all belligerents. It is the general way of forcible actions after the War, so *jus in bello* may well be encouraged as the basis of any armed actions, including enforcement. In fact, the United Nations has, since the 1960s, taken the policy of developing "humanitarian law," which comprises the series of the Hague Conventions in 1907, Protocol for the Prohibition of Poisonous Gases in 1925, Geneva Conventions in 1949, and Protocols Additional to Them in 1977.

Under these circumstances, there is no support for legalization of the use of weapons of mass destruction.[91] This situation is different from that of total war fought for an ideological cause inconsistent with that of the enemy. To win a war, any belligerent would use every means available at the time, with no regard to international law, which is an achievement of human civilization. The Axis states would not have hesitated to use nuclear weapons had there been no technological barrier to their doing so. It was natural that traditional international law did not survive such a war fought without any supposition of freedom of conscience.

So long as the system of the United Nations is an exact formulation of the acts in the Second World War, it is conceived as the "public" entity of international society. It goes without saying that the "public" system is more severe in its treatment of violators than "civil law," in which humanitarian treatment may hardly be possible in the interest of public purposes.

The fact is that the postwar international regime is enforced differently from the strict provisions of the UN Charter. As long as its practices are maintained, the United Nations will not force its ideology upon states whose ideology is conceived differently. Under these circumstances, humanitarian treatment develops, as the Charter structure of enforcement returns to the traditional way of conducting transactions between sovereign states.

Viewed in this light, the postwar international regime is recognized to adopt the following elements: disarmament of weapons of mass destruction, including nuclear weapons; development of *jus in bello* or humanitarian law at the time of armed conflicts; peaceful co-existence in the face of opposing ideologies, such as occurred during the Cold War; and consistency between agencies and arrangements on a regional scale, upon which collaborations for security develop most efficiently. They would not be developed without the wartime doctrine found in provisions of the Charter and some practices thereon lessening their strictness.

It is no coincidence that the "enemy clauses" of the Charter are invalidated side

[91] Treaties prohibiting destructive weapons, including the Convention on the Prohibition of Bacteriological and Toxin Weapons in 1972 and the Convention on the Prohibition of Chemical Weapons in 1993, have been concluded, following the Hague Conventions in 1898 and 1907. International humanitarian law has been used to discuss these treaties since the United Nations has come to recognize the need for the development of the law of war in the name of humanitarian law in armed conflicts.

by side with impracticality of the Charter structure of enforcement. It may be a result of enemies' total destruction rather than a revival of freedom of conscience. Whichever is the case, the principal members of the United Nations made a compromise with the former enemies beforehand by concluding regional agreements on the basis of self-defense and accepting them into the general international organization as important members.

In this context, it is "enemy states," including Japan and Germany, that have driven the postwar international regime to the present situation, apart from the undeniable fact that the principal executors were the creators of the regime, the Allied Nations.

(2) Self-defense as a modification of ideological characteristics

The members of the United Nations take either an act of self-defense or act against the resurrection of enemy states, free from prior authorization by the Security Council. Self-defense is an individual act conditional upon the occurrence of an armed attack. An act against the "enemy" is not altogether individual, but something public, as enforcement in Chapter VII of the Charter originates from it. The conjugation between the two sorts of act is possible as they have the "public" aspect in common.

Members who are exposed to a threat of the resurrection of enemy states may take action against that enemy, while self-defense is open to every member state. The two concepts differ in that an act against the enemy is released from *jus in bello*, while all other armed acts, including self-defense, are taken under the obligation of *jus in bello*. This difference has been dissolved, partly because every armed action comes under the regulation of "humanitarian law" or *jus in bello* and partly because all armed acts tend to be taken in self-defense.

This is recognition of the fact that states acting under "public" authority are equal to "aggressors" in their need of humanitarian treatment of persons in armed conflicts. It is different from the practice of non-belligerency, in which the law of war and neutrality is applied discriminatorily against "the aggressors."

On the other hand, with respect to *jus ad bellum,* the "chaotic" situation would not disappear unless the rigidity of the "public" character in the international regime was modified. Originally, the United Nations was too ideologically oriented to be a general international organization. This character was disputed between the proposing states and the others at the Conference on International Organization in San Francisco, and this dispute was only brought to an end by the provision of self-defense in the Charter.[92]

International law had developed into a general system of international society in the course of the progress of European civilization by the time the Great War began. It may have been the process of integrating "non-civilized" or colonized nations into

---

[92] Stipulation of "the inherent right of self-defense" is a compromise for "world" organization in order to avoid it disappearing: Dulles, *War or Peace*, p. 91.

the domain of European civilization. It was also the process of generalizing the concepts of respect of life, liberty, independence, religious freedom, human rights and justice, most of which were original to European civilization. The United Nations will need to run the whole course of the generalization of international law or European civilization to be humanitarian on the principle of tolerance.

Self-defense is rooted in the municipal legal system, which is based on civil relations among persons. The international legal regime has modified the rigidity of "public" character by incorporating self-defense into it. As this modification progresses, states will come to fall within the jurisdiction of international law rather than a collective system, the principle of which cannot necessarily be reconciled with traditional principles. They would be afforded less protection by collective security if they depart from the principles, but be compensated with easier participation in a regional system based on the right of self-defense.

Between the two ways of exemption from prior authorization by the Security Council in taking forcible action, self-defense and acts against the enemy, it is a logical consequence that only self-defense is available to the "enemy states." As traditional international law, including the procedures of peace conference and peace treaty, is impractical, conclusion of an arrangement on self-defense, whether bilaterally or multilaterally, is the only possible way for such states to be placed in an ordinary position in international society.

This is the present stage in the development of the international regime unavoidably accepted by every nation. This fact will be proved further by the process of Japan's integration into the international regime, which originates in the practice of the Second World War she fought as a main belligerent.

CHAPTER 3

A POSTWAR INTERNATIONAL REGIME CHARACTERIZED BY "ENEMY" STATUS

I. "Enemy" Status Resulting from the Invalidation of Traditional International Law

a) Under traditional international law, the belligerent against whom a state is fighting is accorded the status of "enemy". During the course of war, belligerents act in accordance with the law of war, as distinct from the law applying during peacetime. Their hostile acts cease according to military and political circumstances, but peaceful relations are not restored until a peace conference is convened at the earliest opportunity after the ceasefire. The conference concludes with a peace treaty giving legal expression to the new power structure resulting from the war.

Prior to the Second World War, any international regime conceived after a war assumed that the vanquished party would serve as a balancer in the new power structure. This was the case with the recovery of peace in Europe after the Napoleonic War, the legal basis of which was provided by the Vienna Conventions in 1815 concluded between the parties to the War, namely Austria, Prussia, Russia, Great Britain and France. It was also the case with the recovery of international order at the Paris Conference in 1856 after the Crimean War, which had been fought to change the power relations in the Middle East, particularly between Russia and Turkey.

The traditional procedure of ending wars is a reflection of the civil law framework of the international legal regime in which vanquished states are placed on an equal footing with the victorious as parties to the transaction. The First World War may have differed from previous wars in excluding the vanquished states from consultations on the framing of the postwar regime, but was no exception from tradition insofar as the consent of every member of the society to it was obtained through the conclusion of a peace treaty. Peace treaties such as the Versailles Treaty with Germany were legal proof of the renewed power balance between Germany and the other parties to the War.

Under the changed circumstances of the Second World War, peace negotiations among belligerents have been reduced to being merely nominal, as enemies have no ground upon which to be consulted on the terms of the termination of war. This demonstrates the fact that international society has lost its civil law base whereby no act has legal effect in the absence of agreement between the parties to it.

It also indicates that the Second World War was fought on different conditions from preceding wars, including the First World War.

First of all, wars were traditionally fought between legitimate forces comprising soldiers who had enlisted according to national law. They followed orders in engaging in hostile action, with little personal antagonism towards the enemy. The warfare developed between such parties was limited to actions against the opposing legitimate forces. Civilians escaped from the action and suffered little damage from it since it was a matter between the legitimate armies.

Secondly, war was fought to achieve the political aims of states, including the enhancement of national honor, expansion of territory, interests and influence, and so forth. It ceased when they achieved their goal or stopped pursuing it. For example, the war in continental Europe from 1740 to 1763 resulted from issues relating to succession to the Austrian throne, and ended on condition of principles of *status quo ante bellum*, which was confirmed at peace conferences in Hubertusburg and Paris.[1]

Thirdly, war was fought by means too limited to destroy the enemy completely. As long as the means of war remained limited, such wars needed to end in compromise, with the political structure, religion and civilization remaining as they had been. Non-European civilized nations ceased to exist because they had no means, physically or normatively, to deter their enemies from fighting destructive warfare against them.

It was inevitable that the postwar regime conceived after a war fought in quite a different way from before would be revolutionary in its construction. The regime would be impractical and ineffective unless it departed from the most recent practices in international society.

In light of the changed circumstances, the postwar international regime was conspicuous in the following respects:

The Second World War was fought on the home front as well as on the battlefield. Civilians were mobilized to support military activities utilizing the latest innovations in scientific knowledge and technology. Their property and everyday lives were open to attack due to the enemy's intention of cutting supplies to the legitimate armies fighting at the battlefront. Under such circumstances, sentiment against the enemy ran so high that civilians were prepared to take hostile action of their own free will.

It is in this situation that atrocities are committed against civilians in the occupied territory under the pretext of the maintenance of public order. Civilians respond with retaliatory action of their own, bringing about unprecedented inhumanity.

After filling their people with antagonism against the enemies, the belligerent governments would not cease the action on condition of *status quo ante bellum*, but rather insist on *debellatio* on the part of the enemy. The difficulty for them in ending such a war in compromise would lead them to destroy the enemy totally, if not cease fire by unconditional surrender.

---

1 Austria and Prussia struggled over Silesia, and Britain and France struggled over overseas territories in India and the American continent. The former struggle was settled in accordance with exact principles, while the latter was done in such a way as to benefit Britain discriminatorily.

As a result of war fought in such a manner, there is no need for a peace conference as peace is not recovered in a balance of power with the vanquished enemies. Having no chance to clear away their war relations as a whole, they leave treaties, declarations, and understandings directed against the enemies in wartime valid until after the cessation of hostilities. The "enemy" states have been perpetuated in the postwar international organization created on the initiative of the victorious states, as their name is fixed in the United Nations Charter, the constituent instrument of "general international organization of the Allied Nations."

In the case of the Russo-Japanese War, the conditions of peace were negotiated in a neutral country, the United States, through the mediation of the President. After settlement of the negotiations, an armistice was agreed, peace conference convened, and peace treaty concluded on 5 September 1905. Under the Treaty, their peaceful relations were recovered on condition of the withdrawal of each force from the occupied area (including Manchuria and the northern part of Sakhalin) and transfer of some territory and interests.

A peace treaty provides for disarmament, reparations and the treatment of war criminals in addition to the transfer of territory and interests. It is an expression of the postwar international regime as well as a clearing away of wartime relations, especially when war is fought on a global scale. All are settled by negotiation between the belligerents, including the vanquished states. In drafting the Covenant of the League of Nations, which was an integral part of the Versailles Peace Treaty ending the First World War, the belligerents listened to the opinions of neutrals who were incapacitated to participate in the peace conference.

The scheme following the Second World War was consolidated before the cessation of hostilities, without being negotiated by all the belligerents. According to the Potsdam Declaration issued on 26 July 1945, Japan had no alternative but to accept the terms of peace dictated by the three main Allies; otherwise she would be utterly destroyed (para 13). The terms included the matters to be negotiated at a peace conference, including the transfer of territory and interests, disarmament, reparations and treatment of war criminals, if the War ended in the conventional way. The nuclear bombings following the Declaration were proof that it was not mere rhetoric, but a schedule to be implemented once she refused to accept the Declaration.[2]

In the light of history, it was not exceptional that one party fell into total destruction as a result of war with an overwhelming enemy since non-European civilized nations fell into *debellatio* in the fight against European powers. By contrast, no states within the European Family fell into total destruction as long as war was fought according to the Law of Family of Nations.[3] This was an effect of

---

2 Japanese military leaders' plans for a decisive battle fought by civilians on the Japanese mainland, as had been fought in Okinawa until June 1945, to bring the final chance of victory proved impracticable as land warfare turned out to be an unnecessary strategy for the United States once she put nuclear weapons to practical use.

3 Annexation of countries of European origin into the British Empire as a result of the war in South Africa from 1899 to 1902 might be an exception to the rule.

membership of the European Civilized Family, which was granted even to non-European civilized nations on condition of their "westernization" and ensured that a state would not fall into subjugation as a result of war.

Ideological dissidence is more critical than differences of civilization, as proven by the struggle between the Bolshevists and the counter revolutionists, and between the Nazis and the anti-Nazis. It is worse when the application of advanced technology to warfare drives non-believers to physical annihilation.

If a state is outlawed by reason of either its civilization or ideology, then its nationals are placed outside legal protection in the armed struggle. As the government is too helpless to protect its nationals, they come to distrust the legal regime based on state sovereignty. Instead of placing their hopes on the national government, they direct their attention towards "world government" or its counterpart, general international organization. This is a key to understanding the sentiment of the Japanese people towards the United Nations after the Second World War, even though it was conceived and created by their wartime enemies and one of its purposes was to prevent "a renewal of their aggressive policy."

b) The Allied Nations made peace with the East European Axis states by 1947, but would not, contrary to the practice of traditional international law, commence peace negotiations with Germany and Japan. A temporary solution was reached in relation to the territory of the two German regimes, which remained in effect until their reunification in 1990.

According to the Potsdam Declaration issued by the United States, China and Great Britain on 26 July 1945 and defining the terms of Japanese surrender, "Until such a new order is established and until there is convincing proof that Japan's war-making power is destroyed, points in Japanese territory to be designated by the Allies shall be occupied to secure the achievement of the basic objectives we are here setting forth" (para 7). It depends on the termination of occupation, or making peace with Japan, upon accomplishment of the aim of occupation set by the Allied Nations.

The entire claim against Japan could have been accomplished in substance at the time of her acceptance of the Potsdam Declaration since a turning of the tide of war in her favor was hardly conceivable. Among the basic objectives stated in the Declaration, transfer of the territories in accordance with paragraph 8 was almost realized, as the Allied Forces seized all Japanese territory, including the mainland, soon after the Declaration was accepted.

Assuming the validity of traditional international law, however, armed entry to land in the course of warfare does not necessarily result in a legal transfer of that territory to the occupier. A peace treaty creates legal possession of some occupied land. The withdrawal of occupation forces from other land is realized if it is acceptable to the victorious states from the standpoint of the balance of power. Peace in San Francisco in 1952 brought no withdrawal of Allied forces from Japanese territory, including the mainland, because that would have threatened the balance of power in the Far East.

The Japanese believe the seizure of certain parts of her territory by her former enemy, Russia, who was excluded from the Peace Treaty signed in 1951, was unjustified. In their opinion, the Soviets should have withdrawn from them as soon as the objective of the Potsdam Declaration was fulfilled since they are the native lands of Japanese nationals, of which the Cairo Declaration of 27 November 1943, integrated into the Potsdam Declaration, declares they are not to be deprived.[4]

If she had the chance to conclude a peace treaty with Russia in accordance with the traditional rules of international law, she would argue the inherency of "the four Northern Islands" in response to the *uti possidetis* claimed by the Russians.[5] It would be too much to expect the Russians to take the exact same view on the existing legal situation.

In view of the fact that the Allies made peace with the East European Axis by 1947, peace could also have been achieved with the two main Axis states, Germany and Japan, provided they adhered to the traditional procedures of international law. The fact is that they placed more importance on the power situation around Germany and Japan, the increasing confrontations between East and West, or the split of the Allied Nations than the traditional procedure of making peace.[6]

This forms a contrast with the way in which territories were disposed as a result of the First World War. A peace conference was held following the armistice, the most hotly disputed issue of which was distribution of the deprived territories. In the changed situation of the Second World War, the most important subject at a peace conference, if one could have been convened, would have been the status of the enemies after occupation.

b) In spite of the Charter provision that the United Nations is based on rules and principles of international law, including the principle of the sovereign equality of states (art 1 para 1 and art 2 para 1), the structure and doctrine of the postwar international regime are not necessarily consistent with traditional international law. In the system of the United Nations, the "enemy states" are, as a result of two articles of the Charter, placed unequally in an exceptional position in relation to the Organization and its members (arts 53 and 107).

Article 107 of the Charter provides that "nothing in the present Charter shall invalidate or preclude action, in relation to any state which during the Second World War has been an enemy of any signatory to the present Charter, taken or authorized as a result of that war by the Government having responsibility for such action." Article 53 states that enforcement action may exceptionally be taken without

---

4 The Cairo Declaration states, "They (the United States, Great Britain and China) covet no gain for themselves and have no thought of territorial expansion." Japan believes there is no valid reason for her being deprived of the two disputed Kurile Islands and two other islands off Hokkaido since they have never belonged to any country other than Japan.

5 At the peace conference held by the Western Allies in San Francisco in September 1951, Japan renounced the Kurile Islands without reservation, although the Japanese chief delegate mentioned the specific status of the two southern islands.

6 Civil war in China resulted in the birth of the Communist regime in place of the Nationalists. Even Western nations were divided into supporters of the Nationalists, including the United States, and those who recognized the Communist regime, including the United Kingdom.

authorization of the Security Council provided it is taken under regional arrangements directed against a renewal of aggressive policy on the part of an enemy state.

Those provisions of the Charter might be reasoned on the assumption of "public law" in relations between the Allies and their enemies. In fact, there was such practice as the Axis states' personnel were discriminately punished for war crimes through a procedure unilaterally established by the Allied Nations. However, it does not justify all the Allies' acts of discrimination against their enemies as the Charter is not so comprehensive as to provide a ground for all relations between them. States are still subject to the rule of sovereign equality in other international fields, just as people are subject to both civil and public law in municipal society. The Charter does not deny the fact that members are under the rule of sovereign equality in addition to the rule of collective security.

Under the international regime, any member may be placed in a discriminatory position by being counted among the "enemy states." Under traditional international law, enemy states have the chance to alter the discrimination since the peace treaty comes into effect on condition of the consent of all the belligerents. Japan was denied the chance of restoring her territorial rights in relation to Russia because of the struggle for leadership of postwar politics among the victors.

However, the postwar international regime is sufficiently dynamic to extend, through the functions of the Security Council, the scope of "enemy" status beyond the former opponents of the Allied Nations, or original members of the United Nations, to other states regarded as aggressors.[7] If the United Nations based every act on the exact provisions of the Charter, then it would be unable to address the most serious crises in the world at that time.

Immediately after the conclusion of legitimate battles between the Allies and the Axis states, uprisings occurred in the dependent regions of some Allies, including the United Kingdom, France and The Netherlands, claiming independence from them. This is a problem in the gray area of the UN Charter as the Charter has no positive provision on colonial peoples and areas. It is too serious a matter to be excluded from the jurisdiction of the United Nations on account of the domestic jurisdiction of member states (Charter, art 2 para 7).

Hostile actions between legitimate armies may cease on the directive of the United Nations. However, intergovernmental organizations cannot end "wars for national liberation" fought by illegitimate forces by directives of their home governments. Under these circumstances, acts of the Security Council in accordance with Chapter VII of the Charter are not effective enough to recover international peace, though the situation may be deemed to be "threats to the peace" or "breaches of the peace" under article 39 of the Charter.

---

[7] The enemy clauses of the UN Charter are a record that the Second World War was the "public" settlement of the conflicts between the Allies and the Axis states. It was in this context that the representative of the Soviet Union stated in the Sixth Committee of the General Assembly on 19 November 1975 that "the enemy clauses" did not need to be removed because they were a reflection of the historical fact of German Nazism and Japanese militarism.

The term "wars of national liberation" was born in the war regions of the Second World War. It was in this context that the problem was treated in relation to enemy states, which had been given a definite status in the Charter provisions.

As soon as the Security Council was organized in London in early 1946, Ukraine put "the aggression of Japan, the United Kingdom and Holland against Indonesia" on the Council's agenda.[8]

Iran brought up for discussion the issue of the withdrawal of Soviets troops from her territory in accordance with the agreement between them. The Soviets' counter demand was that British troops be withdrawn from Greece, which had been placed under her occupation for the same purpose as the Allies' garrison in Iran.[9]

Notwithstanding that the United Nations excluded both internal matters and enemy matters from its jurisdiction, it dealt with disposition of the Italian territories, the US trusteeship of the Japanese Pacific Islands, the independence and reunification of Korea detached from Japanese rule, and the Berlin situation. All would be dealt with at peace conferences if traditional international law remained valid. Assuming the validity of traditional international law, however, they were too dynamic to be solved under the jurisdiction of a peace conference limited to issues relating to the war just terminated.

Under these circumstances, there is no place other than the United Nations where problems relating to enemy states can be discussed, despite the fact that article 107 of the Charter excludes the matter of peace with "the enemies" from its jurisdiction.[10] This indicates that traditional rules of international society, including those of peace conferences, have lost their social basis, and the United Nations is the only forum to guide the behavior of states in any field of international security after the Second World War.

Taking all of these circumstances into consideration, Japan may well claim rights as a state in transactions with the Allied Nations. In contrast to Germany, which fell into *debellatio* in the course of belligerent action, she would find the chance to argue her rights on the occasion of a peace conference. In the absence of such occasion, Japan has had no other means of multilateral negotiation on her rights than deliberations by the international organization of the Allied Nations, although she is excluded from membership of it.

This may be a natural consequence of the aspiration of the United Nations to be "the world government" after partial invalidation of the principle of sovereign equality on which traditional international law developed. As far as the "enemy states" were concerned, it was in the system of the United Nations that they expected to be treated suitably for their true ability, although they may feel hopeless in light of the terms of the Charter provisions.

---

8 Ukraine maintained that Dutch military operations, in which regular British troops and Japanese forces also participated, were directed against the local population: *Repertoire* 1946-1951, p. 302.

9 See chapter 1, note 62.

10 Indeed, the Italian Peace Treaty entrusted the deal with Italian colonies to four Allied Powers (art 23). The problem was ultimately brought to the General Assembly of the United Nations after the four powers failed to reach agreement.

2. Rehabilitation of an "Enemy" State on the Basis of the Allies' Ideals

(1) The Constitution of Japan 1946 in the postwar international regime

a) The accomplishment of a postwar international security regime is conditional upon two seemingly contradictory concepts: incorporation of different value standards into those of the Allied Nations' and recognition of the increasing diversity of ideologies in international society. The former is fulfilled by restoring the "enemy states" to states with normal status to the extent that the "enemy clauses" of the United Nations Charter come to be meaningless, and the latter is achieved by accepting nations with different ideologies as equal with one another to the extent that international society comes to be recognized as a unification of coexisting regions divided geographically and ideologically.

There was no international regime on the former condition prior to the Second Word War. In that period, states coexisted with different religions, ideologies and civilizations under the rules of traditional international law. The situation changed into one where enemy nations suffered such complete devastation that they were not restored without being reformed according to a designated ideology. War ceased only on condition that one party accepted the doctrine of the other in order to be spared from complete destruction on account of differences in ideology.

Hostile actions against Japan ceased upon acceptance of the Potsdam Declaration on 14 August 1945, which was issued by the United States, Great Britain and China on 26 July 1945 and later joined by the Soviet Union. It included such demands as the removal of all obstacles to the revival and strengthening of democratic tendencies (para 10), establishment of freedom of speech, religion and thought, and respect for fundamental human rights (para 12). They were also the doctrines that had repeatedly been declared by the Allied Nations to be the basis of the postwar general international organization.

The Allied Nations sought to realize the terms of the Declaration by occupying Japanese territory (para 8). In other words, the Declaration indicated the war objectives of the Second World War, which would be ensured through occupation by the Allied Nations. According to the rules of traditional international law, war objectives were attained and confirmed at a peace conference, which would be convened soon after the armistice on the basis of the war situation until then. Realizing the objectives of war through occupation on the terms of the Declaration, the Allied Nations would need no peace conference, thus avoiding the difficulties of meeting on account of the increasing political dissidence among them.

After realizing the objects specified by the Declaration, the Allied Nations would withdraw the occupation forces from Japanese territory (para 12). Before the occupation forces withdrew, Japan would first have to disarm herself completely of all military capabilities.

The Japanese people had sufficed to live within the Japanese archipelago throughout the Edo Period (1603–1867), and it was military forces holding a predominant position in East Asia during those fifty years that drove them to advance overseas. Japanese military forces disappeared through execution of the

Instrument of Surrender signed on Tokyo Bay on 2 September 1945 by four Allied nations, the United States, United Kingdom, China and Soviet Union, jointly and accomplished by the presence of the occupation forces.

The next step for Japan to take was establishment of a "peacefully inclined and responsible government" after the removal of the militarist powers that had supported the Imperial Government throughout the preceding thirteen years.

This situation forms a contrast with that of the First World War fought by the Alliance against Germany and her allies to prevent the hegemony of Germany in continental Europe. The anti-German allies had no ideals for fighting the war until President Wilson of the United States presented "the Fourteen Points" as the common aims of their joint warfare. It ended on fulfillment of the Fourteen Points, which were integrated into peace treaties, including the Versailles Peace Treaties with Germany.

The Potsdam Declaration could have been paralleled to the Fourteen Points in being integrated into a peace treaty had a peace conference been convened with Japan in a reasonable time after the ceasefire. The fact is that peace with Japan was postponed until the conference in San Francisco between the Western Allies and Japan in 1951, after the outbreak of the Korean War. It was based on the Declaration in some parts, but differed substantially from it with regard to the security system adopted in Japan after the restoration of peace.

The Potsdam Declaration claims that Japanese military forces are completely disarmed, but does not indicate how she is secured thereafter. Traditionally, the problem of the security of the vanquished is answered by disarmament to the extent that it will be impossible for them to take retaliatory action in the near future. In the case of wars fought for ideals, it will be answered by the vision of a postwar international regime conceived on the basis of such ideals. The scheme of the international regime of the Allied Nations in the Second World War is known from the instruments and declarations issued during wartime, which are taken into the constituting instrument of the general international organization, or the Charter of the United Nations.

Destroying the enemy powers completely, the Allied Nations made their own value standard the one of postwar international society, which would be executed through the operations of the international organization they created. On the other hand, the UN Charter excludes "the enemy states" from the international regime as a result of two clauses providing for such states.

Considering that the Charter was drafted during wartime, when "prompt and utter destruction" was to be inflicted upon an Axis state, it is only natural that the Charter does not mention anything about the position of "the enemies" in the postwar international regime. However, "the enemy states" would still continue as entities with their own traditions, culture and history even after the surrender of their wartime ideology to the Allied Nations, especially where they had avoided "prompt and utter destruction" by accepting the Declaration.

In this situation, the problem will be how the international regime recognizes the particularity in some fields, including national security, to the extent that unification under the Allies' ideology does not come to be meaningless. Assuming that the Charter is based on traditional international law, it would be referred to a peace conference convened soon after the cessation of hostilities. Under the invalidation of traditional international law, the Allied Nations were required to tell Japan, as an "enemy" state, what system of security she would be under after rehabilitation on the basis of the Allies' ideals, which must be attained soon after the garrison of the occupation forces.

b) The Potsdam Declaration does not mention Japanese constitutional reform, which may be necessary in realizing its terms. As the directives of the General Headquarters (GHQ) representing the Allied Occupation authorities were executed through an Imperial Edict issued by the Japanese Government,[11] the existing legal and administrative system was not detrimental to the administration of the occupation authorities. In fact, the "three big social changes" in postwar Japan – that is, the dissolution of large family trusts or "zaibatsu," agricultural land reform, and purges of officials responsible for the execution of war – were successfully carried out under the existing legal system.

However, in order to achieve political and social reforms through the Occupation administration, it might be necessary for the reforms to be based on the Japanese Constitution, the ultimate foundation of the Japanese legal system.

Japan had been under the rule of the Imperial Constitution promulgated in 1889. It was enacted by the Imperial Government, which established itself after defeating the feudal government that had reigned over the country since the early seventeenth century.

From the perspective of the US Government, it was desirable that Japan should revise the Imperial Constitution to make her political and social systems accord with the Potsdam Declaration. "Reform of the Japanese Government System"[12] asserted on 11 January 1946 that the Japanese system of government should be reformed by drafting and adopting constitutional amendments in a manner which would express the free will of the Japanese people (a(7)). However, the Occupation authorities did not demand that the Japanese Government undertake such constitutional reform, presumably for the following reasons:

Assuming the sovereign equality of all states, even the Occupation authorities could not enforce a revision of the ultimate foundation of the legal system of a country. In reply to a reference by the Japanese Government on 10 August 1945 as to whether the Potsdam Declaration implied abrogation of the Emperor's prerogative or not, the Allied Nations replied that the final political form of Japan would be decided by the freely expressed will of the Japanese people. A demand by the Occupation authorities for a comprehensive revision of the Imperial Constitution of Japan would contravene the Allies' reply.[13]

---

[11] Imperial Edict no. 542, 20 September in the 20th year of Showa (1945), the so-called Potsdam Edicts.

[12] This was forwarded to the Commander in Chief of the US Armed Forces in the Pacific for his "information" (11 January 1946, SWNCC 228): K. Takayanagi, I. Ohtomo and H. Tanaka, *The Making of Constitution of Japan: vol. 1, Documents,* 1972, Annex 1, p. 412.

[13] The Allies' response was that the Emperor and the Japanese Government were subject to the Supreme Commander of the Allied Powers. This was a repetition of words of the Potsdam Declaration rather than an answer to the Japanese reference. Nevertheless, it is also true that they did not expressly deny the prerogative.

The Declaration requires the establishment of a peacefully inclined and responsible government in accordance with the freely expressed will of the Japanese people (para 12). Whether the initiator was the Japanese Government or the Occupation authorities, the constitutional revisions had to be in accordance with freely expressed will of the Japanese people. It would be approved by referendum in appropriate circumstances.

The problem is in the circumstances of revision of the Constitution in accordance with the will of the Japanese people. Aside from the circumstance of foreign occupation, the Japanese people were too preoccupied with their own affairs, including the daily provision of food, to think about social matters.[14] Under these circumstances, it was no wonder that the Japanese Government would not put constitutional reform on the political agenda, though the Kijuro Shidehara Cabinet did establish the Constitutional Problem Investigation Committee (Matsumoto Committee) on 27 October 1945 at the suggestion of General Douglas MacArthur, Supreme Commander of the Allied Powers.[15]

The situation could have changed, however, when the Far Eastern Commission,[16] scheduled to commence in Washington in February 1946, took up revision of the Japanese Constitution in the context of comprehensive Japanese political and social reform. In such a case, the authority of General MacArthur to make decisions on political reform policy would come to be more or less impaired.[17]

Under these circumstances, General MacArthur took the initiative of advancing constitutional reform.[18] Around 4 February 1946, the General ordered his officers to

---

14 In fact, there were no calls in Japanese society for constitutional reform. According to Professor Toshiyoshi Miyazawa of Tokyo Imperial University, the Japanese Imperial Constitution was sufficiently flexible to develop both party and military politics. He did not necessarily propose the revision of the Constitution two months after the beginning of the Occupation (*Mainichi Shimbun*, 19 October 1945), though he actively promoted it later and became a strong supporter of the revised Constitution.

15 Records of negotiations between the Occupation authorities and the Japanese reveal that they were both uncertain as to the scope of each discretion on the matter of constitutional reform in Occupied Japan. General MacArthur suggested revision of the Imperial Constitution to Duke Fumimaro Konoe, a member of Prince Higashikuni's Cabinet (August 1945-October 1945), when he visited the General personally. Later, the General denied a formal relationship with Konoe by reason that he was no longer a Cabinet minister. Konoe continued his own work of revising the Constitution in the belief that it was not a matter appropriate for foreign intervention, and presented the result, a draft Constitution, to the Emperor.

16 A conference of foreign ministers agreed in Moscow in December 1945 to establish the Commission as the supreme organization with jurisdiction over the Occupation policy of Japan. It comprised eleven members, including the four main Allies of the United States, United Kingdom, China and Soviet Union, which held veto power.

17 The General was alarmed to learn from a memorandum of the General Headquarters of the Supreme Commander for the Allied Powers on 1 February 1946 that his decisions upon this matter could not be implemented since some members, including the Soviet Union, disagreed with them: K. Takayanagi et al., *op. cit.,* 1972, no. 6, p. 90.

18 The Japanese Government was drafting a revised constitution, but the work of the Cabinet Committee was proceeding at a slow pace. The motivation for the decision of the General to start his own draft was assumed to be the Japanese Government Draft leaked in a leading newspaper, the *Mainichi Shimbun*, on 1 February 1946. He is thought to have regarded the Japanese Government Draft as being too moderate to be accepted, in light of the policy of the Allied Occupation.

draft a Japanese Constitution on the basis of three principles he noted down, the result of which was handed to the Japanese Government one week later on 13 February 1946.[19]

After making every effort to make do without the General's draft,[20] the Japanese Government decided to accept and publicize it as the Government's own reform draft on 6 March 1946. With some minor changes made in the process of examination by both Houses of the Imperial Diet, the "Government Draft" was adopted as the new Constitution and promulgated on 3 November 1946, to enter into force some six months later.

The process of revision of the Japanese Constitution provides no answer as to whether Japan surrendered on condition of constitutional reform. If the Occupation authorities were confident of that interpretation, then they would not have needed to keep the process strictly secret.

Apart from interpretation of the terms of surrender, the constitutional reforms pushed by the foreign authorities could be discussed in the light of international law.

First of all, it is said that the process of constitutional reform was against the law of war, which limits the right of occupation forces to certain kinds of non-political acts, such as collection of taxes and other monetary contributions, duties, and tolls, necessary to fulfill the absolute needs of the army or the administration of the territory (Regulations Respecting the Laws and Customs of War on Land, 1907, arts 48-49). They must take all measures to ensure public order and safety, while respecting the laws in force in the country, unless absolutely prevented from doing so (art 43).

According to the Government of the United States, the power of the Supreme Commander of the Allied Powers derived not from any contract with Japan, but rather from unconditional surrender. "Indirect rule" by the General Headquarters (GHQ) was adopted not because the existing form of the Japanese Government was sufficiently excellent to be maintained, but because it was convenient to do so.[21] This argument is based not on traditional customs and law, but on the novel concept of "unconditional surrender." As far as the Constitution is concerned, it vests the Occupation authorities with the power of enactment of the Constitution on behalf of the occupied nation.

---

19 It was recorded that an official of the General pressed the draft Constitution on the Japanese Government on 13 February 1946, saying, "If you accept this Constitution, you can be sure that the Supreme Commander will support your position. I cannot emphasize too strongly that acceptance of the draft Constitution is your only hope of survival": Takayanagi et al., *op. cit.*, no. 16, p. 323. He also stated that "acceptance of the provisions of this new Constitution would render the Emperor practically unassailable" and "bring much closer the day of your freedom from control by the Allied Powers": p. 328.

20 Even after acceptance of the GHQ draft, the Japanese authorities endeavored to make the GHQ withdraw it: Exchange of letters between Jiro Shirasu and General Whitney dated 15 February 1946; ibid., no. 17-18, p. 337.

21 The note of 6 September 1945 sent by the Washington Government to General MacArthur, Supreme Commander of the Allied Forces. The same intent was emphasized in the US Early Occupation Policy of 22 September 1945: ibid., no. 1.

It cannot be denied, however, that the Potsdam Declaration took effect after consent by the Japanese Government.[22] As the Declaration is an undertaking among states, it obligates all parties to accord with the articles in action in the same way as other undertakings. Under the Declaration, there was no demand for the Emperor to abdicate, though he was subject to the Supreme Commander during the Occupation, and the Allied Nations abstained from taking such actions as enslavement of the Japanese people as a race or destruction of them as a nation (para 10), would withdraw their forces from Japanese territory within a reasonable period (paras 7 and 12), and so on. The problem is that no ground for requiring revision of the Japanese Constitution is to be found in definite terms in the Declaration.

In the opinion of the Government of the United States, the Supreme Commander based the Occupation policy on the terms of the Declaration, not because they were provided in it, but because they were consistent with the intention of "unconditional surrender." Whether "unconditional surrender" was named properly or not, what was certain was that it was not found in the practice of traditional international law. If it had the function of overriding agreements, including the Hague Convention on Land War, it was not legitimate until traditional international law, which knew no superior norm or *jus cogens* overriding existing contracts,[23] was invalidated.

All doubts regarding revision of the Japanese Constitution will be cleared if we assume that traditional international law and society have been fundamentally changed. In directing the Constitution, GHQ adhered to secrecy, presumably because it was uncertain whether international law had been changed to the extent that it was permitted to press Japan to enact the Constitution, as GHQ wanted.[24]

The fact that almost all the Occupation powers were from the United States gives us a better understanding of the matter. She is most ambitious in propagating national ideals, but least ardent in attaining material gains. Revision of the Japanese Constitution was a process of generalization of the national ideals of the United States taken into those of the Allied Nations or the United Nations.

c) The attitude of the Japanese Government and people was cool towards constitutional reform, partly because they were faced with more serious problems, such as the daily procurement of food, and partly because they were subject to Occupation rule, whether the existing Constitution remained valid or not. They were

---

22 Section 5 of the Declaration uses the phrase "Following are our terms."

23 The Vienna Convention on the Law of Treaties, adopted in 1969 on the basis of the draft of UN International Law Commission of 1966, has two articles providing for jus cogens (arts 53 and 64).

24 The Far Eastern Commission (FEC), which comprised twelve states and was established in Washington after publication of "the Government Draft" of the Constitution, supervised the process of deliberations on the Constitution in the Japanese Diet in its capacity as an Allied Commission with the highest authority on the policy of the occupation of Japan. Nevertheless, its will was barely reflected in the resulting Constitution. The FEC was dissatisfied that the General's encouraging statements to Japanese Government on this subject were taken to be proof of support by all the Allies. At the last stage of parliamentary deliberations on "the Government draft," the FEC adopted a resolution to review the Constitution within three years (FEC Decision, 17 October 1946), which was never executed.

not in a position to conceive state ideals, being closed to foreign relations until peace with the Allied Nations was recovered. If they happened to enact a Constitution by their own hands, the problem was how differently it would be legislated.

It is often the case that a state takes the opportunity of political revolution and war to reform the state system. No states could enact a Constitution without regard to the doctrine prevalent in international society at the time. Reception of foreign legal systems is not exceptional and is frequently found in world history.

So long as the Japanese Government and people expected foreign relations to be friendly with every nation, identification of the state ideal with the Allied Nations' or the United Nations' would be inevitable to prove their qualification for full membership of postwar international society. The new Constitution enacted in the late 1940s would take human rights and war renunciation as its principles, whatever the process of enactment might be.

Japan received the "Western Legal System," including the Constitution of 1889 or Meiji Constitution, throughout the Meiji Era (1868-1912), following a feudal period of more than two hundred years. It was brought about by revolutionists who were anxious about the national crisis caused by the advance of Western powers.

To address the "campaign for liberty and democracy," the Meiji Government declared in 1881 that it would convene a Diet (Parliament) in ten years in accordance with a Constitution to be promulgated by that time. The Government sent research missions to Western nations to study their Constitutions and ultimately adopted the Constitution of the German Empire as a model for the Japanese Empire. Considering that the primary concern of the Meiji Government was external threats, it is understandable that the Government adopted Germany, who unified the nation after a successful war with Austria and France, as a model for her state.

There could not be any constitutional legislation against the trends of the time. The trend at the time when Japan sought to establish her state was in unification of the nation as a state.[25]

The Constitution of Japan of 1946 is distinctive in that it was enacted under the overwhelming pressure of a foreign power. So long as an Allied Nation pressed Japan to take the doctrine of the Allied Nations into the Constitution, it must have been legislated to be conciliatory with the tide in international society after the Second World War.

The manner of enactment is also distinctive in that it was initially drafted by a foreign authority. Bearing in mind the circumstances of its enactment, the Constitution of 1946 comes within the category of the migration of foreign legal systems as a result of conquest. That is not so exceptional since most nations placed

---

[25] Around the world at that time, the Italian Peninsula was unified into the Italian Empire in 1861, the United States of America reunified itself in 1865 after the Civil War, Japan was unified under the restored Imperial Government in 1868, and the majority of German nations were united under the leadership of the Prussian Empire in 1871.

under foreign rule, especially under the rule of Anglo-Saxon countries, have adopted legal systems modeled after that of the ruling country.[26]

d) Whatever the circumstances of enactment of the Constitution may have been, it is meaningless unless democracy and human rights were encouraged to some extent.[27] Since the Imperial Constitution was promulgated in the 22nd year of Meiji (1889), political parties had increased powers to the extent that the head of the most influential party was appointed as Prime Minister. In 1898, the first party government was born under Prime Minister Shigenobu Okuma. In the Taisho period (1912–1925), party government seems to have been customary. What was unusual about the decline of the Meiji (Imperial) Constitution was that it was hampered by militarists suppressing the democratic tendencies increased through the activities of political parties in the Diet.

The Imperial Constitution was abstract and succinct in its provisions, comprising seven chapters and 76 articles, whereas the revised Constitution has eleven chapters and 103 articles. It enabled interpretations favorable to either democratic or aristocratic tendencies.[28] Militarist groups were dissatisfied with the situation that the Constitution was executed in favor of democracy so that the Diet would have a free hand in carrying out military and foreign policy. In 1932, they assassinated Prime Minister Takeshi Inukai, who was leader of the majority party in the Diet. In 1936, a *coup d'etat* of military officers occurred and political leaders were assaulted.[29]

Under these circumstances, military government, rather than party government, became customary. In 1940, all the political parties dissolved into a political association under a Prime Minister from the military. War against the United States and Britain was declared under the Tojo Cabinet in the militarist government.

The United States would not accept a ceasefire with Japan on any condition other than political and social reform, as distinct from the transfer of territories and interests. Her declaration that "the alternative for Japan is prompt and utter

---

26 The peculiar nature of this process of constitutional enactment may stir national sentiment among the Japanese people to have a Constitution enacted of their own violation abrogating the "MacArthur Constitution." Indeed, the Conservatives have a program for constitutional reform on the initiative of the Japanese people, which has not been realized due to their failure to secure the support of a two-thirds majority of the Diet.

27 An official of the Meiji Government proposed to change "the rights and obligations of subjects" into "the social standing of subjects" in the process of drafting the Imperial Constitution of Japan. In refusing the proposal, Hirobumi Ito, the key person in relation to the constitutional enactment, emphasized that the Constitution was meaningful in that it placed restrictions on the prerogative of the monarch in order to promote the rights of subjects.

28 It could be interpreted so the Emperor had the prerogative to decide everything at his discretion. The Fascists contended that revolution was possible by the exercise of the right constitutional powers of the Emperor, but he did not oblige. On the contrary, he suppressed the *coup d'etat* of military officers in 1936 of his own volition. He exercised his power again under the same interpretation in deciding to accept unconditional surrender in 1945. It was ironic that the second opportunity of using his prerogative ultimately brought the Constitution to an end.

29 The Prime Minister, Keisuke Okada, was assaulted by militarists, but escaped assassination on account of his assailants mistaking another person for him.

destruction" was not rhetoric, but practicable by the use of nuclear weapons. Accepting "unconditional surrender," the Emperor could no longer maintain his status as the power from whom all national authority derived, although it may have been nominal anyway under the prevalence of military authorities.

The problem is whether elimination of the authority of "those who have deceived and misled the people of Japan into embarking on world conquest" (Declaration para 6) means simply elimination of the political system prevalent in the later period under the Meiji Constitution – in other words, whether the Allied Nations represented by the United States wanted a political effect or a legal one through enforcement of the Japanese Constitution.

If they desired a legal effect, they were not altogether successful in ascertaining the validity of the international regime deriving from traditional international law through interference in the enactment of the Constitution of an enemy state. Under an international regime superseding sovereign equality as its principle, General MacArthur did not need to make such directions to the Japanese Government and people in secret. This is an indication that the international legal regime is in a phase of disarray between sovereign equality and invalidation, even after the practice of the Second World War, including unconditional surrender.

e) The qualification for membership of postwar international society was proved on the signing of the Declaration by the United Nations on 1 January 1942, so long as that membership coincided with that of the United Nations (UN Charter, art 3). It was limited to the Allied Nations originally, but came to include neutral and enemy states once their capacity had been examined. This situation is similar to that of the non-European nations being accepted as members of international society after their qualifications for civilized nations were examined. This fact is proof that traditional international law has been downgraded from the principal position in the international normative regime to being subsidiary to the Allied Nations'.

The qualification depended exclusively on a state's attitude toward the Allies' ideals rather than the substance of that state. Indeed, Spain was accepted as a member of the United Nations, despite having once been considered a threat to the Allies and the peace as a result of her neutrality during wartime.[30]

Much less could a defeated nation stand in postwar international society without fundamental political and social reform in accordance with the Allies' ideals. They could hardly accept Japan without complete disarmament, social reforms, punishment of war criminals, and so on. Japan would impress the Allies as qualified for membership of international society by reforming the Constitution according to their ideals.

Germany did not take the same process of constitutional reform as Japan because she had no "terms" comparable to the Potsdam Declaration in ending hostilities with the Allied Nations. The German Government fell into *debellatio* in the course of taking hostile action against the Allies. There was no "revision" of the German Constitution, partly because the former Constitution dissipated as the Government

---

[30] General Assembly Resolution, 12 December 1946, 17 November 1947

fell into dissolution and partly because the state itself was divided into several occupation zones.

This does not mean, however, that Japan was different from Germany in being reformed on a contractual basis. They were both reformed domestically, with no basis for international agreements, including the terms of armistice. As far as traditional international law is concerned, there is no norm absolute enough to be beyond transactions between sovereign states.

A norm is positive when practiced to the extent that it is a convincing legal prescription. Demand for reforms embodied in the terms of the Potsdam Declaration will be positive when realized by executive powers. The Declaration has elements of both armistice agreements and *jus cogens*, the contravention of which invalidates other agreements. When it is executed in an imperative way in Japanese society, it will be proved as *jus cogens* rather than as a ceasefire agreement. Such a manner of accepting the Potsdam Declaration is novel in the history of international law and society, which deserves the novel name of "unconditional surrender."

The revolutionary change in Japan's postwar Constitution in the name of revision of the Constitution of 1889 is understandable in the particular circumstances after the War. If the reforms had been made freely by the Japanese Government, they would have been much more moderate and gradual.[31]

It was almost a hundred years before the Second World War that Japan opened the nation by entry into treaty relations with Western powers under the rule of international law. Unconditional surrender was the second phase of her opening the country in the sense that she was situated in the family of nations, but in a manner different from most other nations.

In the middle of the nineteenth century, Japan was unable, as a non-European civilized nation, to enjoy the full benefits of membership of international society. All non-European nations were discriminated against in treaties concluded with the European civilized nations.

In order to revise the "discriminatory treaties," Japan strove to "westernize" herself in every field of society, including adoption of the Western legal system. Likewise, importation of a Constitution in the name of revision of the Meiji Constitution could be expected to bring her full membership of international society.

If the provisions of the United Nations Charter are taken at face value, membership will secure states through the function of collective security. What Japan anticipated most at the time of constitutional reform was the effect that membership of the United Nations would have on national security.

The reality of the United Nations was a paralysis of the function of maintaining peace and security due to conflict between the main Allies. Japan became a member

---

[31] It would be one like the Konoe Draft or Matsumoto Committee's Draft, which were ignored by the Occupation authorities. There were some more similar to the GHQ Draft than the official drafts, including a plan of a private group consisting of seven intellectuals issued on 27 December 1945. In fact, it was so similar that it was assumed to have been influenced by the GHQ officers. However, this fact does not affect the conclusion that the constitutional reforms were an outcome of unconditional surrender.

in December 1956 after an unsuccessful application in the preceding session. Until then, she solved her security problems after peace by allowing American forces to remain stationed in her territory.

Japan had embarked on a great war against "the haves" in disregard of her rights and obligations under traditional international law. If either the security afforded by the United Nations or United States turns out to be ineffective, she may naturally become incredulous again of the international legal regime itself.

This situation will be remedied if a regional system based on self-defense is convincing as an international regime in doctrine and structure. It will be realized when the US-Japan Security Treaty is believed to be not the subsidiary, but rather the primary, means of security in the system of international society, even under the prevailing general collective security regime, the United Nations. In the light of all experience to date, the United Nations is the undisputed international regime at present, under the authority of which Japan estimates her position in relation to the other members of international society.

(2) A US-Japan Security Treaty concluded outside the Constitution

a) What makes the Constitution of Japan of 1946 revolutionary in comparison with those of other nations enacted in ordinary circumstances in the twentieth century is its provision for the "Renunciation of War."

Chapter II of the Constitution, entitled "Renunciation of War," has only one article providing, "The Japanese people forever renounce war as a sovereign right of the nation and the threat or use of force as means of settling international disputes." In order to accomplish this aim, it continues: "Land, sea, and air forces, as well as war potential, will never be maintained" (art 9).

The provision is not so surprising in the sense that it is an exact description of the existing situation in Japan following her surrender and demilitarization. Nor is it so conspicuous in the sense that similar provisions are found in other constitutions enacted immediately after the Second World War.[32] The problem is that it is a provision in the Constitution of a state in accordance with which she must defend herself, even after the present foreign forces are withdrawn.

A unilateral obligation of demilitarization on the part of the vanquished, as the Versailles Treaty imposes upon Germany, is the usual device to prevent resurrection of that power. How long peace lasts after the end of a war depends on the postwar international regime in which the vanquished states are situated. Peace after the First World War broke after twenty years, partly because of the failure in preventing the bellicose government from resurrecting itself in Germany and partly because of the incompleteness of the postwar international regime, including the League of Nations.

---

[32] Preamble of the Constitution of the Republic of France in 1946, article 4 of the Constitution of Brazil in 1946, articles 211 and 212 of the Constitution of Federation of Burma in 1946, article 26 of the Constitution of Federal Republic of Germany in 1949, and article 11 of the Constitution of the Republic of Italy in 1947 A.J.Peaslee, *Constitutions of Nations*, vols 1–3, 1950.

"Nothing could be fraught with greater danger to the composed and stable situation which now exists in Japan than to abrogate all orders and directives, issued both by and to SCAP during the occupation, upon the effectuation of the peace treaty."[33] The Allies would be satisfied that there would be no repetition of Japanese military expansion if a complete disarmament were maintained by the continued presence of the Allied forces in her territory even after the conclusion of a peace treaty.[34]

Assuming the validity of traditional international law based on the sovereign equality of states, the concept of "permanent occupation" was impossible, no matter how effective it might be to prevent a resurrection by the enemy. Disarmament and reparation had been the means of preventing retaliation by the vanquished enemies in previous wars, including the First World War.

"Reform of the Japanese Governmental System" of 11 January 1946 (SWNCC 226)[35] includes revolutionary statements regarding such things as the status of Emperor, but no statement comparable to the "renunciation of war clause" of the revised Constitution. On the contrary, it assumed the existence of future military powers in Japan and indicated that the Emperor was deprived of military powers provided in articles 11 to 14 of the Meiji Constitution, without referring to the organ empowered instead of the Emperor.

According to a plan formulated by the United States Government and circulated to the main Allied Nations in June 1946, Japan would be demilitarized for 25 years under the watch and guard of four nations, the United States, United Kingdom, Soviet Union and China. Should Japan violate her obligation for demilitarization or resume armament, the four states would take appropriate action, including armed actions by air, sea and land forces.[36] This is a plan for "permanent neutrality," so to speak, to be taken by Japan in the future. There could be no state under an obligation of permanent neutrality, without holding military forces necessary for carrying out the obligations of that law of neutrality.

In light of this plan for permanent neutrality, the Allies did not intend to secure Japan in the future by either complete disarmament or continued foreign occupation. In spite of that, the draft Constitution, including the renunciation of war clause, was discussed in the Diet under the supervision of the Far East Commission[37] in parallel with the suggestion of permanent neutrality in June 1946.

"Renunciation of war" is traced to one of the three basic principles for the

---

[33] From General MacArthur to the Secretary General, 1 September 1947, *FRUS* 1947, vol. VI, p. 514.

[34] This was actually proposed. See, for example, "Memorandum by a United States Naval Authority, 18 August 1947, Subject: Draft Treaty of Peace with Japan," *FRUS,* ibid., p. 495.

As the Japanese people did not resist the Occupation powers at all, it was clear that they would not adhere to the cause of war for which they had fought vehemently. This was against the ordinary sentiments of Western people, who would insist on the cause for which they fought or otherwise reflect deeply on their conduct taken for that cause: R. Benedict, *The Chrysanthemum and the Sword: Patterns of Japanese Culture,* 1946.

[35] See also note 21.

[36] *Asahi Shimbun,* 23 June 1946.

[37] See note 24.

forthcoming Japanese Constitution, noted and dictated by General MacArthur to his officers.[38] The General's draft shown to the Japanese Government on 13 February 1946 has a chapter paraphrasing the second point of these principles. Article 9 of the adopted Constitution is a faithful reproduction of an article in the draft.[39]

In the opinion of the GHQ expressed in the course of an exchange of views with the Japanese Government regarding revisions to the Constitution, Japan should adopt drastic means to declare her intention of renouncing war. The GHQ believed that international society would accept Japan as a member once she had convinced the members that she was no longer dangerous in military capacity.[40]

If the clause of the Constitution requires that Japan be disarmed as she was under the Occupation, there would be no need to discuss disarmament at a peace conference between the Allies and Japan. Indeed, in the power situation of international society immediately following the War, the vanquished took a small role in any case. This did not mean, however, that the vanquished remained negligible in military power permanently. The most important function of a peace conference is the establishment of a postwar security regime on the initiative of the victorious states, into which the vanquished is integrated. There could no longer be a balance of power, so the security system would be conceived to be sufficiently revolutionary to position the vanquished in an unprecedented way.

---

[38] The three basic points stated by Supreme Commander to be "Musts" in the revised Constitution were as follows: 1 Emperor is at the head of the state. 2 War as a sovereign right of the nation is abolished. Japan renounces it as an instrumentality for setting its disputes and even for preserving its security. It relies upon the higher ideals which are now stirring the world for its defense and its protection. 3 The feudal system of Japan will cease: see Appendix 5(2) and Takayanagi et al, *op. cit.*, no. 7, pp. 99-100.

There is evidence to the contrary that the "renunciation of war" in the Japanese Constitution was proposed on the Japanese side. According to the Memoirs of Prime Minister Shidehara, it was he who proposed that the clause be inserted into the Constitution, with which General MacArthur was in full agreement. They depict a scene on 24 January 1946 when they confirm their common conviction in the righteousness of the renunciation of war. Nevertheless, it is hardly probable that the Prime Minister did not know that the Japanese Government Draft (Matsumoto Draft), already completed at that time, had no such clause. There is much evidence to the contrary that the Japanese side made every attempt to weaken the effect of the clause, or, if possible, have the clause itself withdrawn by the GHQ. For example, Dr. Matsumoto wanted the clause to be inserted somewhere in the Preamble rather than be given a Chapter of its own, which was strongly opposed by a GHQ officer: *ibid.*, no. 23, p. 293.

[39] Some writers take the view that the war renunciation clause in the Japanese Constitution is a product of joint work by the General and Prime Minister Shidehara. This may be the view of the majority of writers specializing in the Japanese Constitution: see Y. Higuchi (ed.), *Five Decades of Constitutionalism in Japanese Society*, 2001, p. 30. However, this majority view overlooks the fact described in note 38.

[40] Dr. Matsumoto, chairman of the Constitutional Problem Investigation Committee, pointed out at a meeting with GHQ staff on 22 February 1946 that such a provision for the renunciation of war would better be provided in the Preamble of the Constitution than in the body of it. General Whitney rejected this proposal, arguing that enunciation of this principle should be so prominent as to be provided in Chapter I, but they agreed to provide it in Chapter II next to the chapter on the status of the Emperor: Takayanagi et al, *op. cit.*, no. 23

Among the questions raised in the debates of the Imperial Diet on the GHQ's "Government Draft," one member enquired whether the war renunciation clause was detrimental to membership of the postwar "peace system." In reply, Prime Minister Shigeru Yoshida stated that the quickest way to restore national sovereignty was believed to be adoption of the clause into the Constitution as proposed. He stressed that they should pay utmost consideration to the earliest independence of the country, so no other factor need be taken into consideration.[41] In that context, he did not explain how the state could be independent without maintaining military forces under the principle of war renunciation.

As far as the terms of the Potsdam Declaration are concerned, the interpretation is not necessarily justified that Japan is prohibited from maintaining any forces of her own, though she is placed under the strict obligation of disarmament. For example, "permanent neutrality" has been a means of securing such small states as Switzerland and Belgium since their independence in the nineteenth century. There is the recent precedent of Austria, which was released from occupation by the Allied Powers in 1955 on condition of her permanent neutrality. Japan could regain independence on the same condition as Austria if circumstances so permitted. In any event, there could be no discharge of obligations of neutrality without some form of armament.

b) As far as article 9 of the Japanese Constitution is taken as provided, it is inconsistent with permanent neutrality in providing for complete disarmament with no reservation for forces necessary to discharge the obligations of neutrality. However, the article is not necessarily contradictory with the system of the United Nations, leaving the treatment of "enemy states" to the discretion of member states. According to article 107 of the Charter, the "responsible government" may take an action for its own security against an enemy state independently of the principles of the Charter. Similarly, enemy states may be directed to participate in actions on the basis of "regional arrangements" in order to prevent a renewal of their "aggressive policy" (art 53 para 1).

Permanent neutrality is a system adapted to the traditional circumstances of the balance of powers. Collective security would not be completed until such a system fell into disuse. In dealing with the "enemy states," the United Nations may not legalize the status of permanent neutrality, but do so without permitting any armament, which is not possible under traditional international law.

According to the Preamble to the Japanese Constitution, "the Japanese people have determined to preserve their security and existence, trusting in the justice and faith of the peace-loving peoples of the world." General MacArthur inserted the phrase in the belief that physical force yields to moral force in the settlement of disputes. Being "peace-loving" is the condition for membership of the United Nations (Charter, art 4). In this context, Japan may have rendered her future

---

[41] The questioner, Dr. Shigeru Nambara, professor of University of Tokyo, pointed out, in his capacity as member of the House of Peers, the absurdity of the clause by citing the enforcement system of the United Nations in the Upper House on 27 August 1946.

security subject to the guard and protection of the United Nations, "the final arbitrator among the nations."[42]

The problem is how a state that has renounced war in its Constitution is guarded and protected by the organization of "the peace-loving peoples."

According to General MacArthur, Japan should advance the fundamental political, social and economic reforms already started, even after the withdrawal of direct military control, "with the right reserved to every Japanese citizen to appeal to the United Nations."[43] This may mean that Japan would be placed under the Trusteeship system, which was available for supervision of Japanese political reforms.

If Japan were placed under the Trusteeship system, she could not, however, be a member of the United Nations as the trusteeship system should not apply to any UN member's territory (Charter, art 78). It contradicts the situation where the security and existence of the people of Japan depend on "the justice and faith" of "the peace-loving peoples of the world."

In view of the initial activities of the United Nations, MacArthur may be correct in placing no confidence in its ability to preserve the Japanese people's security and existence. The renunciation of war or "pacifism" of the Constitution may have needed to be maintained until after the Occupation in order to prove that Japan was willing to accept the international regime rehabilitated by the Allied Nations, but it was another thing whether the renunciation of war was practical to secure Japan once she had regained independence.

In the long run, the situation may make it correct to conclude that any traditional means of security was available in place of an international regime established for postwar international society. In fact, MacArthur once expressed support for "permanent neutrality" as means of achieving security for Japan, stating that he wanted Japan to be "Switzerland in the Far East."[44]

c) In any case, article 9 of the Japanese Constitution would not, in the absence of support from some other system, be maintained as provided once the Occupation forces were withdrawn. At some time or other, Japan would seek membership of the United Nations. On the basis of the provisions of the UN Charter, any member would be required to assist enforcement actions by contributing military forces.

---

[42] Memorandum by General MacArthur, 21 March 1947; *FRUS* 1947, vol. VI, p. 456. The draft peace treaty by the US Department of State, according to which the demilitarized Japan was placed under the control of four powers, should be amended in accordance with the above concepts: ibid., p. 454. It was incumbent that "the Allied Nations for their part, in the spirit of this [Japanese] constitutional provision, should undertake to guarantee the neutrality of Japan, with the view to the transfer of such undertaking to the stewardship of the UN, where the responsibility properly should rest." His views on this matter were not necessarily consistent. By the time of the outbreak of the Korean War, he had begun to say, "Japan's integrity and sovereignty should be guaranteed by all the Powers concerned, which are placed under the UN framework": *FRUS* 1950, vol. VI, p. 1171.

[43] *FRUS* 1947, vol. VI, p. 455.

[44] In an interview with a journalist on 3 March 1949, he stated that the United States would not form an alliance with Japan, and what the United States wanted was Japanese neutrality in the case of an outbreak of war.

In sessions of the Imperial Diet relating to revisions to the Constitution, there was some doubt as to whether the "renunciation of war" clause was detrimental to possible cooperation with "the peace-loving nations."[45] In seeking membership of the League of Nations, Germany sought exemption from the duty of sanctions to be imposed under article 16 of the Covenant by reason that she was under too heavy an obligation of disarmament.[46]

The fact is that Japan acceded to the United Nations with no reservation of enforcement action in relation to article 9 of the Constitution prohibiting maintenance of "land, sea, and air forces as well as other war potential." It was a natural consequence in view of the precedent that Austria was accepted as a member on condition of her retaining a policy of neutrality.

Considering that "enemy states" were originally excluded from the regime of the Allied Nations, they might be best positioned in the status of neutrality, theoretically and practically, under the strong guard of a vigilant organization.[47] Under a strict application of the Charter, however, members of the United Nations could not maintain a state of neutrality as they are required to give the Organization every assistance in any action it takes in accordance with the Charter (art 2 para 5).

This dilemma will be removed if the United Nations discharges the task of maintenance of international peace and security in a neutral manner between the disputants. Neutral activities in the name of peacekeeping have come to be recognized as the principal activities for peace and security since the 1950s. They were not a necessary development of enforcement under Chapter VII of the Charter, but rather an alternative to enforcement, amid political tensions between the main members.

The United Nations Emergency Forces were sent to Suez in 1956 to observe the armistice reached by the parties to the Suez Crisis. They were sent with the consent of all states involved in the conflict and carried out their observation duties in a neutral manner. They did not correspond to United Nations forces based on article 43 of the Charter, which would be one-sided in enforcing the will of the Security Council or some members, as in fact occurred during the Korean War in 1950 and the Gulf War in 1990.

Any states having a keen interest in Japan's security would not accept the garrison of forces of any leading state in her territory after attainment of the Allies' objectives. If international forces were stationed there to discharge their duty in a "neutral" manner, they would be free of apprehension about employment of Japanese power for the benefit of the garrisoning state.

Unlike peacekeeping forces, enforcement forces are organized ad hoc to counter unforeseen aggressors. The Allied Nations Forces was organized ad hoc to counter aggression by the Axis states. The United Nations was a formulation of such actions

---

45 Mr. Sanzo Nonaka, a Communist member of the Diet, pointed out that article 9 would render assistance to a "right war" or enforcement action taken by the United Nations impossible. He proposed that the article be amended to renounce a war of aggression rather than every sort of war. Prime Minister Yoshida refuted him, saying that every war was commenced on the pretext of legitimate defense: Plenary Session, House of Representatives, 28 June 1946. See also note 41.

46 Walters, *op. cit.*, p. 279.

47 Yasuo Yamashita, "Eisei Churitsu ni tsuite" (On permanent neutrality), *Chuokoron*, April 1950.

by the Allied Nations. The occupation forces in the enemies' territory were, so to speak, United Nations forces, as understood according to the provisions of the Charter themselves. The ground for the Allied occupation of enemy states would be Chapter VII; otherwise, the "enemy" clauses of the Charter.

It is a matter of traditional international law that Allied occupation is terminated by the conclusion of a peace treaty. Under the legal regime created by the Allied Nations, their forces would, in order to prevent the resurrection of the enemy, not withdraw from that enemy's territory.

The UN Forces in Korea were supported by a state leading one bloc of the Cold War, and opposed by states in favor of the other. By contrast, the UN Forces in Suez were tolerated by all states on account of their "neutral" function. It came to be contended that Japan should find the solution to her means of security by retaining article 9 of the Constitution as it was and accepting United Nations Forces in her territory along the same lines as the UN Emergency Forces in Suez.[48]

However, the organization of the forces would not necessarily remain the same throughout the operation. It would be changed from one of "peacekeeping" to sanction. After the outbreak of the Korean War in June 1950, the American Occupation forces in Japan engaged in hostilities on the Peninsula under the banner of the United Nations Forces. From that time, it was necessary for Japan to be placed under the protection of "the United Nations Forces," the commander-in-chief of which was General MacArthur, also Supreme Commander of the Allied Forces.

At the outbreak of the Korean War, five years after the armistice with Japan, the Government of the United States moved to convene a peace conference in accordance with the rules of traditional international law. As far as it followed the traditional procedure, recovery of peace would bring the Allied Occupation to termination. What was certain was that the peace attained did not bring the United States forces to withdraw from Japanese territory, under whatever concept the continuous presence of such forces might be grounded.

d) In view of the practice of traditional international law, it was an abnormal prolongation for the Occupation to continue for more than six years with no chance of a peace conference. The Japanese Government and people waited patiently for the conclusion of a peace treaty to free them from the Occupation. The outbreak of hostilities on the Korean Peninsula was a chance for the Occupation powers to set a date for a peace conference.

It depended upon political and military circumstances whether the outbreak of hostilities was the chance for a peace conference. In the event, the United States opted to end the enemy status of Japan at the earliest opportunity.[49] It was this policy that drove the Western Allies to hold a peace conference to make Japan participate publicly in their bloc.

---

48 The idea that UN forces be stationed in place of US forces was taken from the experience of UNEF: Yoshikazu Sakamoto, "Churitsu Nippon no boei koso" (A Security Plan of Neutralized Japan), *Sekai*, 164, 1959.

49 If the United States lost the war on the Peninsula, the ceasefire could have been conditional upon the withdrawal of forces from Japan: *FRUS* 1950, vol. VI, p. 1388.

As the peace conference was convened in the midst of hostilities in Korea, the Eastern Allies would not join in making peace with Japan in San Francisco. The conference was held according to the established custom of traditional international law and ended in the conclusion of a peace treaty on 8 September 1951. Among every abnormality in the light of traditional international law, the two main belligerent states supporting the North Korean regime, the Soviet Union and mainland China, were absent from the conference. The Treaty could not be a peace treaty in the strict sense of traditional international law without the participation of two of the main belligerents against the vanquished, but 46 of the Allied Nations who had been at war with Japan did participate.

Another extraordinary factor in view of traditional international law was the grant of the right to continuing garrison to the former enemy by the vanquished. It was based on the following article of the Peace Treaty in San Francisco: "All the occupation forces shall be withdrawn from Japan as soon as possible after the Peace Treaty comes into force. Nothing in this provision shall, however, prevent station or retention of foreign armed forces in Japanese territory under or in consequence of any bilateral and multilateral agreements which have been or may be made between one more of the Allied Powers, on the one hand, and Japan on the other" (art 6).[50] The US-Japan Security Treaty was concluded simultaneously with the Peace Treaty on the basis of this article in the Peace Treaty.

Whether this article is legally justifiable or not depends on one's view of the postwar international regime. Separation of the Security Treaty from the Peace Treaty may signify that Japan has negotiated an agreement on an equal footing with the United States. In view of traditional international law, however, there could be no negotiation between the occupying and the occupied in equal terms.[51] Also, there could be no peace treaty tolerating continued garrison of the former enemy forces. The situation would be legitimated only if an international legal regime replaced traditional international law after its invalidation through the practice of the Second World War.

So what international legal regime replaced traditional international law? Japan was not in a position to claim the rights of the United Nations Charter. In fact, Japan's claim in the process of negotiations that action taken on the Treaty should be clearly based on the articles of the United Nations Charter, including article 51, was not accepted by the United States.[52]

---

[50] By providing this, they paid regard to the rules of traditional international law. In fact, the Allied forces other than those of the US, most of which were from the Commonwealth, withdrew within 90 days, as stipulated in the Treaty.

[51] In the same context, there could be no negotiation between an occupying state and a puppet government in equal terms. The Protocol between Japan and Manchukuo, signed and promulgated on 15 September 1932, recognized that any threat to the territory or to the peace and order of either of the contracting parties constituted at the same time a threat to the safety and existence of the other and agreed that Japanese forces would be stationed in Manchukuo.

[52] According to a Japanese government official, Kumao Nishimura, the United States took the position that Japan had no ability to conclude the Security Treaty on an equal footing since she could not give any military assistance to the United States, but rather received it from the United States: *Anzenhoshojoyakuron* (On the US-Japan Security Treaty), 1959, p. 18.

This is a literal consequence of the fact that the provision of the Japanese Constitution, having almost the same phrase as the War Renunciation Pact, implies the right of self-defense, although the Constitution does not mention the right expressly. In light of the practice under the Pact, there could be no principle of war renunciation without reservation of self-defense. The problem is that it is practically impossible to exercise the right under a Constitution prohibiting maintenance of "land, sea, and air forces, as well as other war potential" (art 9 para 2).

As the right of self-defense is "inherent" to any state, the practical impossibility of exercising such a right will result in the loss of normal status of that state in international society. The situation is the same when the ability to defend oneself is supplemented by foreign powers.[53]

If *de facto* permanent occupation of Japan were the solution, it would be contrary to the Potsdam Declaration stipulating that the Allied forces would be withdrawn from Japan as soon as the objectives of the Declaration had been accomplished (art 12). It would be detrimental to Japan's membership of the United Nations since the UN Charter stipulates that the Organization is based on the principle of the sovereign equality of all its members (art 2 para 1).

So far as the provisions of the Charter are concerned, the United Nations is a system for outlawry by "enemy states." In this context, it is only natural that they should seek the means of security among those established under traditional international law, including "permanent neutrality," instead of some other system under the UN Charter.

However, "permanent neutrality" would drastically change the relationship that existed between Japan and the United States at the time of conclusion of the Peace Treaty. If it were taken as the means of securing Japan after her release from Occupation, the close cooperation between the two countries in countering invasion by North Korea would be handicapped. Her neutral status would not fail to be encroached and end in her integration into an Eastern sphere in opposition to the West.

The peace conference in San Francisco and the US-Japan Security Treaty were the solution to the means of securing Japan after termination of their war status, without stipulating an exact ground in either traditional international law or the collective security of the United Nations. The American forces in Japan had the nominal status of United Nations Forces in accordance with resolutions adopted at the outbreak of the Korean War. In spite of that capacity, the Forces would not secure Japan, but expose her to greater threat from the opposing powers, the Soviet Union and mainland China. As the powers that would not take part in the peace conference in San Francisco were still in a state of war with Japan, any state allying Japan, including the United States, could be an enemy against the two states within the meaning of the UN Charter.

---

[53] According to India's preliminary view on the U.S. Memorandum on the Japanese Peace Treaty, "If bases are to be maintained in Japan for the defense of the Japanese islands they will practically constitute military occupation of Japan and thus limit free exercise of sovereignty by Japan": *FRUS* 1950, vol. VI, pp. 1382-1383. As a matter of fact, India refused to participate in the Peace Treaty in San Francisco.

A Soviet representative attended the conference in San Francisco, but did not sign the Treaty. The Soviet Government did not attach importance to the Peace Treaty under the changed normative circumstances of international society. Rather, the Soviet Union placed greater importance, in legitimating her war gains, on her agreement with the United States and United Kingdom at Yalta than Japan's consent at a peace conference.[54]

A similar situation applied in relation to the other Allied Nations, including the United States and United Kingdom. What was important to them was execution of the Potsdam Declaration, which entailed withdrawal from territories which Japan had occupied and the surrender of other rights relating to them.

In this context, the Peace Treaty yields importance to the US-Japan Security Treaty, on the basis of which Japan is integrated into the postwar international regime, the creation of the Allied Nations. It accounts for the Soviets' behavior in acquiescing to the Peace Treaty, but not recognizing the US-Japan Security Treaty. When the original Security Treaty was strengthened, the Soviet Union reproached Japan for her willingness to be integrated into the Western bloc in opposition to the East and canceled the 1956 agreement under which she had agreed to transfer the two groups of islands under Soviet occupation to Japan once a peace treaty between the Soviets and Japan entered into force.

Whether the Soviets have reason for their contention depends on the answer to the following problems: whether the "enemy states" remain outlaws from the international legal regime after the Second World War, and if so, whether traditional international law is still valid in dealing with the hostile relations with "the enemies.[55]

e) As far as the war with Japan was concerned, the Allied Nations in the Western bloc adhered to the procedure of a peace conference to publicize the recovery of their peaceful relations with their former enemy. One result of a peace conference is the conclusion of a peace treaty, which was believed valid under the international legal regime prevailing at that time, not to mention traditional international law.

In basing Japan's means of security on any system of international society, the United States would not take the collective system of the United Nations because it should be independent of the Security Council, a permanent member of which was the Soviet Union. According to article 2 paragraph 6 of the UN Charter, "the Organization shall ensure that states which are not Members of the United Nations act in accordance with these Principles." The Peace Treaty with Japan makes her accept the obligations set out in article 2 of the UN Charter (Treaty art 5 a). In concluding the Peace Treaty, the United States acted in accordance with the

---

54 H.W. Briggs, "The Leaders' Agreement of Yalta," 40*AJ*, 1946, p. 376.

55 Occupation of Japan might not be a belligerent occupation under the law of war, but rather be an act under a contract, the Potsdam Declaration, between the Allied Nations and Japan. If it was the latter, then it was not necessarily regulated by the law and customs of war formulated into the Hague Regulations. Even if it was an act under a contract between the belligerents, it could not be independent of the law of war as it was an act taken in the process of making war. Nevertheless, it could not be distinguished without reference to the postwar international order, under which part of the law of belligerent occupation was still valid.

provision of the UN Charter, although she would not base the means of security in Japan on the security system of the Charter.

After the armistice on the Korean Peninsula in 1953, the restoration of diplomatic relations between Japan and the Soviet Union was declared in 1956, pending the conclusion of a peace treaty. According to a provision of the Joint Declaration, the Soviets supported Japan's proposed membership of the United Nations. It did not make abrogation of the US-Japan Security Treaty a condition for recovery of their peaceful relations.

Japan had already joined the United Nations when she sought revision of the US-Japan Security Treaty of 1951. She sought to become an equal partner with the United States in the same way that members of the North Atlantic Treaty are in relation to one another.

The Peace Treaty with Japan contains a clause providing that Japan conforms to the principles of the UN Charter and is recognized to possess the inherent right of individual and collective self-defense referred to in article 51 of the Charter (art 5). If they sought to realize this clause, the Security Treaty of 1951 should have taken self-defense as the basis of the action. The fact is that a Japanese proposal to provide the right of self-defense in the text was rejected by the United States by reason that Japan was unable to engage in mutual defense action by military forces.[56]

By contrast, the Treaty revised in 1960 provides that they will act on the ground of self-defense recognized by article 51 of the UN Charter on condition that they maintain and develop their capacities to resist armed attack, "by means of continuous and effective self-help and mutual aid" (art 3).

Development of means of "self-help" was effected by a build-up of the Japan National Defense Forces originating in the National Police Reserve established under a GHQ directive in August 1950, which was motivated by the outbreak of hostilities in Korea. Directives of the Occupation authorities took precedence over the Constitution, so the creation of military forces regarded almost as an army could not be disputed on the ground of inconsistency with the "Peace Constitution."

The situation could not be changed once peace had been attained as Japan recognized the validity of all acts and omissions done during the period of Occupation under or in consequence of directives of the Occupation authorities (Peace Treaty, art 19 (d)). In logical consequence of the provisions of the Peace Treaty, even acts inconsistent with each other, including the provision of article 9 of the Constitution and the establishment of the National Defense Forces, shall be maintained after peace, so long as they are made under the Occupation authorities. The argument against the legality of the National Defense Forces on the ground of its inconsistency with article 9 of the Constitution could not be sustainable without invalidation of the Peace Treaty.[57]

---

56 The Vandenberg Resolution, 11 June 1948, states, inter alia, "(3) Association of the United States, by constitutional process, with such regional and other collective arrangements as are based on continuous and effective self-help and mutual aid, and as affect its national security." See also note 52.

57 The argument against the legality of the National Defense Forces voiced by opponents to the Liberal Democratic Government cannot be persuasive as it fails to mention non-recognition of the validity of the Peace Treaty.

The dissolution of the National Defense Forces would also violate the Security Treaty with the United States, which provides that they would cope with "an armed attack against either party in the territories under the administration of Japan, recognizing that such an attack would be dangerous to its own peace and safety" (revised art 5). The Constitution, National Defense Forces, and US-Japan Security Treaty may be be inconsistent with each other in view of municipal law and traditional international law, but could be consistent on the assumption of the postwar international regime.

Reinforcement of the Defense Forces in accordance with the Security Treaty was a condition of the revision of the original Security Treaty rather than a tribute to Japanese security. According to the Soviets' observation, Japan demonstrated a willingness to support the military acts of the United States in renewing the Security Treaty in 1960, which deteriorated the political situation in East Asia. According to the same observation, Japan incurred another danger of destruction by nuclear attack, as she had experienced in Hiroshima and Nagasaki.[58]

The Soviets maintained that Japan was against the eternal renunciation of war pledged by adoption of the Peace Constitution thirteen years earlier. In response to this lack of fidelity, the Soviets stated that their agreement on the return of the islands made in the Soviet-Japan Joint Declaration in 1956 was duly canceled.[59]

The increased threat from the Soviets should be compensated for by an improvement achieved through the revision of a treaty in favor of state sovereignty.

The Treaty of 1951 contains a provision for US forces to be utilized to put down large-scale internal riots and disturbances in Japan caused through instigation or intervention by an outside power or powers (art 1). This would need to be removed from the text of the revised Treaty for Japan to enjoy ordinary status in international society.

The stipulation on termination of the Treaty (art 10), which is not seen in the preceding text, is necessary to publicize the fact that Japan has regained ordinary status in international society.

The most conspicuous benefit conferred upon Japan is found in the ascertainment that it would be exercised on the right of self-defense "inherent" to any party. In basing acts taken in relation to the Security Treaty on this right, Japan is linked to the normal members of international society whose security depends upon self-defense agreements. In other words, her status of outlawry is dissolved despite the opposition of the Soviet Union and the existing enemy clauses of the UN Charter. There could be no such dissolution if the US-Japan Security Treaty were replaced by any other means, including permanent neutrality and complete disarmament under supervision by the Security Council of the United Nations.

Indeed, the Soviets would not accept any system as long as it was schemed by "the Capitalists" and their affiliates as enemies of "the people." However, the Soviets

---

[58] Memorandum of the Soviet Union to the Japanese Government, 27 January 1960, issued immediately after signature of the revised US-Japan Security Treaty.

[59] This Memorandum was refuted by the Japanese Government on 2 February 1960.

could not deny the right of self-defense on which the Communist bloc was also developing a network of security treaties.

f) The US-Japan Security Treaty is an indication that the Allied Nations, including the United States, agree to give an enemy due place in an international regime they have conceived and established. In granting it that status, they revise the regime as time demands. The US-Japan Security Treaty, whether the original one or the revised, has a provision on "the Far East," which is not found in any comparable agreements, including the North Atlantic Treaty. An analysis of the provision reveals how they necessitate a revision in the international regime, as circumstances change from one of collaboration to opposition among the Allies.

The Japanese Government had difficulty in persuading its opponents to accept the US-Japan Security Treaty as a counterpart to the North Atlantic Treaty on account of the Far East clause. On the other hand, it was undeniable that the provision was practicable to meet the existing danger in the Far East, which no international organization, including the United Nations, could adequately address.

The Security Treaty grants the United States the use of Japanese territory for the purpose of contributing to the security of Japan on the one hand, and "for the purpose of maintenance of international peace and security in the Far East" on the other (revised Treaty, art 6). The American forces act on the right of self-defense for the former purpose, but it is unclear which provision of the Charter they act on for the latter.[60]

The United States may deem an armed attack directed against a third state in the Far East to be an attack against herself to be responded against by her own right of collective self-defense. It need not necessarily be deemed to be an attack on Japan if Japan has her own diplomatic and military policy independent of the United States'. However, under the Security Treaty with the United States, Japan could not be free of the policy of the United States taken for the purpose of "the maintenance of international peace and security in the Far East." If the US-Japan Security Treaty obligates Japan to take the same act as the United States, then Japan cannot reject it by reason that she does not deem the attack to be directed against herself.

A member of NATO may be placed in a similar position to Japan in the event of an armed attack against another member. However, the North Atlantic Treaty cannot be same as the US-Japan Security Treaty because it has no provision comparable to the Far East clause. In the case of NATO, only an attack directed towards any member or members is responded against in accordance with the Treaty. By contrast, the situation in a "third state" located in the Far East can be the subject of a military operation by American forces in Japanese territory as a result of the US-Japan Security Treaty.[61]

---

[60] Japanese writers point out the contradiction between the Far East clause and the system of self-defense under the UN Charter: see, for example, Yuichi Takano, "Kokusairengo Kenshou tono Kankei" (Relationship to the Charter of the United Nations), 59 *Kokusaihogaikozasi,* no. 1-2.

[61] As is pointed out later, NATO followed the example of the US-Japan Security Treaty in responding to the situation of a non-member state in Eastern Europe without any provision comparable to the Far East clause.

The operations are taken in accordance with US policy regarding the Far East, with which Japan may not necessarily agree. In order to amend this excessively one-sided relationship, they exchanged a note concerning implementation of article 6 of the Treaty. According to this note, "major changes in the deployment into Japan of the United States armed forces, major changes in their equipment, and the use of facilities and areas in Japan as bases for military combat operations to be undertaken from Japan other than those conducted under article 5 of the said Treaty, shall be the subjects of prior consultation with the Government of Japan" (Washington, 19 January 1960).

In spite of this note, it is not clear whether the changes in the deployment of the American armed forces depend on the consent of Japan. In other words, the question is whether she can refuse such activity at the consultation. If Japan is not free to answer, then the prior consultation will necessarily involve Japan in the American operations, regardless of what she really desires.

As far as the express provisions of the Japanese Constitution are concerned, there is no provision for self-defense, whether individual or collective. The Japanese Government takes the view that collective self-defense is prohibited by the Constitution, so any assistance given the United States in action in the Far East cannot be collective self-defense on the part of Japan.

The Japanese Government is clever in adopting this interpretation in order to avoid the situation where an armed attack against the United States is automatically regarded as being against Japan. Nevertheless, Japan cannot remain indifferent to military action by the United States, the bases for which are offered of Japan's own free will.

Under traditional international law, Japan could not be neutral under the US-Japan Security Treaty in a conflict in which the United States participates by the use of military force. The law of neutrality prohibits a neutral state from granting the use of military bases to any belligerent states. Thus, Japan was involved in the Vietnam War until 1975 and the Gulf War in 1990 fought with American forces sent from Japanese bases.

In light of the practice in the prewar period, the status of Japan under the US-Japan Security Treaty is exactly the same as "non-belligerency" in relation to the United States and her enemies. Bearing in mind that the organization of the Allied Nations, or the United Nations, is an outcome of the practice of "non-belligerency," it is noteworthy that the postwar situation of "non-belligerency" is based on the US-Japan Security Treaty, which is executed independently of the United Nations Charter.

The status under the US-Japan Security Treaty is not a creation of the Charter system, but rather an outcome of the "partial peace" in San Francisco, which is accorded with neither the procedure of traditional international law nor that of the United Nations Organization.[62] The Treaty was accepted not because it accorded

---

[62] Most leading Japanese writers in the 1950s argued that in order to gain independence, they should not intensify the conflict by taking sides with any conflicting power: Abe Nozei, "Shinzen to Fuso to Dokuritsu to" (Amity, no Struggle and Independence), *Sekai*, December 1950, p. 53. Nevertheless, they fell into contradiction in supporting early peace, the possibility of which was found only in "partial peace" with the Western powers.

with any established international normative regime, but because it was effective to meet the realities of international society in the 1950s.[63]

In examining the constitutional basis of the American forces in Japan, a district court has held that the US-Japan Security Treaty violates the Constitution prohibiting the Government from maintaining any military forces within Japanese territory.[64] However, the Court did not discuss how the apparent inconsistency between law and reality is settled in practice.

This judgment was reversed and remanded by the Supreme Court by reason that the US forces are not regulated by the Japanese Constitution. The Court did not, however, mention the responsibility of the Japanese Government as party to an international agreement for creating this situation under the Security Treaty. The Court held that a matter of security is left to the exclusive jurisdiction of the Government, and is not justiciable as "an act of the Government" (16 December 1959).

In stipulating "the Far East Clause" in the US-Japan Security Treaty, there is no evidence that they seek to base it on any provision of the United Nations Charter, including article 51, or the Constitution. On the contrary, it is assumed that the United States places the Treaty out of the system of the United Nations, to operate under no decision of the Security Council and no condition of self-defense or occurrence of an "armed attack" in the Far East. In doing so, the United States makes tactful use of article 107 of the Charter validating action taken in relation to an enemy state during the Second World War.

Assuming invalidation of every "enemy clause" in the Charter, the consistency of US-Japan Security Treaty with article 51 of the Charter would be questioned. That is to say, an act on the Treaty may be in violation unless taken on condition of collective self-defense. If any armed response of the United States is conciliatory with the UN Charter, then Japan must be aligned with the United States by recognizing the original attack as an "armed attack" against both.

However, Japan would not always invoke the right of self-defense in cooperating with the United States in armed action in the Far East. That is because the Japanese Government insists on the view that the Constitution prohibits her from recourse to the right of collective self-defense.

This situation may have been the intention, rather than the oversight, of General MacArthur regarding the Constitution, who declared that he would not form an alliance with Japan, but make her remain neutral in the US strategy in the Pacific (3 March 1949). Soon after this declaration, however, he must have changed his mind when, in response to the outbreak of hostilities in the Far East, including Korea, he directed the Japanese Government to establish the National Police Reserve.

The Peace at San Francisco came into effect in 1952, the Cold War ended in 1989,

---

[63] After reopening diplomatic relations with Japan in 1972, China would not align herself with the Soviets on this matter. She will support the US-Japan Security Treaty insofar as it prevents Japan from rising to become a military power. With respect to the renewal of the Guidelines for US-Japan Defense Cooperation, she warned Japan in 1999 that it must not lead to the full-scale rearmament of Japan.

[64] Tokyo District Court, 30 March 1959.

and the situation is now slowly departing from the international regime originating in the Second World War. In this situation, Japan has not moved to end the stationing of American forces within her territory. Nor has the United States has changed her position towards invoking the clause of the US-Japan Security Treaty "for the purpose of maintenance of international peace and security in the Far East" in mobilizing her forces in Japanese territory.

Far from it, they have improved their Guidelines for defense cooperation, leaving the rights and obligations under the US- Japan Security Treaty unchanged. This cooperation continues, just as the Japanese Constitution's requirement of "complete disarmament" as a result of the loss of the Second World War also remains unchanged.

The problem is how Japan's behavior serves to interpret the postwar international regime, which has survived landmark events in postwar history.

3. The US-Japan Security Treaty in a Regional International Regime

(1) A US-Japan Security Treaty unprejudiced by the UN Charter

a) During the Cold War, states found no ground other than self-defense upon which base their acts of force in the face of inaction by collective organizations competent to distinguish parties of an armed conflict into right and wrong. Since the end of the Cold War, they have been able to ground their acts on bases other than self-defense since the Security Council of the United Nations has come to examine conflicts and recommend that members assist one side to them.

Under these circumstances, the Japanese Government is moving to free herself from the handicap she has borne since losing the Second World War, namely her inability to act abroad by force even in situations where other states act jointly for the benefit of the party declared to be right in a conflict. She is also unable to take effective measures in times of crisis for the protection of her nationals abroad.

In this situation, Japan has had no choice other than to depend on the collective self-defense taken by foreign states on her behalf. At the same time, she could not exercise the right of collective self-defense for the benefit of other states under the current interpretation of her Peace Constitution. To act as a "normal member" of international society, it would be necessary for Japan to collaborate with the United Nations in a more progressive way when, for example, it declared that members should take joint forcible action to counteract a circumstance recognized as a "threat to the peace" or such.

On the occasion of the Gulf Crisis, when the Security Council authorized members to take all necessary measures to remove the invaders from Kuwait, the Japanese Government introduced a draft bill for a "Law on Cooperation with Peace Activities of the United Nations" in the Diet in October 1990.

Under the proposed legislation, Japan would have cooperated with foreign states in taking forcible action in compliance with resolutions of the United Nations. The law would make such cooperation dependent on resolutions of the United Nations. They would not be limited to those of the Security Council, but also include those of other organs of the United Nations, such as the General Assembly and its subsidiary organs. They would not necessarily be specific, as the law would permit the Government to act not only to fulfill United Nations resolutions, but also to ensure their effectiveness (clause 3).

It was pointed out that the Government's real intention in proposing the law was to facilitate closer cooperation with the United States in taking action in response to resolutions of the United Nations. Resolution 665 of the Security Council calls upon member states to halt all inward and outward maritime shipping to meet the Gulf Crisis, and Resolution 678 authorizes them "to use all necessary means" to implement the preceding resolutions. In taking action in compliance with the resolutions, the United States mobilized forces stationed in Japanese territory in accordance with the US-Japan Security Treaty. If the law were adopted by the Diet, Japan would extend wider assistance to the United States as the combined effect of the law and the US-Japan Security Treaty.

Under the proposed law, Japan would assist the blockade of ports in the Middle East by the US Navy, as authorized by the Security Council. This was not possible in the absence of such legislation, partly because it overstepped the limitation of "the Far East" in the US-Japan Security Treaty and partly because it was practically the same action as collective self-defense, the right to which the Japanese Government had long believed was inconsistent with the Constitution.

The vagueness in the scope and nature of the cooperation to be provided under the law was not solved in deliberations before the Diet. After three weeks of debate, the Government abandoned the proposed legislation and did not attempt to revive it in subsequent sessions.

One year after the withdrawal of the proposed "Law on Cooperation with Peace Activities of the United Nations," the Government introduced a bill in 1992 for a "Law Concerning Cooperation for United Nations Peacekeeping Operations and Other Operations (The Peacekeeping Cooperation Law)".[65] This Act was enacted in June 1992 and entered into force in August of the same year.

Sections 3 and 6 of the Act stipulate that Japan shall only cooperate with UN Peacekeeping Operations and international humanitarian relief operations in circumstances where the following basic conditions are satisfied:

1 Agreement between the conflicting parties to a ceasefire and maintenance of the cessation of hostilities;
2 Consent by the parties to an armed conflict and the host countries both to deployment of the PKOs and Japanese participation in such operations; and
3 Impartiality of the PKOs,

In addition to the above three principles, the following two principles must be observed:

---

[65] With respect to the circumstances of the withdrawal and adoption of these bills, see Wakamizu Tsutsui, "Conceptions of Japan's Security Affecting Cooperation with the United Nations," (1997) 27 *Victoria University of Wellington Law Review* 1.

4 Termination of the dispatch of personnel if any of the above principles is not satisfied; and
5 Limitation of the use of arms to the extent deemed reasonable and necessary for self-defense.

These mostly correspond to "peacekeeping," as described in a report by the Secretary General of the United Nations.[66] In contrast to the withdrawn Bill, the Law centers cooperation on "peacekeeping operations," the concept and practice of which seem to have been established without serious procedural difficulties in the Security Council.

In enacting this legislation, Japan finally adopted a policy of sending personnel, whether civil or military, overseas to assist activities understood to be "peacekeeping operations of the United Nations" or international humanitarian relief operations.[67] Since the Law entered into force on 10 August 1992, Japan has participated in peacekeeping operations in Angola, Cambodia, Mozambique, El Salvador and Golan Heights and international humanitarian relief operations in Rwanda.

Nevertheless, section 2 of Additional Provisions to the Peacekeeping Cooperation Law excludes some operations from implementation for the time being. They are:

1 Monitoring of whether the agreement on the cessation of armed conflicts is observed;
2 Patrolling in buffer zones; and
3 Collection of abandoned weapons.

That is because they overstep the constitution prohibition on the use of force on the part of Japan.[68]

On the occasion of the terrorists attacks in the United States on 11 September 2001, when the Security Council called upon all states to work together to bring the perpetrators to justice (Resolution 1368 (2001)), the Japanese Government brought a bill for a "Special Law to Deal with Terrorism," or the Antiterrorism Law, before the Diet.

The Law is effective for only two years and applies only to Self-Defense Force activities supporting the fight, authorized by the Security Council, against the terrorist assaults on the United States on 11 September 2001.[69] Subject to these

[66] Supplement to an Agenda for Peace, January 1995, para 33.

[67] Japanese civil personnel had already participated in operations not involving force on the basis of UN resolutions, including international election monitoring activities. The gist of International Peace Cooperation is the possibility of the Self-Defense Forces participating in activities abroad.

[68] Indeed, the Constitution renounces warlike action by use of the term, "the threat or use of force." However, the UN Charter also prohibits members from warlike action by use of the same term. It is absurd that the Japanese Government should argue Japan's special status on the basis of the same phrase as the UN Charter!

[69] At the same time as the adoption of the Anti-terrorism Bill, the Self-Defense Law was revised to enable troops to guard American bases in Japan from possible terrorist attacks and the Japan Coast Guard Law was amended to allow Coast Guard personnel to fire at vessels that invade Japanese territorial waters.

limitations, Self-Defense Force personnel will be sent abroad to extend logistical support to states fighting terrorism (including the United States) away from battle zones, on search and rescue missions, and in providing relief to refugees.

"Neutrality" characterizes peacekeeping, to which the Self-Defense Forces have extended help under the Peacekeeping Cooperation Law. By contrast, an antiterrorism campaign is an action taken on behalf of those in "the right," the distinction of which is recognized by the United Nations. In other words, Japan will be taking action overseas on a ground other than self-defense, which has long been believed to be the only legitimate and practical ground of forcible action under the UN system.

b) From a theoretical standpoint, the Peacekeeping Cooperation Law differs from the US-Japan Security Treaty in that it bases overseas activities of the Self-Defense Forces on UN resolutions. In this respect, it is the same as the Antiterrorism Law. By contrast, the US-Japan Security Treaty assumes the right of self-defense, which is exercised independently of UN resolutions and is the ground upon which action is taken.

From a practical standpoint, however, there is little difference in the conditions for action by the Self-Defense Forces, on whatever law it is based, insofar as it is linked to action by the United States. An action under the Peacekeeping Cooperation Law may be taken independently of the United States, but does not involve hostile action as long as it remains within the limitations of peacekeeping. By contrast, actions under the Antiterrorism Law are linked to those of the United States developed in Afghanistan, and the US-Japan Security Treaty will be executed in relation to American armed action occurring in the Far East.

As a matter of practice after the Cold War, the United States acts on resolutions by the United Nations, without prejudice to the right of self-defense. It is also quite possible that Japan will not be able to stand aloof from hostilities in "the Far East" by virtue of her obligations under the US-Japan Security Treaty, even if no UN resolutions are adopted with respect to them.

As long as the power structure in international society cannot be changed, the US-Japan Security Treaty regime continues to prevail over the United Nations system. The Soviet Union and Communist China naturally opposed the provisions of the US-Japan Security Treaty, which may serve to emasculate the veto powers of the permanent members of the Security Council to be exercised in a situation arising in the Far East.

The United Nations would not deny the fact that it does not necessarily prevail over a regional system based on the right of self-defense. Resolution 1368 of the Security Council, on the basis of which the Antiterrorism Law was enacted, provides that the existence of threats to international peace and security are to be met by all means, "recognizing the inherent right of individual and collective self-defense."

In municipal society, public authorities do not fail to move to punish a crime through criminal procedure, just as individuals bring lawsuits through civil procedure. By contrast, public authorities in international society do not move to punish offenders through established procedures distinct from individual actions.

Notwithstanding that article 51 of the UN Charter foresees a taking over of acts in self-defense by the United Nations, the Gulf War in 1990 under Resolution 661 and the counteractions against the terrorist attacks on the United States in 2001 under Resolution 1368 were developed by the US forces and their affiliates based on self-defense throughout the period they were taken.[70]

Acts of assistance under the Antiterrorism Law have characteristics of a collective or public act as well as collaboration with an individual act of the United States. The collaboration with an individual act is based on the right of collective self-defense. The Japanese Government takes the view that collective self-defense is inconsistent with the Constitution. Accordingly, there can be US-Japanese military collaboration on condition that the United Nations endorses the action of the United States as being in response to "a threat to international peace and security."

In legislating for overseas action, the Japanese Government has no discretion to choose the ground on which it is taken between the resolutions and self-defense. A resolution of the United Nations is acknowledged as a presentation of the will of "the peace-loving peoples of the world" described in the Constitution. In choosing the former, the Japanese Government must take into consideration, in addition to the situation above, the fact that the UN resolution is authoritative enough to make the people accept such potentially dangerous activity as the dispatch of the Self-Defense Forces abroad.

c) Cooperation with the United Nations is not complete insofar as the US-Japan Security Treaty regime takes precedence over the others. In opposition to this state of affairs, the following arguments prevail among writers:

Any act under the US-Japan Security Treaty is conditional upon self-defense, such as is provided for in article 51 of the UN Charter, "if an armed attack occurs against a member." In this context, action taken under the Far East clause of the US-Japan Security Treaty must be taken on the occurrence of "an armed attack," though the Treaty contains no express provision of that condition. In other words, American forces in Japan cannot take action in the Far East in the absence of an armed attack directed against the United States or Japan.[71]

This argument does not oppose US-Japanese cooperation based on the collective resolutions of the United Nations. In the rivalry between East and West, the United

[70] It may be asked whether additional resolutions are necessary to approve forcible actions specifically in taking further action to meet "a threat to international peace and security." With respect to the attacks against Iraq, which refused weapons inspections after ceasefire, see J. Lobel and M. Ratner, "Bypassing: Ambiguous Authorizations to Use Force, Cease-fires and the Iraqi Inspection Regime," 93 *AJ*, 1999, p. 124. However, it seems that the practice of taking further action on the original resolution without the specific approval of the Security Council has almost been established as far as the United Nations is concerned.

[71] In this context, opposition to the closer link with the United States is based more on the United Nations Charter. It intends to check the arbitrariness of the United States by being sympathetic to the Soviet and Chinese permanent membership of the Security Council. The Japanese Government does not dare deny this argument because it takes "close collaboration with the United Nations" as one of its fundamental postwar foreign policies. See, for example, Yuichi Takano, op. cit.

Nations rarely made such resolutions. In that situation, the argument would be nothing other than one against the US-Japan Security Treaty itself.

The argument fails, first of all, in overlooking the intrinsic nature of self-defense. In both theory and practice, an act in self-defense may be recognized as being collective. Article 51 of the UN Charter recognizes collective action taken by the Security Council as "measures necessary." Some resolutions of the Security Council have a phrase directing members to take action in accordance with Chapter VII of the UN Charter, affirming the right of self-defense of each member.

Cooperative acts under the US-Japan Security Treaty are not necessarily individual, but can be collective, depending on the will of international society. This is presumed from authoritative acts, including decisions of the Security Council. In being recognized to be collective, cooperative acts need not necessarily be based on a resolution specifying the means and manner of the action. Any resolution recognizing them as according with the intent of the United Nations is sufficient qualification for collective action so long as they are based on self-defense.

In the same context, any activity commenced as peacekeeping can develop into enforcement by the United Nations. The conversion may be declared publicly, as was the case with peacekeeping in Somalia in the 1990s. Although the procedures are not found in the exact provisions of the UN Charter, there is no reason why internationally organized forces cannot be deemed to be social forces engaging in sanctions.

The Peacekeeping Cooperation Law of 1992 grounds overseas action of the Self-Defense Forces of Japan on "peacekeeping," which is conditional upon ceasefire and the consent of the disputing parties. In light of the theory and practice of peacekeeping, it may be converted into enforcement action. A sanction or enforcement is, by definition, taken without ceasefire and consent. Opposition to US-Japanese security cooperation would not be persuasive so long as such opposition was based on the system of the United Nations recognizing the very provisions of the Charter, with no stipulation of the peacekeeping and self-defense practiced for more than half a century.

If the argument adhered to the Charter provisions, it had to take into consideration the clause that an action taken by an Allied Government in relation to an enemy state was excluded from the Charter provisions (art 107). The Peace Treaty and the US-Japan Security Treaty would be exempted from criticism by invoking the "enemy clauses" so long as the criticism was laid without regard to Japan's status as an "enemy state." Considering that the United Nations outlaws enemy states from the system, it is not surprising that the occupation authorities perceive an enemy's security system to fit its outlawed status.

It was of little concern to the Allied Nations whether the Peace Treaty and US-Japan Security Treaty, including the Far East clause, were consistent with the structure of the UN Charter. Whether they were contrary to traditional international law or not was contested even less.

Notwithstanding its extraordinariness and extra-UN nature, the US-Japan Security Treaty has survived the Cold War and will be strengthened to meet situations different from the confrontations between the Capitalists and Communists. It is noteworthy that the foundation of US-Japanese cooperation to meet the changed circumstances is not necessarily self-defense.

Procedural difficulties having been removed, the Security Council has come to authorize members' action more often, whether taken individually or jointly on the basis of security treaties. On the other hand, the causes and number of conflicts have increased with the greater diversity of value standards. There will be less argument about the exact application of article 51 of the Charter requiring the occurrence of "an armed attack against a member."

Throughout postwar history, the regional treaties system has remained unprejudiced by the general international organization, at least in the sense that no states can be indifferent to the situation in adjacent areas. In conceiving an international regime beyond the present, they may find the coordination of regional regimes a step towards it. The positive basis of such a regime would be bilateral treaties for regional security comparable to the US-Japan Security Treaty as well as international organizations such as the Organization for Security and Cooperation in Europe, European Union, League of Arab States, Organization of African Unity, and Organization for American States.[72]

(2) Constitutional pacifism undermined by US-Japanese cooperation

a) The Governments of the United States and Japan agreed on a comprehensive framework for cooperation under the US-Japan Security Treaty in the form of "Guidelines for Defense Cooperation." They originally agreed to this in 1978 in order to address the situation after the Vietnam War, and renewed it in 1997 to address the situation following the dissolution of the threat from the Soviet Union in the Far East.

In parallel with legislation for cooperation with the activities of the United Nations, the Japanese Government sought to increase cooperation with the United States on the basis of the US-Japan Security Treaty. The Guidelines Law was proposed by the Japanese Government in 1999, and supplemented by the Ship Search Law in 2000 in order to strengthen the internal structure for implementation of the renewed Guidelines.

The renewed Guidelines provide that the rights and obligations under the US-Japan Security Treaty and related arrangements as well as the fundamental framework of the US-Japanese alliance remain unchanged under any circumstances (II 1). They detail how the two governments will take steps to prevent a further deterioration of the situation whenever Japanese territory is under imminent attack, and how they will act when she is attacked.

The US-Japan Security Treaty has the purpose of contributing to the maintenance of international peace and security in "the Far East" as well as to the security of Japan. The Guidelines paraphrase the purpose in a different way, creating a basis for cooperation "in case of an armed attack against Japan, and in situations in areas surrounding Japan."

---

[72] See also chapter 2, note 68.

According to the Guidelines, "areas surrounding Japan" is not a geographic concept, but situational (V). The Japanese Government substituted that phrase for "the Far East," which had proven unsuitable as a concept for cooperating in humanitarian activities, the evacuation of civilians in armed conflicts, and actions giving effect to economic sanctions.[73]

Conflicts are highly probable in that area, as there persists the potential for instability and uncertainty even after the Cold War. Whichever conventional or unconventional means the parties to a conflict may take, Japan will not be able to remain aloof from such conflict if the United States has an interest in it.

The Guidelines state that Japan will conduct all action within the limitations of the Constitution (II 2). Accordingly, Japan would not engage in such operations as she excluded from implementation for the time being under the Peacekeeping Cooperation Law, even if she were under pressure to be discharged from the obligation of the Guidelines. The Guidelines do not expressly mention unconventional attacks on the United States and her nationals, but Japan could not remain indifferent to such attacks, though they may be responded against only by means beyond the limitations of the Constitution.

An increase in adoption of resolutions by the Security Council of the United Nations has not led the United States to cease basing her actions on self-defense, but rather to adopt a more liberal interpretation of it, taking advantage of the phrasing of resolutions. However, the Japanese Government and people would not abandon the strict doctrine of self-defense, on which they have developed arguments about their Constitution. In this situation, resolutions of the Security Council do not break the deadlock between the increasing need for cooperation with the United States and the restriction imposed by the Constitution.

However, there is a growing tendency to envisage a matter practically, leaving untouched the question of what doctrine they would take. The Antiterrorism Law was adopted after three weeks of deliberation by the Diet, in contrast to the Peacekeeping Cooperation Law, which took two years after rejection of the original draft. At the same time, operations hitherto excluded for the time being from implementation under the Peacekeeping Cooperation Law have now become possible as a result of amendments to the Law in December 2001.

b) With the outbreak of war on the Korean Peninsula, the United States moved to settle the status of the area by concluding a peace treaty between Japan and the states joining her in opposing the Communists. At the same time, she also sought to establish a regional system for security in Asia and the Pacific. In relation to Japan, the United States supplemented the Peace Treaty with the US-Japan Security Treaty. A tripartite security arrangement modeled after NATO was concluded between Australia, New Zealand and the United States in San Francisco on 1 September 1951. The US-Korea Mutual Defense Treaty of 1 October 1953 and the US-China (Taiwan) Mutual Defense Treaty of 2 December 1954 followed ANZUS.

In the original framework of the United Nations, such a system would best be

---

[73] Statement of the Japanese Government in the Diet, 140th session, Commission of Foreign Relations.

organized by a regional arrangement or agency under Chapter VIII of the Charter. The United Nations was deadlocked at the time under the paralysis of the Security Council. Under these circumstances, all the regional agreements took the right of self-defense under article 51 of the Charter as the legal basis for their action, except the US-Korea Mutual Defense Treaty, one party of which was not a member of the United Nations at the time of its conclusion.

As the systems for security in East Asia and the Pacific were motivated by the need to prevent the resurrection of Japan after her attainment of peace with the Allies, they could be exempted from the authorization of the Security Council in taking action on the basis of paragraph 1 of article 53, the "enemy clause" of the UN Charter. Nevertheless, the United States would not base the treaties for security in East Asia and the Pacific on the "enemy clause" since she was seeking a link with Japan, an enemy state, in order to accomplish a system that would be truly regional.

As the US-Japan Security Treaty is part of the regional security system conceived by the United States, it must cover all of East Asia and the Pacific without exception. In spite of this, the sphere of defense cooperation under the US-Japan Security Treaty is disputed for uncertainty, as "the Far East" is not defined in the text. The Guidelines for US-Japan Defense Cooperation of 1997 replace "the Far East" with "situations in areas surrounding Japan" in order to clarify the circumstances in which the Japanese Self-Defense Forces will act jointly with the American forces. What is important to the United States is the establishment of a regional security system having jurisdiction over the entire Asia-Pacific area.

"Situations" imagined at the time of renewal of the Guidelines were clashes around the armistice demarcation line of the Korean War and the straits between mainland China and Taiwan and around the Japanese mainland itself. Most of the "areas" were within the former Japanese Empire, the status of which would be settled by the consent of all the belligerents assembled at a peace conference, had the War ended according to the traditional procedure of international law. The United Nations will not "invalidate and preclude" the settlement if it is authorized "by the Governments having responsibility for such action" (art 107).

Nevertheless, a system exercised on the right of self-defense was established for the security of East Asia and the Pacific independently of the Peace Treaty of the Second World War. Basing the system's operations on this right, it is placed within the postwar general international organization.

During the Cold War, they conceived a regional system independently of general international organization, making favorable use of the "enemy clauses" and the provision of self-defense. As a matter of fact, any regional system was created to protect regional interests against the rival bloc. The security treaty network of East Asia and the Pacific, including the San Francisco Peace Treaty supplemented by the US-Japan Security Treaty, was also a regime protecting regional interests throughout the Cold War.

They act on the right of self-defense because it is the only concept independent of the veto power of the permanent members of the Security Council. Unless the US-Japanese joint actions in accordance with the Guidelines were grounded on enforcement or self-defense, whether in "the Far East" or surrounding areas, they would not be consistent with "basic principles of international law and relevant international agreements such as the Charter of the United Nations" (II 3).

According to the Guidelines, each government may conduct activities at its own discretion, such as relief activities and measures to deal with refugees, search and rescue, noncombatant evacuation operations, and activities for ensuring the effectiveness of economic sanctions for the maintenance of international peace and stability (V 2). In the case of an armed attack against Japan, she has primary responsibility to take action to repel it. The American forces will provide appropriate support to Japan through their own command-and-control channels in a coordinated manner with the Self-Defense Forces (IV 2).

All should have been regional actions rightly taken in the postwar international regime, rather than self-defense taken exceptionally in the framework of general international organization. The problem is that the postwar international regime was conceived as a general international regime, placing "regional arrangements or agencies" in a wrong position within it.

c) NATO spanning the Atlantic Ocean corresponds to the US-Japan Security Treaty in East Asia and the Pacific. Their histories differ, but they both include former enemy states within their membership with a view to rehabilitating them in the postwar international regime. They have successfully integrated Germany and Japan, as proven by German participation in regional action, including that in the former Yugoslavia and peacekeeping thereafter, and Japan's pledges of closer involvement in regional affairs under the reinforced arrangements with the United States.

Through such regional systems, an act taken by the former enemies can be collective in character. It depends on the political circumstances as to whether an act taken by the old enemies is authorized explicitly by collective organizations, as the veto power of the permanent members of the UN Security Council is exercised for political or other reasons.[74] Irrespective of the existence and procedural specification of the authorization, an act can be public, provided it is based on self-defense.

NATO took forcible action in former Yugoslavia in 1999 in a situation that the Security Council of the United Nations had recognized as deplorable. In the same resolution, the Council recalled provisions of Chapter VIII of the Charter and the role of the European Union (757, 30 May 1992). NATO could be accused by members of overriding the constituting instrument providing the condition that the organization should act on the right of self-defense, since none of the members had been attacked from outside when it took forcible action in former Yugoslavia. It could not be blamed, on the other hand, for overriding any norms of international society as the Security Council encouraged international organizations to take part in sanctions in the area.[75]

---

[74] China vetoed the military observation mission in Guatemala in 1997 on account of Guatemala's friendly relations with Taiwan.

[75] The OAS, EU, and NATO envisage external sanctions, irrespective of their respective constituting instruments: H. McCoubrey and N.D. White, *International Organizations and Civil Wars*, 1995, ch. 10.

What is certain is that exercise of force is left to individual states in international society, without entities corresponding to governments in municipal society. This situation has not changed, even with the increase of international organizations in number and powers.[76]

The legislation implementing the Guidelines in 1999 makes it easier for the Japanese Self-Defense Forces to take action in cooperation with the American forces, whether based on collective resolutions or not. "The surrounding area" in the Guidelines paraphrases "the Far East" in the Security Treaty, the original provision of which does not make the deployment of US forces from military bases on Japanese territory conditional upon self-defense.

The series of legislation, including the enactment of the Peacekeeping Cooperation Law, the Law to implement the Guidelines and the Antiterrorism Law, were attempts to fit the defense scheme established since Peace in San Francisco into the postwar international legal regime. It can hardly be denied that the Japanese Government has, throughout this process, drifted into invalidation of the "pacifism" of the Constitution in order to resume her "normal position" in international society. Another interesting characteristic of this progress is that it has been made by reinforcement of her cooperation with the United States.

4. "Enemy" Status Liquidated through Integration into a Regional Regime

(1) The international regime into which Japan was taken after peace

a) The United Nations was conceived and agreed upon by the Allied Nations as the general international organization in the course of the belligerent action of the Second World War. Under the Atlantic Charter, Cairo Declaration and the United Nations Charter, they called for the Axis nations to be "punished" as well as "expelled" from certain territories to be transferred to the Allied Nations.

As war was fought in the name of ideology, it would end in total destruction or unconditional surrender on the part of the enemies. The territory of the enemy was occupied in the process of war fought in that way, for the purpose of reforming that government and society along the lines of the victor's ideology rather than for the purpose of securing material interests. As the Cairo Declaration states, "The Three Great Allies covet no gain for themselves and have no thought of territorial expansion."

The Japanese Constitution, drafted by the Occupation authorities in the name of "revision" of the preceding Imperial Constitution, is revolutionary in two principles, namely democracy and pacifism. The party Cabinet system and respect for human

[76] Even in municipal society, public authority is not distinguished among entities fighting a civil war until one belligerent party turns out to be powerful enough to be recognized as the legitimate government. This particular point does not indicate any fundamental difference between international and municipal law.

rights are deduced from the principle of democracy, and the renunciation of war is a materialization of "internationalism" or pacifism to be followed by all members of international society, whether vanquished or not.

The outbreak of hostilities off the Japanese mainland on the Korean Peninsula led the Occupation authorities to hold a peace conference among the non-Communist Allies. It was the latter principle that brought the United States and Japan to conclude a Security Treaty since the Occupation powers would not withdraw from a war-renouncing Japan without adequate measures to prevent infiltration by neighboring Communist powers.[77] The US-Japan Security Treaty filled the power vacuum created on Japanese territory under a Constitution forbidding the "maintenance of land, sea and air forces as well as other war potential."

The Peace Treaty, supplemented by the US-Japan Security Treaty, did not change the existing situation whereby Japan was completely disarmed and had US forces stationed within her territory, but documented her integration into part of the postwar international regime. The Treaty was a counterpart to the North Atlantic Treaty concluded between Western European nations, the United States and Canada in 1949 and participated in by another principal former enemy, Germany. It was followed by bilateral defense agreements between the United States and other Asian-Pacific nations. The postwar international regime could not be completed if Japan were freed from Allied Occupation after a peace conference participated in by all the belligerents in accordance with the rules of traditional international law.

Notwithstanding a Constitution presupposing security by international organization of "the peace-loving peoples" or the United Nations, Japan entrusted her security not to a general or collective security system, but to self-defense or a regional system. This situation did not change once she was granted membership of the United Nations. On the contrary, she maintained a firm ground of self-defense after gaining membership as the UN Charter acknowledged the right of individual and collective self-defense as "inherent," indifferent to the status of a former enemy.

The original US-Japan Security Treaty negotiated under the Allied Occupation contained no provision relating to the basis of action, but reserved the obligations of the UN Charter on the part of the United States. When the Treaty was revised to address the intensification of the Cold War, it provided self-defense as the basis of the action, citing provisions in the UN Charter. The revised Treaty did not entirely clarify the ground of action taken thereupon, especially action taken in the Far East. This situation has not improved, even after the Treaty was supplemented by the Guidelines exchanged between the two governments.

Matters are further complicated by the interpretation of the Constitution adopted by the Japanese Government. According to the Government, the Constitution does not legitimate the right of collective self-defense to be exercised by Japan. If the right

---

[77] Under the circumstances of the hostilities on the Korean Peninsula, Japan could not follow the example of Austria, from which foreign forces withdrew on condition of her "permanent neutrality." This was partly because obligations of neutrality could not be discharged without military means held to a certain degree by the country and partly because foreign forces would not withdraw from Japan while they were using Japanese territory as a rear front to fight in Korea.

of collective self-defense did not justify an action under the US-Japan Security Treaty, then there would be a void filled by no other theory or practice beyond the UN Charter.

Arguments against the US-Japan Security Treaty have been developed politically, especially during the Cold War, as the Soviets and their allies opposed the peace attained in San Francisco in 1951 and reproached the revision of the Security Treaty in 1960. Such arguments have been politically orientated, without espousing any view on the postwar international regime.

Anyone, whether sympathizers with Communist ideology or not, would find it difficult to embrace this view while adhering to a UN system recognizing the exact provisions of the Charter. There would be no prospect of a regime beyond the present unless a positive view is taken of the present regime based on its practices from the start.[78]

b) According to article 6 of the US-Japan Security Treaty, the United States is granted use of Japanese territory "for the purpose of contributing to the maintenance of international peace and security in the Far East." In this context, an armed attack limited to American military bases is not necessarily deemed to be an attack against Japan.[79] If Japan responds to such attack, she has no other right than that of collective self-defense upon which to ground such response. According to the Japanese Government, however, she will not respond to any attack on the basis of the right of collective self-defense because it is inconsistent with the Japanese Constitution.

This interpretation is political insofar as it provides an excuse for not collaborating with American forces engaging in action not according with her interest.[80] However, she will not be deemed differently from the United States by third countries for the very reason that she permits the United States to use her territory as a military base.

Almost the same situation existed in the prewar period when "neutral" states stood on the side of one of the belligerents under the concept of "non-belligerency." That practice has developed into the postwar collective system, abrogating rules of traditional international law, including those of permanent neutrality. The UN Charter provides the organizational procedure to recognize extra-legal acts as being

---

[78] The general tone of comments by the press regarding the Guidelines Law has been severe. Most writers have opposed it by reason of its perceived inconsistency with the Constitution rather than with international law, including the principles of the United Nations as understood from the provisions of the Charter.

[79] There is some question as to whether Japan has sovereignty over the bases apart from limited title reserved for her. With respect to some islands including Okinawa, the Peace Treaty recognized this fact outright, stipulating that the United States is exercising "all and any powers of administration, legislation, and jurisdiction over the territory and inhabitants" (art 3).

[80] In relation to the support extended by Japan to the United States during the Gulf War, a writer observed, "The Constitution was drafted and imposed upon the Japanese by the United States, which is now finding that the restriction intended to prevent a resurgence of Japanese imperialism is working to its own disadvantage": L.C. Green, "The Gulf 'War', the UN and the Law of Armed Conflict," 28 *Archiv des Völkerrecht*, 1990, p. 396.

collective, in light of previous anti-enemy practice. At the same time, the Charter provides the same function for collective self-defense or defense action for another state, which is legitimately taken without organizational examination.

It is into this regime of collective self-defense that the "enemy states" are integrated through agreements concluded for the defense of each region. Development of such agreements has reduced the provisions in Chapter VIII of the Charter for "regional arrangements and agencies" as the regional counterpart of the United Nations to a dead letter.

The Covenant of the League of Nations contained an article excluding "regional understandings like the Monroe doctrine" from regulation (art 21), with no provisions according such understandings their due place within the system. In incorporating Germany into the League of Nations system, the system of Locarno Pacts, the regional counterpart of the League of Nations, was established among European states independently of the League in order to compensate for the lack of completeness of the League in that respect.

In the system of the United Nations, NATO has been the most effective inter-state defense system in Europe, and had the Organization for American States and the security treaty system between the United States and her affiliates in the Far East and Pacific as its counterparts. Most of them have a strict provision making an action conditional upon the right of self-defense exercised in the case of an armed attack against one or more of the members' territory (Rio Pact art 3, NATO art 5).

Regional organizations remain dependent on the alliance of their members, which is inconsistent with the collective principle. In fact, they base their actions on individual actions of self-defense, which is contrasted with collective action. Non-belligerency led to collective systems by superseding systems of alliance and neutrality. By contrast, regional organizations depend heavily on alliance and neutrality discarded in the interest of collective security. They have not abstained from actions beyond self-defense, but dared to overstep the United Nations scheme proved by the Charter provisions. NATO has attacked territory outside its treaty jurisdiction in the absence of an armed attack against any member. It committed itself to the war against terrorism triggered by the attacks against the United States on 11 September 2001 by regarding them as an action covered by article 5 of the Treaty on the assumption that they were directed from abroad against a member of it.[81]

The existing regional systems are effective not because of their link to the United Nations, but rather because of the necessity of the mutual defense of each region. The Charter of the United Nations is binding on non-members, as seen in article 2 paragraph 6, because it is based on the powers of one party to the Second World War overwhelming its opponents. If the postwar international regime truly desired

[81] The North Atlantic Council, 12 September 2001. This commitment may be regarded as unusual in that it dealt with terrorism rather than an attack by legitimate forces. However, it was not exceptional in regarding an attack against one member, the United States, as an attack against all the other members, which was legitimately based on the right of collective self-defense.

to be positive without intermediation by the United Nations, it could not fail to position each existing regional system in its structure in an effective way.

On the basis of practices discriminatory toward the enemies, the United Nations includes "public" characteristics in its structure. In its capacity as an original member of the United Nations, every state can be placed in a public position by invoking the "enemy clauses."[82] If the wartime practice taken in disregard of the enemies' rights could not be retained in the international regime into which enemy states are integrated, then the principle should be corrected to revive the principles of traditional international law, including neutrality and the sovereign equality of all states, just as regional organizations and treaties have had such correction.

The corrected regime would not necessarily be accorded with the UN Charter, as regional organizations and treaties have provisions like the Far East clause and practices such as the bombing of Kosovo, which are deviations from the requirement of the UN Charter that an armed act is legal on either the condition of self-defense or enforcement.

Japan is situated within a postwar international regime given effect by acts of self-defense, holding her Constitution up as proof of her acceptance of the Allies' ideology. If the Japanese Government comes to understand the Constitution differently from the intent of the drafters so that the nation is permitted to exercise the right of collective self-defense, then the postwar international regime will have come to a turning point in principle and structure evidenced by the practice of the Allied Nations.

c) In the context that an act against "enemy states" is *ipso facto* deemed to be public or collective, a forcible act taken under regional arrangements against a renewal of aggressive policy by the "enemies" is exempted from authorization by the Security Council (Charter art 53, latter part of para 1). Bearing in mind that not every member is necessarily in a position to invoke article 53 of the Charter, the "inherent right of self-defense" to every member is ascertained in the process of concluding the drafting of the UN Charter. According to an article added to the Proposal – article 51 of the present Charter – every member may act independently of the Security Council provided such action is in self-defense.

The frequent invocation of the right of self-defense is evidence that the postwar international regime is situated midway between the individual or sovereign regime and the public. As international organization created by the Allied Nations tolerates membership by their former enemy states, regional international organization and arrangements hesitate even less to accept them as indispensable members. On the occasion of the Gulf War in 1991, for example, the Security Council of the United

---

[82] State actions taken jointly by the five main powers are conceived to be those of the United Nations merely because they are taken by the said powers (art 106). Individual states' actions can be self-defense or collective actions, depending on the procedural conditions of the particular organization. There is no established procedure to distinguish between individual and public actions. In the Korean War, the Security Council adopted a resolution authorizing the forces engaged in opposing action to be United Nations Forces under the flag of the United Nations. This precedent does not restrict the nature or activities of future United Nations Forces.

Nations, an authentic organ of international society, specifically declared the act initiated by "the multinational forces" composed of the United States, United Kingdom and France "public." On other occasions, it will not declare so, leaving the act to continue to be an individual act or self-defense without the conviction that it is collective in character.

A national act commenced as an individual act may be converted into a collective or public one, with no change in personnel, equipment or command, provided it is based on the right of self-defense inherent to each state. The "enemies" in the Second World War, such as Germany and Japan, may be recognized as having "public" status by the competent organ, the decision of which is left to the discretion of the main Allies, provided they act on the condition of self-defense.[83]

The Gulf War ceased with the achievement of the initial aim of the release of the victim state from aggression, without the total destruction of the aggressor. This situation makes the presumption possible that the postwar international regime is not so biased as to depart from the original principle of international society, "freedom of conscience," on the basis of which traditional international law developed.

The postwar international regime is not just a system created by the Allied Nations, but one subsequently corrected to address the realities of an international society with diverse histories, religions, cultures, economies, political doctrines and military capabilities. It is a system corrected to address the reality that states that have lost a total war are rehabilitated after loss of the traditional means of recovery of peace as a consequence of the invalidation of traditional international law in that respect.

(2) Regional regimes to be taken into the future general regime

a) In joining the League of Nations, Germany claimed to be immune from military burdens, while insisting on her permanent membership of the Council.[84] In joining the United Nations, Japan did not attempt similar as she believed she would not be asked to contribute to enforcement actions by virtue of her Peace Constitution. Considering her handicapped position, it may be natural to assume that Japan would claim no privileges, including permanent membership of the Security Council, even after rising to become an economic power.

After gaining membership of the United Nations, Japan continuously renewed

---

[83] In addition, Japan funded the activities of the multinational forces to the tune of 13 billion dollars.

[84] In contrast with Japan, which was eager to become a member of the United Nations, Germany was indifferent to acceptance by the League of Nations. In 1924, Foreign Minister Stresemann addressed his memorandum to each member of the Council, contending that Germany had to be assured of immediately receiving a permanent seat on the Council, allowed to take no part in economic and military sanctions, not be asked to repeat the admission of responsibility for the war, and given a share in the mandatory system: Walters, *op. cit.*, p. 279. Japan's application for membership of the United Nations was rejected once due to veto by the Soviets, in return for nationalist China's veto against the Mongolian People's Republic. In 1956, the Soviets abstained from the veto against Japanese membership in accordance with their agreement in the Joint Declaration between the Soviet Union and Japan.

her membership of the Council until she lost the election in 1978 to a newly independent state, Bangladesh. As Japan's financial contribution to the United Nations came to be second only to the United States, she sought permanent membership of the Security Council on the basis of her contribution to purposes of the Organization other than the maintenance of international peace and security (Charter, art 23 para 1).[85]

If the "enemy states" rose to a privileged position within the Organization because of their contribution to purposes other than the principal one, it could be deemed to have turned into the same situation as the League of Nations, in which the non-original members of Germany and the Soviet Union gained privileged membership. The principle of sovereign equality invalidated to the detriment of the "enemy states" would almost revert to its former status if the United Nations placed them on an equal footing with the main Allies in terms of privilege.

Japan ended her war with the Allied Nations on the terms of the Potsdam Declaration and restored her sovereign status by concluding a peace treaty after the Allied Occupation following the agreed armistice. The process appeared to accord with the rules of traditional international law, especially in comparison with the process of recovery of Germany, which had been divided into East and West until the end of the Cold War.

Germany had no basis for ending the War as she had, at the time of cessation of hostilities, no government competent to accept terms comparable to the Potsdam Declaration. In other words, Germany fell into *debellatio*, though not in the strict sense of the concept, which was not possible as a result of warfare between the members of the Family of Civilized Nations.

By contrast, Japan ended the War by concluding a peace treaty, although only some of the belligerents were represented among the parties to that Treaty and the Occupation preceding the peace was extraordinarily long. The situation was also unusual in that no obligation of disarmament was imposed on the vanquished, unlike other peace treaties such as the Versailles Treaty at the end of the First World War. This is not surprising in view of the fact that Japan had already been destroyed so completely that further disarmament was impossible.

The process as a whole could be persuasive enough to prove the invalidation of traditional international law. It also provides evidence of the nature of the postwar international regime, albeit indirectly.

Amid increasing confrontation between East and West, the postwar international regime survived rather than being invalidated, thanks to the original structure of the Organization of the Allied Nations. The veto power vested in the original main Allies has prevented the Organization from dissolving as a result of

[85] The defeat of an economic power, ranked third in the world to the United States and Soviet Union by her financial contributions, in the election by a newly independent state, was symbolic of the ideological character of the United Nations. She sought permanent membership of the Council on the basis of her contribution to purposes other than the maintenance of international peace and security, including financial contributions, as cited as conditions of membership in article 23 of the Charter: Speech by Foreign Minister K. Aichi in the General Assembly on 15 September 1970.

their withdrawal.[86] It was also the cause of the Allied Organization's loss of status as the main forum of public sanction. Since the end of the Second World War, any main powerful member, including the United States, has responded to "armed attacks" against member states, whether such attacks were conventional or unconventional.

A regional security organization or treaty is more reliable than the mechanism of Chapter VII in the UN Charter. It is put into effect by making the right of collective self-defense certain to be exercised by the parties. This is the situation under which "the peace-loving peoples of the world," to whom Japan's "security and existence" are entrusted under her Peace Constitution, can be a regional security system rather than the United Nations. In such circumstances, the position she holds in the regional security system is more important than the one she does in the general collective international organization, the United Nations. Taking notice of this effect, the Soviets did not hesitate to justify their cancellation of the return of the islands agreed to in the Joint Declaration in 1956 on the basis of the innovations of the regional security system or the US-Japan Security Treaty in 1960.

Tensions in Europe and the outbreak of the Korean War in the Far East led the Allies to associate with their former enemies on the basis of self-defense in their competition with each rival bloc.[87] The two German regimes and Japan were thus placed in responsible positions in each regional regime prior to gaining membership of the general international organization.

In light of the process through which they regained sovereign status after total devastation in the Second World War, it is to the regional regimes that they give priority in entrusting their security. Germany has relied more on NATO and the EU than the United Nations in ensuring her security. Japan hesitates to place more importance upon regional arrangements, including the US-Japan Security Treaty, but appears to have become aware of their importance, as seen in the series of enactments on the overseas operations of the Self-Defense Forces.

Communism was claimed to be general, but no true Communist community ever existed in the real sense. The basis of the Warsaw Pact was the military forces of the

---

86 By contrast, permanent members of the Council of the League of Nations withdrew from it due to their displeasure with its reproach of their policies. There cannot be a similar withdrawal of the major members of the United Nations as they have recourse to the veto power to prevent any decisions unfavorable to them and their affiliates.

87 The ultimate cause was the limitation of the United Nations, the general international organization, to the Allied Nations' jurisdiction. In this context, it was wrong for General MacArthur to draft the "renunciation of war clause" of the Japanese Constitution in connection with "the justice and faith" of "the peace-loving peoples of the world." The General's second basic "Must" in the revised Constitution had a negative implication for the right of self-defense to be conferred upon Japan. The adopted Constitution is not free of that original idea. In deliberations in the Diet, Prime Minister Yoshida's statement had a connotation that Japan renounced the right of self-defense as well as that of making war. In reply to a question by a Communist member, he stated words to the effect that the clause does not indeed specify the right of self-defense to be renounced, but achieves a renouncement of that right as a result of disarmament and the renunciation of "the right of belligerency" of the State as well as war. In doing so, the suspicion that a rearmed Japan will engage in a war of retaliation will be completely removed: see note 45.

Soviet Union, rather than the ideological persuasiveness of Communism. By contrast, the existence of the North Atlantic community may be proven. The European Union is developing on the basis of economic interdependencies and historical and cultural identity, rather than a united force.

The furtherance of regional unification in East Asia would be difficult due to the lack of regional solidarity. Unlike Europe, East Asia has no common civilization under which it can be united. On the other hand, East Asia does share a common history of prosperity under the prevalence of Chinese civilization and subjugation under Western colonialism. It is also clear that East Asia cannot do without the Oceania area, where the presence of the United States continues. Until such time as solidarity forms over a wider region, the current network of bilateral security arrangements will induce the region to act jointly in every field, as international organizations such as NATO and OAS have done in other regions.

b) Regionalism is believed to be at variance with peace as it tends to lead to wars fought to seize hegemony in the region. This was the case with both World Wars and the Cold War in the twentieth century. The United Nations was conceived as the general international organization because the United States, which was the only world power among the belligerents, took the initiative in the postwar international regime. Any international regime is positive provided it is renewed after the practice taken just before. In this context, the Dumbarton Oaks Proposals were correct in taking regional arrangements and agencies into the proposed system, as was the practice of regional cooperation in wartime.

At the last stage of drafting the UN Charter, the members amended the original scheme of the Proposals by providing an article confirming the right of self-defense. The postwar international regime has developed on the basis of regional arrangements on the right of self-defense, as well as general instruments, such as the UN Charter, and related instruments of general character, including those of "specialized agencies."

The "enemy states" were rehabilitated by being integrated into each opposing bloc of the Allied Nations, instead of concluding peace treaties with all the other belligerents. Similarly, newly independent states began their presence in international society by being accepted into one or more regional blocs in Southeast Asia, Africa and the Islamic world as well as the general international organization.

The Soviets united the East European nations under the Warsaw Pact and used it to suppress defiant states that threatened to break away from that bloc. NATO, the Western counterpart of the Warsaw Pact, has predominated over the United Nations in dealing with local struggles in Europe. In some cases, it has taken forcible action as if it has replaced the Security Council.

The United States and Japan have developed their defense cooperation since 1951, reinforcing the provision of self-defense on which it is based in the Security Treaty and supplementing it with Guidelines in order to address tensions in East Asia, around China, Taiwan and the Korean Peninsula after the Cold War.

With the activation of regional cooperation, general international organization has a lesser role to play in the maintenance of international peace and security. Japan is not an indispensable member of the United Nations, apart from her substantial financial contributions second only to the United States, but is indispensable to security in East Asia, which has also relied most heavily on American support.

It is no coincidence that international organizations based on real communities have disregarded the UN Charter openly. NATO, overlapping with the European Union, intervened in the former Yugoslavia without prior authorization of the Security Council under article 53 paragraph 1 of the Charter. Furthermore, it disregarded the North Atlantic Treaty itself by using armed force in the absence of an armed attack to be responded against with bombing (art 5).

NATO sought to justify its extra-legal acts on the ground of humanitarian necessity. Violations of humanitarian law may reasonably be responded against by forcible means.[88] Judging from the provisions of the UN Charter, however, members have no excuse for taking forcible means for humanitarian necessity.

Treaties are corrected without literal amendment through practice contrary to the provisions. International law consists of treaties and custom developed from practices. The international legal regime is not free of modifications to the existing international society. If humanitarian needs were repeatedly met by practices contrary to treaty provisions, they would not, in the ultimate interest of international society, remain valid. As inhumanity in racial tensions has become so acute as to necessitate some timely response, so the international regime should be modified to accord with the practices of NATO.[89]

The postwar international regime may have survived the Cold War, but will not necessarily survive clashes resulting from differences in culture, levels of development in economics and democracy, and other social beliefs. Nations sharing a common value, such as Western-style democracy, may find conciliation with one another easier to attain than with nations having Islamic teachings, cultures under strong Confucian influence and so on, which have clashed with each other over such differences. What may lead to global catastrophe is a clash resulting from differences in beliefs.

Under the system of the United Nations Charter, the only possible basis for conciliation is self-defense, apart from certain theories and policies propounded on this concept. The problem is whether that concept is sufficiently established to form the basis of conciliation, which is extremely difficult in view of the greater diversity of value standards.

c) Peace was recovered among the belligerents of the Second World War on the basis of regional conciliation despite the loss of the means of recovery of peace on a general basis. Solidarity of regions has progressed in every region, such as Western

---

88 See, for example, "Editorial Comments: NATO's Kosovo Intervention," 93 *AJ*, 1999, pp. 824-862.

89 The NATO alliance's exemption from the rule of no use of force in action in Kosovo may not be convincing in the absence of an express mandate by the Security Council: Javier Solana, "NATO's Success in Kosovo," 78 *Foreign Affairs*, no. 6, p. 118. However, it cannot be denied that the role played by a region in giving effect to humanitarian principles, the ultimate norm of international society, has been clarified by the definite action of NATO, taken in disregard of the interests of each disputing party.

Europe, the United States and Japan, Southeast Asia, the other newly independent nations, and so on. The lower incidence of confrontations between East and West may be a result of the progress in regionalism in the decades since the Second World War.

On the basis of regional integrity, the international regime has come to be stable and positive since the War. General international organization conceived on the initiative of the United States has been amended to strengthen its positive basis by meeting the claims of members for autonomy in each region.

As far as international lawyers are concerned, the ineffectiveness of norms of international society is most serious. This may lead to the resurrection of a "medieval" situation in contemporary international society, which was superseded by the advent of "modern international society."

International law was not conceived until nations were recognized as equals without discrimination on the basis of belief, culture, race, politics and so forth. There was indeed a phase in modern international society in which non-European civilized nations were excluded from the benefits of international law. The way they were treated was "medieval" in the sense that they fought a war without knowing the humanitarian principles involved in international law. The situation came to be improved through recognition of some foreign civilizations as being equal to the Europeans', just as Japan was recognized as a member of the "civilized" family in the mid-nineteenth century.

In this context, regionalism has been denounced as a cause of disorder in international society. At the same time, however, it has been taken in every attempt to create a general international organization. The situation may be criticized by reason of its encouragement of disunity in international society. This criticism is incorrect if it overlooks the fact that, apart from wartime alliance, no union has ever existed in international society.

As a matter of fact, the United Nations originates in the wartime union of the Allied Nations in the Second World War. The contribution to victory in the Second World War is the source of privilege and authority in the Organization. It is "public" because it is organized on the basis of discriminatory practices in favor of the sanctioning states against the aggressors – in other words, in favor of the victors against the vanquished. The problem is that the successful operation of sanctions necessarily involves inhumanity and devastation not only on the vanquished, but also on the part of the victorious.[90] In this situation, there is every reason to accept the contention that they take a forcible action in the cause of humanity.

The Second World War terminated in an indistinctive way between war and peace, without expression of the will of all the belligerents for conciliation.

---

[90] It has been reported that 260,000 Japanese civilians perished and another 420,000 were wounded by air attacks upon Japanese cities. Some 920,000 suffered war damage: *Yomiuri Shimbun*, 24 August 1945. Other statistics reveal even greater loss of civilian life. Significantly more civilians are believed to have been killed during the War in the Soviet Union and China. The total loss of life among nationals of the major Allied Nations, including soldiers and civilians, exceeded that of the Axis states: Q. Wright, A Study of War , Appendix A, p. 1542.

Rehabilitation of Japan, an enemy state to the Allied Nations, was not given consent through negotiations among the belligerents, but implied by the entry into force of the US-Japan Security Treaty, keeping the Constitution valid as an international instrument in substance.[91] The San Francisco Peace Treaty was too incomplete in terms of the parties to it and its contents to provide an adequate foundation for Japan in postwar international society.

One reason why the Second World War concluded in such an indistinctive way between war and peace was because the involvement of the people was too great for them to be persuaded to accept the conditions of ceasefire agreed between the governments.[92] In fact, the hostilities continued in an irregular way and developed into "wars for national liberation" after they terminated between regular forces.

There could not be a just and stable international regime without paying due regard to the need for such regional regimes. Bearing in mind the circumstances to date, there may be good reason to seek replacement of the United Nations by some other regime beyond it. In a future phase of international society, elements of public law will necessarily be adopted more than they are at present, with sovereign equality remaining as the guiding principle.

Not only aggression, but also international crimes such as terrorism, must be dealt with effectively in order to maintain international peace and security. In the capacity of an international public authority, any state may take the task of suppressing international crimes in the most effective way. In spite of the law and practice of the postwar international regime, any concept better than self-defense could ground an individual act taken in international society in the near future.[93]

Regionalism will necessarily assume its due position more than it does at present in light of the past practice and future possibility of more intercultural confrontations. In whatever way a general international organization may be conceived, self-defense could not be the best choice of concept to ground individual action, despite the adoption of that practice in the postwar international regime.

5. Concluding Remarks

The Second World War has been the most significant impetus to change in the

[91] To keep the policy of Japan in check, foreign governments often remind the Japanese Government of the constitutional principle of "war renunciation," just as President Kim Dae-jung of South Korea did to Prime Minister Junichiro Koizumi in the course of examining the Antiterrorism Law in October 2001. Such practice is extraordinary insofar as the Constitution is a domestic law in the true sense.

[92] At the fiftieth anniversary of the San Francisco Peace Treaty in September 2001, both the US and Japanese Governments confirmed the settlement of war claims, and the Japanese Foreign Minister apologized for the ill treatment of American prisoners of war.

[93] The United States based her actions in response to the terrorist attacks on New York and Washington on 11 September 2001 on self-defense rather than resolutions of the United Nations. In view of the nature of terrorist activities, they must be responded against socially or publicly rather than individually, regardless of resolutions by the United Nations. As procedural difficulties create problems for their adoption, other law and practice should be established as a basis for an instant response by the victim states.

international legal regime over the past two centuries. It brought unprecedented destruction to a world that could no longer be under traditional international law. Opposing ideologies cancelled out the effect of the principle of no discrimination against civilizations, which had brought every nation to be equal under international law.

Destruction is the other side to construction. Great war brings international organization to fruition. The United Nations is a public entity or the "world government" for one reason or another. The postwar international legal regime is one of war renunciation to be executed by the United Nations.

Any international regime cannot be effective without being based on the practice from which it came into existence. In fact, the Allied Nations was a collection of wartime collaborations in each region. The provision of self-defense in the UN Charter reflects this reality.

Japan, as a main enemy of the Allied Nations, escaped from dissolution as a state on condition that she would enact a "Peace Constitution." If general international organization were effective enough to sustain the independence of any state, then Japan would be independent, "trusting in the justice and faith of the peace-loving peoples of the world," as provided by the Constitution. In fact, she concluded a Security Treaty with the United States based on the right of self-defense. This was regarded as necessary in order to meet the particular circumstances of the Cold War. After the conclusion of the Cold War, however, they have continued to strengthen the Treaty system rather than give effect to the Peace Constitution.

Under the circumstances existing around the turn of the century, the UN Charter does not preclude action considered to be justified, such as action by NATO outside the Treaty area, including the bombing of Kosovo, and the United States' war of counteraction against terrorism, including military attacks in Afghanistan. There may be U.S.-Japan joint action in "the Far East" without the clear authorization of the United Nations. Both NATO and the U.S.-Japan Security Treaty system have "enemy" states as core members, unlike the United Nations in which the main Allies continue to enjoy the prerogative.

This series of events may be a sign that the postwar international legal regime itself is heading towards another regime. Whatever regime should follow the present one, it will need to be more collective or "public" in order to address the increasingly common interests of the international community, including the harmonious development of each nation, eradication of international crime, establishment of the rule of law, and so forth.

Such a regime would be effective when its institution is one of regional cooperation recognizing the equal value of each civilization. In such a regime, self-defense would not be the main concept on which to base "public" actions, as it is in the postwar international legal regime. Rather, it would be based upon a concept closer to social action, departing from individual concepts such as "necessity" and self-defense.

On whatever concept it might be based, it would draw more on the fundamental principles of traditional international law, including the humanity principle based on "freedom of conscience," the superiority of which has been doubted in the postwar international regime.

SELECT BIBLIOGRAPHY

* indicates that the work has not been cited, but was referred to in writing this book.

Abe, N., Shinzen to Fuso to Dokuritsu to (Amity, no Struggle and Independence), *Sekai*, December 1950.

Akehurst, M., Reprisals by Third States, *British Yearbook of International Law*, 1970.

Akindele, R. A., From the Covenant to the Charter: Constitutional Relations between Universal and Regional Organizations in the Promotion of Peace and Security, *Israel Law Review*, 1973.

Amador, G., Sohn, L. and Baxter, R. R., *Recent Codification of the Law of State Responsibility for Injuries to Aliens,* 1974. *

Ariga, N., *La guerre Sino-Japonaise au point de vue droit international, 1896 and La guerre Russo-Japonaise au point de vue droit international*, 1908.

Asprey, R. B., *War in the Shadows: The Guerrilla in History*, 1975, 2 vols.

Badr, G. M., The Exculpatory Effect of Self-Defense in State Responsibility, 10 *Georgia Journal of International Comparative Law*, 1980.*

Bailey, S. D., Veto in the Security Council, 566 *International Conciliation*, 1968.

Beckett, W. E., *The NATO, Brussels Treaty and the Charter of the United Nations.**

Benedict, R., *The Chrysanthemum and the Sword: Patterns of Japanese Culture*, 1946.

Bertrand, M., *Refaire L'UNO*, 1991.

Boutros-Ghali, B., *An Agenda for Peace*, 1955.

Bowett, D. W., Collective Self-defence under the Charter of the United Nations, *British Yearbook of International Law*, 1955–1956.*

Bowett, D. W., *Self-defense in International Law*, 1958.

Bowett, D. W., *United Nations Forces*, 1964.

Bowett, D. W, Reprisals Involving Recourse to Armed Force, 66 *American Journal of International Law*, 1972.

Brierly, J. L., *The Law of Nations*, (6th ed.), 1963.

Briggs, H. W., The Leaders' Agreement of Yalta, 40 *American Journal of International Law*, 1946.

Brownlie, I., The Use of Force in Self-defense, *British Yearbook of International Law*, 1961.

Brownlie, I., *International Law and the Use of Force by States*, 1963.

Caron, D. D., The Legitimacy of the Collective Authority of the Security Council, 87 *American Journal of International Law*, 1993.*

Cassese, A. (ed.), *The Current Legal Regulation of the Use of Force*, 1986.*

Churchill, W. S., *The Second World War*, vol. 4; The Hinge of Fate, 1951.
Colbert, E. S., *Retaliation in International Law*, 1948.*
Crawford, J., *The Creation of States in International Law*, 1979.
Dinstein, Y. D., *War, Aggression and Self-defense*, 1988.*
Dore, I. I., *International Law and the Super Powers,* 1984.*
Dulles, J. F., A First Balance Sheet of the United Nations, 420 *International Conciliation*, 1946.
Dulles, J. F., *War or Peace*, 1950.
Eagleton, C., The Needs of International Law, 34 *American Journal of International Law*, 1940.
Eagleton, C., *International Government* (rev. ed.), 1948.
Elagab, O. Y., *The Legality of Non-forcible Counter-Measures in International Law*, 1988.*
Falkenstein, W. T., *Bedeutung der Feindstaatenartikel für Deutschland*, 1975.*
Feinberg, N., *The Legality of a "state of war" after the cessation of hostilities: Under the United Nations and the Covenant of the League of Nations*, 1961.*
Fenwick, C. G., Neutrality on the Defensive, 34 *American Journal of International Law* 1940.
Fitzmaurice, G., General Principle of International Law, *Recueil des cours de l'Académie de droit international*, 1957, vol. 2.*
Fukuzawa, Y., *Gakumon no susume (An Exhortation to Learning)*, 1873.
Garner, J. W., *International Law and the World War*, 2 vols, 1920.
Genoni, M. A. M., *Die Notwehr im Völkerrecht*, 1987.*
Gietz, A., *Die Neue Alte Welt: Roosevelt, Churchill und die Europäische Nachkriegsordnung*, 1986.*
Giraud, E., La théorie de la légitime défense, *Recueil des cours de l'Académie de droit international*, 1934, vol. 3.*
Goulding, M., The Evolution of United Nations peacekeeping, *International Affairs,* 1993–3.
Gowlland-Debbas, V., Security Council Enforcement Action and Issues of State Responsibility, 43 *International and Comparative law Quarterly*, 1994.
Green, L. C., The Gulf "War", the UN and the Law of Armed Conflict, 28 *Archiv des Völkerrecht*, 1990.
Greig, D.W., Self-defence and the Security Council: What does article 51 require? 40 *International and Comparative law Quarterly*, 1991.
Grotius, H., *De Jure Belli ac Pacis* ,1925, translation in J.B. Scott (ed.), *The Classics of International Law.*
Hall, W. E. A., *Treatise on International Law*, 1909.
Hemleben, S. J., *Plans for World Peace Through Six Centuries*, 1943.
Higgins, R., The Legal Limits to the Use of Force by Sovereign States: United Nations Practice, *British Yearbook of International Law*, 1961.*
Higgins, R., *United Nations Peacekeeping 1946-1967: Documents and Commentary*, 3 vols, 1970.
Higgins, R., The New United Nations and former Yugoslavia, *International Affairs* 1993–3.

Higuchi, Y., (ed.), *Five Decades of Constitutionalism in Japanese Society*, 2001.
Hilderband, R. C., *Dumbarton Oaks: The Origin of the United Nations and the Search for Postwar Security*, 1990.*
Hill, N. L., *International Administration*, 1931.
Hudec, R. E., *Developing Countries in the GATT System*, 1987.
Huntington, S. P., The Clash of Civilizations, *Foreign Affairs*, Summer 1993.
Jennings, R. Y. The Caroline and McLeod Cases, 32 *American Journal of International Law*, 1938.
Jessup, P. C., *A Modern Law of Nations*, 1950.
Kant, I., *Zum ewigen Frieden*, 1795, translated by Hastie, W., *Kant's Eternal Peace*, 1914.
Kaplan, L. S., *The United States and NATO*, 1984.*
Kelsen, H., *The Law of the United Nations*, 1951.
Kelsen, H. and Tucker, R. W., *Principles of International Law*. 1966.*
Kempeski, J., *Der Überfall auf Kopenhagen*, 1940.
Klein, E., Völkerrechtliche Aspekte des Golfkonflikts 1990/91, 29 *Archiv des Völkerrechts*, 1991.*
Korovin, E. A., *International Law of the Time of Transition*, 1925.
Kotzsch, L., *The Concept of War in Contemporary History and International Law*, 1956.*
Kozai, S., *Kokuren no Heiwaijikatsudo (United Nations Peacekeeping Operations)*, 1991.
Kulsrud, C. J., The Seizure of Danish Fleet 1807, 32 *American Journal of International Law*, 1938.
Kunz, J. L., *The Changing Law of Nations: Essays on International Law*, 1968.
Lapidoth, R., Some Reflections on the Law and Practice Concerning the Imposition of Sanctions by the Security Council, 30 *Archiv des Völkerrechts*, 1992.*
Lavalle, R., The Law of the United Nations and the Use of Force, under the Relevant Resolutions of 1990 and 1991, to Resolve the Persian Gulf Crisis, 23 *Netherlands Yearbook of International Law*, 1992.
Lissitzyn, O. J., International Law in a Divided World, 542 *International Conciliation*, 1963.
Lobel J. and Ratner M., Bypassing the Security Council: Ambiguous Authorizations to Use of Force, Cease-fires and the Iraq Inspection Regime, 93 *American Journal of International Law*, 1999.
Lyons, G.M., A New Collective Security: The United Nations and International Peace, *Washington Quarterly*, Spring 1994.
McCoubrey, H. and White, N. D., *International Organizations and Civil Wars*, 1995.
McWhinney, E., *Judge Shigeru Oda and the Progressive Development of International Law*, 1993.
Moore, J. B., *A Digest of International Law*, vol. 2.
Moore, J. N., *Neutrality Law and the Indo-China War*, 1972.
Murphy, S. D., *Humanitarian Intervention*, 1996.
Nishimura, K., *Anzenhoshojoyakuron (On the US-Japan Security Treaty)*, 1959.
Okuni, T., *Shin shin kohoron (New and True Public Law)*, 1867.

Peaslee, A. J., *Constitutions of Nations*, 3 vols., 1950.
Poblador, A. J., The Defense of Necessity in International Law, *Philippine Law Journal*, 1982.*
Przetacznik, F., The Basic Ideas of the Philosophical Concept of War and Peace, 66 *Revue de Droit International de Sciences Diplomatiques et Politiques*, 1988.
Radke, K., *Der Staatsnotstand im Modernen Friedensvölkerrecht*, 1988.*
Range, W., *Franklin D. Roosevelt's World Order*, 1959.
Reves, E., *Anatomy of Peace*, 1945.
Rodick, B.C., *The Doctrine of Necessity in International Law*, 1928.
Rostow, N., The International Use of Force after Cold War, 32 *Harvard International Law Journal*, 1991 Spring.*
Rowles, L. P., "Secret Wars", Self-Defense and the Charter – A Reply to Professor Moore, 80 *American Journal of International Law*, 1986.
Russell, R. B., *A History of the United Nations Charter: the Role of the United States, 1940–1945,* 1958.
Sainsbury, K., *The Turning Point: Roosevelt, Stalin, Churchill and Chang-Kai-Shek: 1945 The Moscow, Cairo and Teheran Conference*, 1985.*
Sakamoto, Y., Churitsu Nippon no boei koso (A Security Plan of Neutralized Japan), *Sekai*, July 1959.
Schacter, O., The Right of States to Use Armed Force, *Michigan Law Review*, 1984.*
Schmitt, C., Grossraum gegen Universalismus, Der völkerrechtliche Kampf um die Monroedoktrin, 6 *Zeitschrift der Akademie für Deutsches Recht*, Heft 10, 1939.
Schmitt, C., *Völkerrechtliche Grossraumordnung*, 1941.
Schneider, H.C., *Die Charter der Vereinten Nationen und das Sonderrecht für die im Zweiten Weltkrieg unterlegenen Natione (Artikel 53 und 107),* 1967.*
Seyersted, F., *United Nations Forces in the Law of Peace and War*, 1966.*
Shoham, U., The Israel Aerial Raid upon the Iraqi Nuclear Reactor and the Right of Self-defense, *Military Law Review*, 1985.
Siekmann, R., *Basic Documents on UN and Related Peacekeeping Forces*, 1984.
Sofaer, A.D., International Law and Kosovo, 36 *Stanford Journal of International Law*, 2000.
Sohn, L., *Cases and Materials on World Law*, 1950.
Solana, J., NATO's Success in Kosovo, *Foreign Affairs*, November/December, 1999.
Spinedi, M. and Simma, B., (ed.), *United Nations Codification of State Responsibility*, 1987.*
Takano, Y., Kokusairengo Kenshou tono Kankei (Relationship to the Charter of the United Nations), 59 *Kokusaihogaikozasi*, 1960.
Takayanagi, K., Ohtomo, I. and Tanaka, H., *The Making of Constitution of Japan*, vol. 1, Documents, 1972.
Taoka, R., *Self-defense in International Law*, 1978.
Temperley, H. W. V., (ed.), *A History of the Peace Conference of Paris*, vol. VI, 1924.
Toynbee, A., *A Study of History,* 1921–1954.
Tsutsui, W., Conceptions of Japan's Security Affecting Cooperation with the United Nations, 27 *Victoria University of Wellington Law Review*, 1997.

Tsutsui, W., Japan's Role in the International Organizations with Particular Reference to the United Nations, 25 *Archiv des Völkerrechts*, 1987.

Tucker, R. W., Reprisal and Self-defense: The Customary Law, 66 *American Journal of International Law*, 1972.*

UN Department of Public Information, *The Blue Helmets: A Review of United Nations Peace-keeping* (3rd ed.), 1996.

Viner, J., *Customs Union Issue*, 1950.

Vitoria, F., *De Indis et de jure belli relectiones* 1532 translation in J.B. Scott (ed.), *Classics of International Law*.

Walters, F. P., *A History of the League of Nations*, 1952.

Watkins and Robinson, *General International Organization: A Source Book*, 1956.

Weightman, M. A., Self-defense in International Law, *Virginia Law Review*, 1951.

Wheeler-Bennett, J. W., *Information on the Renunciation of War: 1927–1928* (reissued in 1973).

White, N. D., *Keeping the Peace*, 1997.

Wilcox, F.W., Regionalism and the United Nations, *International Organization*, 1965.

Williams, B., *State Security and the League of Nations*, 1927.

Wiseman, H., (ed.), *Peacekeeping: Appraisal and Proposal*, 1983.*

Wright, Q., The Transfer of Destroyers to Great Britain, 34 *American Journal of International Law*, 1940.

Wright, Q., *A Study of War* (2nd ed.), 1965.

Yamashita, Y., Eisei Churitsu ni tsuite (On permanent neutrality), *Chuokoron*, April 1950.

Yokota, K., *Anzenhosho no Mondai (Problems on Security)*, 1949.

Yoshida, S., Japan and the Crisis in Asia, *Foreign Affairs*, January 1951.

Zacher, M. W., *International Conflicts and Collective Security, 1946–77*, 1979.*

APPENDIX

1. Wartime Documents Relating to Japan

(1) The Cairo Declaration
(2) The Yalta Agreement
(3) The Potsdam Declaration

2. The Constitution of Japan 1946

(1) Reform of the Japanese Governmental System (SWNCC228)
(2) The three basic points stated by the Supreme Commander
(3) The Constitution of Japan (extract)

3. The Treaty of Peace with Japan (extract)

4. US-Japan Security Arrangements

(1) The US-Japan Security Treaty of 1951 (extract)
(2) The US-Japan Security Treaty of 1960
(3) The Guidelines for US-Japan Defense Cooperation (extract)

5. The Peacekeeping Cooperation Law (extract)

I. Wartime Documents Relating to Japan

(1) The Cairo Declaration

Signed at Cairo, November 27, 1943
Statement Issued Following the Conference of President Roosevelt, Generalissimo Chiang Kai-shek and Prime Minister Churchill

The several military missions have agreed upon future military operations against Japan. The Three Great Allies expressed their resolve to bring unrelenting pressure against their brutal enemies by sea, land, and air. This pressure is already rising.

The Three Great Allies are fighting this war to restrain and punish the aggression of Japan. They covet no gain for themselves and have no thought of territorial expansion. It is their purpose that Japan shall be stripped of all the islands in the Pacific which she has seized or occupied since the beginning of the first World War in 1914, and that all the territories Japan has stolen from the Chinese, such as Manchuria, Formosa, and the Pescadores, shall be restored to the Republic of China. Japan will also be expelled from all other territories which she has taken by violence and greed. The aforesaid three great powers, mindful of the enslavement of the people of Korea, are determined that in due course Korea shall become free and independent.

With these objects in view the three Allies, in harmony with those of the United Nations at war with Japan, will continue to persevere in the serious and prolonged operations necessary to procure the unconditional surrender of Japan.

(2) The Yalta Agreement

AGREEMENT REGARDING ENTRY OF THE SOVIET UNION INTO THE WAR AGAINST JAPAN

Signed at Yalta, February 11, 1945

Agreement

The leaders of the three Great Powers – the Soviet Union, the United States of America and Great Britain- have agreed that in two or three months after Germany has surrendered and the war in Europe has terminated the Soviet Union shall enter into the war against Japan on the side of the Allies on condition that:

1. The *status quo* in Outer-Mongolia (The Mongolian People's Republic) shall be preserved;
2. The former rights of Russia violated by the treacherous attack of Japan in 1904 shall be restored, viz:
   (a) the southern part of Sakhalin as well as all the islands adjacent to it shall be returned to the Soviet Union,
   (b) the commercial port of Dairen shall be internationalized, the preeminent interests of the Soviet Union in this port being safeguarded and the lease of Port Arthur as a naval base of the USSR restored,
   (c) the Chinese-Eastern Railroad and the South-Manchurian Railroad which

provides an outlet to Dairen shall be jointly operated by the establishment of a joint Soviet-Chinese Company it being understood that the preeminent interests of the Soviet Union shall be safeguarded and that China shall retain full sovereignty in Manchuria;

3. The Kuril islands shall be handed over to the Soviet Union.

It is understood, that the agreement concerning Outer-Mongolia and the ports and railroads referred to above will require concurrence of Generalissimo Chiang Kai-Shek. The President will take measures in order to obtain this concurrence on advice from Marshal Stalin.

The Heads of the three Great Powers have agreed that these claims of the Soviet Union shall be unquestionably fulfilled after Japan has been defeated.

For its part the Soviet Union expresses its readiness to conclude with the National Government of China a pact of friendship and alliance between the USSR and China in order to render assistance to China with its armed forces for the purpose of liberating China from the Japanese yoke.

И. СТАЛИН
FRANKLIN D. ROOSEVELT
WINSTON S. CHURCHILL

FEBRUARY 11, 1945.

(3) The Potsdam Declaration

PROCLAMATION DEFINING TERMS FOR JAPANESE SURRENDER

Signed at Potsdam, July 26, 1945

(1) We – The President of the United States, the President of the National Government of the Republic of China, and the Prime Minister of Great Britain, representing the hundreds of millions of our countrymen, have conferred and agree that Japan shall be given an opportunity to end this war.

(2) The prodigious land, sea and air forces of the United States, the British Empire and of China, many times reinforced by their armies and air fleets from the west, are poised to strike the final blows upon Japan. This military power is sustained and inspired by the determination of all the Allied Nations to prosecute the war against Japan until she ceases to resist.

(3) The result of the futile and senseless German resistance to the might of the aroused free peoples of the world stands forth in awful clarity as an example to the people of Japan. The might, that now converges on Japan is immeasurably greater than that which, when applied to the resisting Nazis, necessarily laid waste to the lands, the industry and the method of life of the whole German people. The full application of our military power, backed by our resolve, *will* mean the inevitable and complete destruction of the Japanese armed forces and just as inevitably the utter devastation of the Japanese homeland.

(4) The time has come for Japan to decide whether she will continue to be controlled by those self-willed militaristic advisers whose unintelligent calculations have brought the Empire of Japan to the threshold of annihilation, or whether she will follow the path of reason.

(5) Following are our terms. We will not deviate from them. There are no alternatives. We shall brook no delay.

(6) There must be eliminated for all time the authority and influence of those who have deceived and misled the people of Japan into embarking on world conquest, for we insist that

a new order of peace, security and justice will be impossible until irresponsible militarism is driven from the world.

(7) Until such a new order is established *and* until there is convincing proof that Japan's war-making power is destroyed, points in Japanese territory to be designated by the Allies shall be occupied to secure the achievement of the basic objectives we are here setting forth.

(8) The terms of the Cairo Declaration shall be carried out and Japanese sovereignty shall be limited to the islands of Honshu, Hokkaido, Kyushu, Shikoku and such minor islands as we determine.

(9) The Japanese military forces, after being completely disarmed, shall be permitted to return to their homes with the opportunity to lead peaceful and productive lives.

(10) We do not intend that the Japanese shall be enslaved as a race or destroyed as a nation, but stern justice shall be meted out to all war criminals, including those who have visited cruelties upon our prisoners. The Japanese Government shall remove all obstacles to the revival and strengthening of democratic tendencies among the Japanese people. Freedom of speech, of religion, and of thought, as well as respect for the fundamental human rights shall be established.

(11) Japan shall be permitted to maintain such industries as will sustain her economy and permit the exaction of just reparations in kind, but not those industries which would enable her to re-arm for war. To this end, access to, as distinguished from control of, raw materials shall be permitted. Eventual Japanese participation in world trade relations shall be permitted.

(12) The occupying forces of the Allies shall be withdrawn from Japan as soon as these objectives have been accomplished and there has been established in accordance with the freely expressed will of the Japanese people a peacefully inclined and responsible government.

(13) We call upon the government of Japan to proclaim now the unconditional surrender of all Japanese armed forces, and to provide proper and adequate assurances of their good faith in such action. The alternative for Japan is prompt and utter destruction.

2. The Constitution of Japan 1946

(1) Reform of the Japanese Governmental System (SWNCC228)

"Reform of the Japanese Governmental System" Approved by SWNCC, January 7, 1946. Forwarded to Commander in Chief, U.S. Army Forces, Pacific, for his "information," January 11, 1946.

Conclusions

"a. The Supreme Commander should indicate to the Japanese authorities that the Japanese governmental system should be reformed to accomplish the following general objectives:

(1) A government responsible to an electorate based upon wide representative suffrage;

(2) An executive branch of government deriving its authority from and responsible to the electorate or to a fully representative legislative body;

(3) A legislative body, fully representative of the electorate, with full power to reduce, increase or reject any items in the budget or to suggest new items;

(4) No budget shall become effective without the express approval of the legislative body;

(5) Guarantee of fundamental civil rights to Japanese subjects and to all persons within Japanese jurisdiction;

(6) The popular election or local appointment of as many of the prefectural officials as practicable;

(7) The drafting and adoption of constitutional amendments or of a constitution in a manner which will express the free will of the Japanese people.

"b. Though the ultimate form of government in Japan is to be established by the freely expressed will of the Japanese people, the retention of the Emperor institution in its present form is not considered consistent with the foregoing general objectives.

"c. If the Japanese people decide that the Emperor Institution is not to be retained, constitutional safeguards against the institution will obviously not be required but the Supreme Commander should indicate to the Japanese that the constitution should be amended to conform to the objectives listed in *a* above and to include specific provisions;

(1) That any other bodies shall possess only a temporary veto power over legislative measures, including constitutional amendments approved by the representative legislative body, and that such body shall have sole authority over financial measures;

(2) That the Ministers of State or the members of a Cabinet should in all cases be civilians;

(3) That the legislative body may meet at will.

"d. The Japanese should be encouraged to abolish the Emperor Institution or to reform it along more democratic lines. If the Japanese decide to retain the Institution of the Emperor, however, the Supreme Commander should also indicate to the Japanese authorities that the following safeguards in addition to those enumerated in *a* and *c* above would be necessary:

(1) That the Ministers of State, chosen with the advice and consent of the representative legislative body, shall form a Cabinet collectively responsible to the legislative body;

(2) That when a Cabinet loses the confidence of the representative legislative body, it must either resign or appeal to the electorate;

(3) The Emperor shall act in all important matters only on the advice of the Cabinet;

(4) The Emperor shall be deprived of all military authority such as that provided in Articles XI, XII, XIII, and XIV of Chapter I of the Constitution;

(5) The Cabinet shall advise and assist the Emperor;

(6) The entire income of the Imperial Household shall be turned into the public treasury and the expenses of the Imperial Household shall be appropriated by the legislature in the annual budget."

Only as a last resort should the Supreme Commander order the Japanese Government to effect the above listed reforms, as the knowledge that they had been imposed by the Allies would materially reduce the possibility of their acceptance and support by the Japanese people for the future.

The effectiveness of governmental reforms in preventing the resurgence of military control in Japan will depend in a large measure upon the acceptance by the Japanese people of the entire program. In the implementation of allied policy on the reform of the Japanese Government, the Supreme Commander for the Allied Powers must take into account the problems of sequence and timing, as well as measures which might be adopted to prepare the Japanese people to accept the changes, in order to insure that the reforms are lasting in strengthening representative government in Japan.

This paper should not be released for publication. The eventual release of a statement of allied policy on the reform of the Japanese Government should be coordinated with the Supreme Commander for the Allied Powers in order not to impede the accomplishment of such reforms in Japan itself.

(2) The three basic points stated by the Supreme Commander

TOP SECRET

Three basic points stated by Supreme Commander to be "Musts" in constitutional revision. Government Section paper prepared about 4 Feb 1946.

I

Emperor is at the head of the state.

His succession is dynastic.

His duties and powers will be exercised in accordance with the Constitution and responsive to the basic will of the people as provided therein.

II

War as a sovereign right of the nation is abolished. Japan renounces it as an instrumentality for settling its disputes and even for preserving its own security. It relies upon the higher ideals which are now stirring the world for its defense and its protection.

No Japanese Army, Navy or Air Force will ever be authorized and no rights of belligerency will ever be conferred upon any Japanese force.

III

The feudal system of Japan will cease.

No rights of peerage except those of the Imperial family will extend beyond the lines of those now existent.

No patent of nobility will from this time forth embody within itself any National or Civic power of government.

Pattern budget after British system.

(3) The Constitution of Japan (extract)

Promulgated 3 November 1946

THE CONSTITUTION OF JAPAN

1. We, the Japanese people, acting through our duly elected representatives in the National Diet, determined that we shall secure for ourselves and our posterity the fruits of peaceful co-operation with all nations and the blessings of liberty throughout this land, and resolved that never again shall we be visited with the horrors of war through the action of government, do proclaim that sovereign power resides with the people and do firmly establish this Constitution. Government is a sacred trust of the people, the authority for which is derived from the people, the powers of which are exercised by the representatives of the people, and the benefits of which are enjoyed by the people. This is a universal principle of mankind upon which this Constitution is founded. We reject and revoke all constitutions, laws, ordinances, and rescripts in conflict herewith.

2. We, the Japanese people, desire peace for all time and are deeply conscious of the high ideals controlling human relationship, and we have determined to preserve our security and existence, trusting in the justice and faith of the peace-loving peoples of the world. We desire to occupy an honored place in an international society striving for the preservation of peace, and the banishment of tyranny and slavery, oppression and intolerance for all time from the earth. We recognize that all peoples of the world have the right to live in peace, free from fear and want.

3. We believe that no nation is responsible to itself alone, but that laws of political morality are universal; and that obedience to such laws is incumbent upon all nations who would sustain their own sovereignty and justify their sovereign relationship with other nations.

4. We, the Japanese people, pledge our national honor to accomplish these high ideals and purposes with all our resources.

CHAPTER II. RENUNCIATION OF WAR

Article 9

1. Aspiring sincerely to an international peace based on justice and order, the Japanese people forever renounce war as a sovereign right of the nation and the threat or use of force as means of settling international disputes.

2. In order to accomplish the aim of the preceding paragraph, land, sea, and air forces, as well as other war potential, will never be maintained. The right of belligerency of the state will not be recognized.

NOTE ON THE TRANSLATION

The English text reproduced here is an official translation, and therefore no attempt has been made to revise it.

3. The Treaty of Peace with Japan (Extract)

Signed 8 September 1961

CHAPTER I

PEACE

Article 1

(a) The state of war between Japan and each of the Allied Powers is terminated as from the date on which the present Treaty comes into force between Japan and the Allied Power concerned as provided for in Article 23.

(b) The Allied Powers recognize the full sovereignty of the Japanese people over Japan and its territorial waters.

CHAPTER III

SECURITY

Article 5

(a) Japan accepts the obligations set forth in Article 2 of the Charter of the United Nations, and in particular the obligations.

(i) to settle its international disputes by peaceful means in such a manner that international peace and security, and justice, are not endangered;

(ii) to refrain in its international relations from the threat or use of force against the territorial integrity or political independence of any State or in any other manner inconsistent with the Purposes of the United Nations;

(iii) to give the United Nations every assistance in any action it takes in accordance with the Charter and to refrain from giving assistance to any State against which the United Nations may take preventive or enforcement action.

(b) The Allied Powers confirm that they will be guided by the principles of Article 2 of the Charter of the United Nations in their relations with Japan.

(c) The Allied Powers for their part recognize that Japan as a sovereign nation possesses the inherent right of individual or collective self-defense referred to in Article 51 of the Charter of the United Nations and that Japan may voluntarily enter into collective security arrangements.

Article 6

(a) All occupation forces of the Allied Powers shall be withdrawn from Japan as soon as possible after the coming into force of the present Treaty, and in any case not later than 90 days thereafter. Nothing in this provision shall, however, prevent the stationing or retention of foreign armed forces in Japanese territory under or in consequence of any bilateral or multilateral agreements which have been or may be made between one or more of the Allied Powers, on the one hand, and Japan on the other.

(b) The provisions of Article 9 of the Potsdam Proclamation of July 26, 1945, dealing with the return of Japanese military forces to their homes, to the extent not already completed, will be carried out.

(c) All Japanese property for which compensation has not already been paid, which was supplied for the use of the occupation forces and which remains in the possession of those forces at the time of the coming into force at the present Treaty, shall be returned to the Japanese Government within the same 90 days unless other arrangements are made by mutual agreement.

CHAPTER V

CLAIMS AND PROPERTY

Article 14

(b) Except as otherwise provided in the present Treaty, the Allied Powers waive all reparations claims of the Allied Powers, other claims of the Allied Powers and their nationals arising out of any actions taken by Japan and its nationals in the course of the prosecution of the war, and claims of the Allied Powers for direct military costs of occupation.

Article 19

(a) Japan waives all claims of Japan and its nationals against the Allied Powers and their nationals arising out of the war or out of actions taken because of the existence of a state of war, and waives all claims arising from the presence, operations or actions of forces or authorities of any of the Allied Powers in Japanese territory prior to the coming into force of the present Treaty.

(b) The foregoing waiver includes any claims arising out of actions taken by any of the Allied Powers with respect to Japanese ships between September 1, 1939, and the coming into force of the present Treaty, as well as any claims and debts arising in respect to Japanese prisoners of war and civilian internees in the hands of the Allied Powers, but does not include Japanese claims specifically recognized in the laws of any Allied Power enacted since September 2, 1945.

(c) Subject to reciprocal renunciation, the Japanese Government also renounces all claims (including debts) against Germany and German nationals on behalf of the Japanese Government and Japanese nationals, including intergovernmental claims and claims for loss or damage sustained during the war, but excepting (a) claims in respect of contracts entered into and rights acquired before September 1, 1939 and (b) claims arising out of trade and financial relations between Japan and Germany after September 2, 1945. Such renunciation shall not prejudice actions taken in accordance with Articles 16 and 20 of the present Treaty.

(d) Japan recognizes the validity of all acts and omissions done during the period of occupation under or in consequence of directives of the occupation authorities or authorized by Japanese law at that time, and will take no action subjecting Allied nationals to civil or criminal liability arising out of such acts or omissions.

4. US-Japan Security Arrangements

(1) The US-Japan Security Treaty of 1951 (extract)

Signed 8 September 1951

SECURITY TREATY BETWEEN JAPAN AND THE UNITED STATES OF AMERICA

Japan has this day signed a Treaty of Peace with the Allied Powers. On the coming into force of that Treaty, Japan will not have the effective means to exercise its inherent right of self-defense because it has been disarmed.

There is danger to Japan in this situation because irresponsible militarism has not yet been driven from the world. Therefore Japan desires a Security Treaty with the United States of America to come into force simultaneously with the Treaty of Peace between Japan and the United States of America.

The Treaty of Peace recognizes that Japan as a sovereign nation has the right to enter into collective security arrangements, and further, the Charter of the United Nations recognizes that all nations possess an inherent right of individual and collective self-defense.

In exercise of these rights, Japan desires, as a provisional arrangement for its defense, that the United States of America should maintain armed forces of its own in and about Japan so as to deter armed attack upon Japan.

The United States of America, in the interest of peace and security, is presently willing to maintain certain of its armed forces in and about Japan, in the expectation, however, that

Japan will itself increasingly assume responsibility for its own defense against direct and indirect aggression, always avoiding any armament which could be an offensive threat or serve other than to promote peace and security in accordance with the purposes and principles of the United Nations Charter.

Accordingly, the two countries have agreed as follows:

Article I

Japan grants, and the United States of America accepts, the right, upon the coming into force of the Treaty of Peace and of this Treaty, to dispose United States land, air and sea forces in and about Japan. Such forces may be utilized to contribute to the maintenance of international peace and security in the Far East and to the security of Japan against armed attack from without, including assistance given at the express request of the Japanese Government to put down large-scale internal riots and disturbances in Japan, caused through instigation or intervention by an outside power or powers.

Article II

During the exercise of the right referred to in Article I, Japan will not grant, without the prior consent of the United States of America, any bases or any rights, powers or authority whatsoever, in or relating to bases or the right of garrison or of maneuver, or transit of ground, air or naval forces to any third power.

Article III

The conditions which shall govern the disposition of armed forces of the United States of America in and about Japan shall be determined by administrative agreements between the two Governments.

Article IV

This Treaty shall expire whenever in the opinion of the Governments of Japan and the United States of America there shall have come into force such United Nations arrangements or such alternative individual or collective security dispositions as will satisfactorily provide for the maintenance by the United Nations or otherwise of international peace and security in the Japan Area.

(2) The US-Japan Security Treaty of 1960

Signed 19 January 1960

TREATY OF MUTUAL COOPERATION AND SECURITY BETWEEN JAPAN AND THE UNITED STATES OF AMERICA

Japan and the United States of America,

Desiring to strengthen the bonds of peace and friendship traditionally existing between them, and to uphold the principles of democracy, individual liberty, and the rule of law,

Desiring further to encourage closer economic cooperation between them and to promote conditions of economic stability and well-being in their countries,

Reaffirming their faith in the purposes and principles of the Charter of the United Nations, and their desire to live in peace with all peoples and all governments,

Recognizing that they have the inherent right of individual or collective self-defense as affirmed in the Charter of the United Nations,

Considering that they have a common concern in the maintenance of international peace and security in the Far East,

Having resolved to conclude a treaty of mutual cooperation and security,

Therefore agree as follows:

Article I

The Parties undertake, as set forth in the Charter of the United Nations, to settle any international disputes in which they may be involved by peaceful means in such a manner that international peace and security and justice are not endangered and to refrain in their international relations from the threat or use of force against the territorial integrity or political independence of any state, or in any other manner inconsistent with the purposes of the United Nations.

The Parties will endeavor in concert with other peace-loving countries to strengthen the United Nations so that its mission of maintaining international peace and security may be discharged more effectively.

Article II

The Parties will contribute toward the further development of peaceful and friendly international relations by strengthening their free institutions, by bringing about a better understanding of the principles upon which these institution are founded, and by promoting conditions of stability and well-being. They will seek to eliminate conflict in their international economic policies and will encourage economic collaboration between them.

Article III

The Parties, individually and in cooperation with each other, by means of continuous and effective self-help and mutual aid will maintain and develop, subject to their constitutional provisions, their capacities to resist armed attack.

Article IV

The Parties will consult together from time to time regarding the implementation of this Treaty, and, at the request of either Party, whenever the security of Japan or international peace and security in the Far East is threatened.

Article V

Each Party recognizes that an armed attack against either Party in the territories under the administration of Japan would be dangerous to its own peace and safety and declares that it would act to meet the common danger in accordance with its constitutional provisions and processes.

Any such armed attack and all measures taken as a result thereof shall be immediately reported to the Security Council of the United Nations in accordance with the provisions of Article 51 of the Charter. Such measures shall be terminated when the Security Council has taken the measures necessary to restore and maintain international peace and security.

Article VI

For the purpose of contributing to the security of Japan and the maintenance of international peace and security in the Far East, the United States of America is granted the use by its land, air and naval forces of facilities and areas in Japan.

The use of these facilities and areas as well as the status of United States armed forces in Japan shall be governed by a separate agreement, replacing the Administrative Agreement under Article III of the Security Treaty between Japan and the United States of America, signed at Tokyo on February 28, 1952, as amended, and by such other arrangements as may be agreed upon.

Article VII
This Treaty does not affect and shall not be interpreted as affecting in any way the rights and obligations of the Parties under the Charter of the United Nations or the responsibility of the United Nations for the maintenance of international peace and security.

Article VIII
This Treaty shall be ratified by Japan and the United States of America in accordance with their respective constitutional processes and will enter into force on the date on which the instruments of ratification thereof have been exchanged by them in Tokyo.

Article IX
The Security Treaty between Japan and the United States of America signed at the city of San Francisco on September 8, 1951 shall expire upon the entering into force of this Treaty.

Article X
This Treaty shall remain in force until in the opinion of the Governments of Japan and the United States of America there shall have come into force such United Nations arrangements as will satisfactorily provide for the maintenance of international peace and security in the Japan area.

However, after the Treaty has been in force for ten years, either Party may give notice to the other Party of its intention to terminate the Treaty, in which case the Treaty shall terminate one year after such notice has been given.

EXCHANGE OF NOTES

Washington, January 19, 1960

Excellency:

I have the honour to refer to the Treaty of Mutual Cooperation and Security between Japan and the United States of America signed today, and to inform Your Excellency that the following is the understanding of the Government of Japan concerning the implementation of Article VI thereof:

> Major changes in the deployment into Japan of United States armed forces, major changes in their equipment, and the use of facilities and areas in Japan as bases for military combat operations to be undertaken from Japan other than those conducted under Article V of the said Treaty, shall be the subjects of prior consultation with the Government of Japan.

I should be appreciative if Your Excellency would confirm on behalf of your Government that this is also the understanding of the Government of the United States of America.

I avail myself of this opportunity to renew to Your Excellency the assurance of my highest consideration.

Nobusuke Kishi

His Excellency
Christian A. Herter,
Secretary of State of the United States of America.

January 19, 1960

Excellency:

I have the honor to acknowledge the receipt of Your Excellency's Note of today's date, which reads as follows:

"I have the honour to refer to the Treaty of Mutual Cooperation and Security between Japan and the United States of America signed today, and to inform Your Excellency that the following is the understanding of the Government of Japan concerning the implementation of Article VI thereof:

> Major changes in the deployment into Japan of United States armed forces, major changes in their equipment, and the use of facilities and areas in Japan as bases for military combat operations to be undertaken from Japan other than those conducted under Article V of the said Treaty, shall be the subjects of prior consultation with the Government of Japan.

"I should be appreciative if Your Excellency would confirm on behalf of your Government that this is also the understanding of the Government of the United States of America.

"I avail myself of this opportunity to renew to Your Excellency the assurance of my highest consideration."

I have the honor to confirm on behalf of my Government that the foregoing is also the understanding of the Government of the United States of America.

Accept, Excellency, the renewed assurances of my highest consideration.

Christian A. Herter
Secretary of State of the United States of America

His Excellency
Nobusuke Kishi,
Prime Minister of Japan.

(3) The Guidelines for US-Japan Defense Cooperation (extract)

Approved and Issued by U.S.-Japan Security Consultative Committee,
September 23, 1997

I. The aim of the guidelines
The aim of these Guidelines is to create a solid basis for more effective and credible U.S.-Japan cooperation under normal circumstances, in case of an armed attack against Japan, and in situations in areas surrounding Japan. The Guidelines also provide a general framework and policy direction for the roles and missions of the two countries and ways of cooperation and coordination, both under normal circumstances and during contingencies.

II. Basic premises and principles
The Guidelines and programs under the Guidelines are consistent with the following basic premises and principles.

1. The rights and obligations under the Treaty of Mutual Cooperation and Security between the United States of America and Japan (the U.S.-Japan Security Treaty) and its related arrangements, as well as the fundamental framework of the U.S.-Japan alliance, will remain unchanged.
2. Japan will conduct all its actions within the limitations of its Constitution and in accordance with such basic positions as the maintenance of its exclusively defense-oriented policy and its three non-nuclear principles.
3. All actions taken by the United States and Japan will be consistent with basic principles of international law, including the peaceful settlement of disputes and sovereign equality, and relevant international agreements such as the Charter of the United Nations.
4. The Guidelines and programs under the Guidelines will not obligate either Government to take legislative, budgetary or administrative measures.

However, since the objective of the Guidelines and programs under the Guidelines is to establish an effective framework for bilateral cooperation, the two Governments are expected to reflect in an appropriate way the results of these efforts, based on their own judgements, in their specific policies and measures. All actions taken by Japan will be consistent with its laws and regulations then in effect.

III. Cooperation under normal circumstances
Both Governments will firmly maintain existing U.S.-Japan security arrangements. Each Government will make efforts to maintain required defense postures. Japan will possess defense capability within the scope necessary for self-defense on the basis of the "National Defense Program Outline." In order to meet its commitments, the United States will maintain its nuclear deterrent capability, its forward deployed forces in the Asia-Pacific region, and other forces capable of reinforcing those forward deployed forces.

Both Governments, based on their respective policies, under normal circumstances will maintain close cooperation for the defense of Japan as well as for the creation of a more stable international security environment.

Both Governments will under normal circumstances enhance cooperation in a variety of areas. Examples include mutual support activities under the Agreement between the Government of Japan and the Government of the United States of America concerning Reciprocal Provision of Logistic Support, Supplies and Services between the Self-Defense Forces of Japan and the Armed Forces of the United States of America; the Mutual Defense Assistance Agreement between the United States of America and Japan; and their related arrangements.

1. Information Sharing and Policy Consultations

Recognizing that accurate information and sound analysis are at the foundation of security, the two Governments will increase information and intelligence sharing, and the exchange of views on international situations of mutual interest, especially in the Asia-Pacific region. They will also continue close consultations on defense policies and military postures.

Such information sharing and policy consultations will be conducted at as many levels as possible and on the broadest range of subjects. This will be accomplished by taking advantage of all available opportunities, such as SCC and Security Sub-Committee (SSC) meetings.

2. Various Types of Security Cooperation

Bilateral cooperation to promote regional and global activities in the field of security contributes to the creation of a more stable international security environment.

Recognizing the importance and significance of security dialogues and defense exchanges in the region, as well as international arms control and disarmament, the two Governments will promote such activities and cooperate as necessary.

When either or both Governments participate in United Nations peacekeeping operations or international humanitarian relief operations, the two sides will cooperate closely for mutual support as necessary. They will prepare procedures for cooperation in such areas as transportation, medical services, information sharing, and education and training.

When either or both Governments conduct emergency relief operations in response to requests from governments concerned or international organizations in the wake of large-scale disasters, they will cooperate closely with each other as necessary.

3. Bilateral Programs

Both Governments will conduct bilateral work, including bilateral defense planning in case of an armed attack against Japan, and mutual cooperation planning in situations in areas surrounding Japan. Such efforts will be made in a comprehensive mechanism involving relevant agencies of the respective Governments, and establish the foundation for bilateral cooperation.

Bilateral exercises and training will be enhanced in order not only to validate such bilateral work but also to enable smooth and effective responses by public and private entities of both countries, starting with U.S. Forces and the Self-Defense Forces. The two Governments will under normal circumstances establish a bilateral coordination mechanism involving relevant agencies to be operated during contingencies.

IV. Actions in response to an armed attack against Japan

Bilateral actions in response to an armed attack against Japan remain a core aspect of U.S.-Japan defense cooperation.

When an armed attack against Japan is imminent, the two Governments will take steps to prevent further deterioration of the situation and make preparations necessary for the defense of Japan. When an armed attack against Japan takes place, the two Governments will conduct appropriate bilateral actions to repel it at the earliest possible stage.

1. When an Armed Attack against Japan is Imminent

The two Governments will intensify information and intelligence sharing and policy consultations, and initiate at an early stage the operation of a bilateral coordination mechanism. Cooperating as appropriate, they will make preparations necessary for ensuring coordinated responses according to the readiness stage selected by mutual agreement. Japan will establish and maintain the basis for U.S. reinforcements. As circumstances change, the two Governments will also increase intelligence gathering and surveillance, and will prepare to respond to activities which could develop into an armed attack against Japan.

The two Governments will make every effort, including diplomatic efforts, to prevent further deterioration of the situation.

Recognizing that a situation in areas surrounding Japan may develop into an armed attack against Japan, the two Governments will be mindful of the close interrelationship of the two requirements: preparations for the defense of Japan and responses to or preparations for situations in areas surrounding Japan.

2. When an Armed Attack against Japan Takes Place

(1) Principles for Coordinated Bilateral Actions

(a) Japan will have primary responsibility immediately to take action and to repel an armed attack against Japan as soon as possible. The United States will provide appropriate support to Japan. Such bilateral cooperation may vary according to the scale, type, phase, and other factors of the armed attack. This cooperation may include preparations for and execution of coordinated bilateral operations, steps to prevent further deterioration of the situation, surveillance, and intelligence sharing.

(b) In conducting bilateral operations, U.S. Forces and the Self-Defense Forces will employ their respective defense capabilities in a coordinated, timely, and effective manner. In doing this, they will conduct effective joint operations of their respective Forces' ground, maritime and air services. The Self-Defense Forces will primarily conduct defensive operations in Japanese territory and its surrounding waters and airspace, while U.S. Forces support Self-Defense Forces' operations. U.S. Forces will also conduct operations to supplement the capabilities of the Self-Defense Forces.

(c) The United States will introduce reinforcements in a timely manner, and Japan will establish and maintain the basis to facilitate these deployments.

(2) Concept of Operations

(a) Operations to Counter Air Attack against Japan

U.S. Forces and the Self-Defense Forces will bilaterally conduct operations to counter air attack against Japan.

The Self-Defense Forces will have primary responsibility for conducting operations for air defense.

U.S. Forces will support Self-Defense Forces' operations and conduct operations, including those which may involve the use of strike power, to supplement the capabilities of the Self-Defense Forces.

(b) Operations to Defend Surrounding Waters and to Protect Sea Lines of Communication

U.S. Forces and the Self-Defense Forces will bilaterally conduct operations for the defense of surrounding waters and for the protection of sea lines of communication.

The Self-Defense Forces will have primary responsibility for the protection of major ports and straits in Japan, for the protection of ships in surrounding waters, and for other operations.

U.S. Forces will support Self-Defense Forces' operations and conduct operations, including those which may provide additional mobility and strike power, to supplement the capabilities of the Self-Defense Forces.

(c) Operations to Counter Airborne and Seaborne Invasions of Japan

U.S. Forces and the Self-Defense Forces will bilaterally conduct operations to counter airborne and seaborne invasions of Japan.

The Self-Defense Forces will have primary responsibility for conducting operations to check and repel such invasions.

U.S. Forces will primarily conduct operations to supplement the capabilities of the Self-Defense Forces. The United States will introduce reinforcements at the earliest possible stage, according to the scale, type, and other factors of the invasion, and will support Self-Defense Forces' operations.

(d) Responses to Other Threats

(i) The Self-Defense Forces will have primary responsibility to check and repel guerilla-commando type attacks or any other unconventional attacks involving military infiltration in Japanese territory at the earliest possible stage. They will cooperate and coordinate closely with relevant agencies, and will be supported in appropriate ways by U.S. Forces depending on the situation.

(ii) U.S. Forces and the Self-Defense Forces will cooperate and coordinate closely to respond to a ballistic missile attack. U.S. Forces will provide Japan with necessary intelligence, and consider, as necessary, the use of forces providing additional strike power.

(3) Activities and Requirements for Operations

(a) Command and Coordination

U.S. Forces and the Self-Defense Forces, in close cooperation, will take action through their respective command-and-control channels. To conduct effective bilateral operations, the two Forces will establish, in advance, procedures which include those to determine the division of roles and missions and to synchronize their operations.

(b) Bilateral Coordination Mechanism

Necessary coordination among the relevant agencies of the two counties will be conducted through a bilateral coordination mechanism. In order to conduct effective bilateral operations, U.S. Forces and the Self-Defense Forces will closely coordinate operations, intelligence activities, and logistics support through this coordination mechanism including use of a bilateral coordination center.

(c) Communications and Electronics

The two Governments will provide mutual support to ensure effective use of communications and electronics capabilities.

(d) Intelligence Activities

The two Governments will cooperate in intelligence activities in order to ensure effective bilateral operations. This will include coordination of requirements, collection, production, and dissemination of intelligence products. Each Government will be responsible for the security of shared intelligence.

(e) Logistics Support Activities

U.S. Forces and the Self-Defense Forces will conduct logistics support activities efficiently and properly in accordance with appropriate bilateral arrangements.

To improve the effectiveness of logistics and to alleviate functional shortfalls, the two Governments will undertake mutual support activities, making appropriate use of authorities and assets of central and local government agencies, as well as private sector assets. Particular attention will be paid to the following points in conducting such activities:

(i) Supply
The United States will support the acquisition of supplies for systems of U.S. origin while Japan will support the acquisition of supplies in Japan.

(ii) Transportation
The two Governments will closely cooperate in transportation operations, including airlift and sealift of supplies from the United States to Japan.

(iii) Maintenance
Japan will support the maintenance of U.S. Forces' equipment in Japan; the United States will support the maintenance of items of U.S. origin which are beyond Japanese maintenance capabilities. Maintenance support will include the technical training of maintenance personnel as required. Japan will also support U.S. Forces' requirement for salvage and recovery.

(iv) Facilities
Japan will, in case of need, provide additional facilities and areas in accordance with the U.S.-Japan Security Treaty and its related arrangements. If necessary for effective and efficient operations, U.S. Forces and the Self-Defense Forces will make joint use of Self-Defense Forces facilities and U.S. facilities and areas in accordance with the Treaty and its related arrangements.

(v) Medical Services
The two Governments will support each other in the area of medical services such as medical treatment and transportation of casualties.

V. Cooperation in situations in areas surrounding Japan that will have an important influence of Japan's peace and security (situations in areas surrounding Japan)

Situations in areas surrounding Japan will have an important influence on Japan's peace and security. The concept, situations in areas surrounding Japan, is not geographic but situational. The two Governments will make every effort, including diplomatic efforts, to prevent such situations from occurring. When the two Governments reach a common assessment of the state of each situation, they will effectively coordinate their activities. In responding to such situations, measures taken may differ depending on circumstances.

1. When a Situation in Areas Surrounding Japan is Anticipated

When a situation in areas surrounding Japan is anticipated, the two Governments will intensify information and intelligence sharing and policy consultations, including efforts to reach a common assessment of the situation.

At the same time, they will make every effort, including diplomatic efforts, to prevent further deterioration of the situation, while initiating at an early stage the operation of a bilateral coordination mechanism, including use of a bilateral coordination center. Cooperating as appropriate, they will make preparations necessary for ensuring coordinated responses according to the readiness stage selected by mutual agreement. As circumstances change, they will also increase intelligence gathering and surveillance, and enhance their readiness to respond to the circumstances.

2. Responses to Situations in Areas Surrounding Japan

The two Governments will take appropriate measures, to include preventing further deterioration of situations, in response to situations in areas surrounding Japan. This will be done in accordance with the basic premises and principles listed in Section II above and based on their respective decisions. They will support each other as necessary in accordance with appropriate arrangements.

Functions and fields of cooperation and examples of items of cooperation are outlined below, and listed in the Annex.

(1) Cooperation in Activities Initiated by Either Government

Although either Government may conduct the following activities at its own discretion, bilateral cooperation will enhance their effectiveness.

(a) Relief Activities and Measures to Deal with Refugees

Each Government will conduct relief activities with the consent and cooperation of the authorities in the affected area. The two Governments will cooperate as necessary, taking into account their respective capabilities.

The two Governments will cooperate in dealing with refugees as necessary. When there is a flow of refugees into Japanese territory, Japan will decide how to respond and will have primary responsibility for dealing with the flow; the United States will provide appropriate support.

(b) Search and Rescue

The two Governments will cooperate in search and rescue operations. Japan will conduct search and rescue operations at in Japanese territory; and at sea around Japan, as distinguished from areas where combat operations are being conducted. When U.S. Forces are conducting operations, the United States will conduct search and rescue operations in and near the operational areas.

(c) Noncombatant Evacuation Operations

When the need arises for U.S. and Japanese noncombatants to be evacuated from a third country to a safe haven, each Government is responsible for evacuating its own nationals as well as for dealing with the authorities of the affected area. In instances in which each decides it is appropriate, the two Governments will coordinate in planning and cooperate in carrying out their evacuations, including for the securing of transportation means, transportation and the use of facilities, using their respective capabilities in a mutually supplementary manner. If similar need arises for noncombatants other than of U.S. or Japanese nationality, the respective countries may consider extending, on their respective terms, evacuation assistance to third county nationals.

(d) Activities for Ensuring the Effectiveness of Economic Sanctions for the Maintenance of International Peace and Stability

Each Government will contribute to activities for ensuring the effectiveness of economic sanctions for the maintenance of international peace and stability. Such contributions will be made in accordance with each Government's own criteria.

Additionally, the two Governments will cooperate with each other as appropriate, taking into account their respective capabilities. Such cooperation includes information sharing, and cooperation in inspection of ships based on United Nations Security Council resolutions.

(2) Japan's Support for U.S. Forces Activities

(a) Use of Facilities

Based on the U.S.-Japan Security Treaty and its related arrangements, Japan will, in case of need, provide additional facilities and areas in a timely and appropriate manner, and ensure the temporary use by U.S. Forces of Self-Defense Forces facilities and civilian airports and ports.

(b) Rear Area Support

Japan will provide rear area support to those U.S. Forces that are conducting operations for the purpose of achieving the objectives of the U.S.-Japan Security Treaty. The primary aim of this rear area support is to enable U.S Forces to use facilities and conduct operations in an effective manner. By its very nature, Japan's rear area support will be provided primarily in Japanese territory. It may also be provided on the high seas and international airspace around Japan which are distinguished from areas where combat operations are being conducted.

In providing rear area support, Japan will make appropriate use of authorities and assets of central and local government agencies, as well as private sector assets. The Self-Defense Forces, as appropriate, will provide such support consistent with their mission for the defense of Japan and the maintenance of public order.

(3) U.S.-Japan Operational Cooperation

As situations in areas surrounding Japan have an important influence on Japan's peace and security, the Self-Defense Forces will conduct such activities as intelligence gathering, surveillance and minesweeping, to protect lives and property and to ensure navigational safety. U.S. Forces will conduct operations to restore the peace and security affected by situations in areas surrounding Japan.

With the involvement of relevant agencies, cooperation and coordination will significantly enhance the effectiveness of both Forces' activities.

5. The Peacekeeping Cooperation Law (Extract)

Law Concerning Cooperation for United Nations Peacekeeping Operations and other Operations

Enacted, 19 June 1992

Table of Contents

Chapter I: General Provisions

(Purpose)

Article I
The purpose of this Law is, with a view to extending an appropriate and prompt cooperation for United Nations Peacekeeping Operations, International Humanitarian Relief Operations and International Election Monitoring Activities, to set forth a framework for the implementation of International Peace Cooperation Assignments by stipulating the procedures for preparing Implementation Plans and Operating Procedures for International Peace Cooperation Assignments, the establishment of the International Peace Cooperation Corps and other matters, to take such measures as those to extend Cooperation in Kind for United Nations Peacekeeping Operations, International Humanitarian Relief Operations and International Election Monitoring Activities, and thereby to enable Japan to actively contribute to efforts for international peace centering upon the United Nations.

(Basic Principles of Cooperation for United Nations Peacekeeping Operations and other Operations)

Article II
1. The Government shall cooperate effectively for United Nations Peacekeeping Operations, International Humanitarian Relief Operations and International Election Monitoring Activities by appropriately coordinating the implementation of International Peace Cooperation Assignments, Cooperation in Kind, cooperation extended by those other than the State related to such implementation and cooperation, and other cooperation under this Law (hereinafter jointly referred to as "the implementation of International Peace Cooperation Assignments and Others"), as well as by mobilizing the creativity and expertise of the personnel engaged in the implementation of International Peace Cooperation Assignments and Others.

2. The implementation of International Peace Cooperation Assignments and Others shall not be tantamount to the threat or use of force.

3. The Prime Minister shall, in the implementation of International Peace Cooperation Assignments and Others, represent the Cabinet and direct and supervise the respective administrative divisions under Implementation Plans for International Peace Cooperation Assignments.

4. To achieve the objective of Article I above, the heads of Administrative Agencies Concerned shall cooperate with the Chief of the International Peace Cooperation Headquarters for the implementation of International Peace Cooperation Assignments and Others.

(Definitions)

Article III
For the purpose of this Law, the following terms shall have the following definitions:

(1) "United Nations Peacekeeping Operations" means operations that are conducted under the control of the United Nations, and upon the basis of resolutions of the General Assembly or the Security Council of the United Nations, to ensure the observance of agreement to prevent the recurrence of armed conflicts among the parties to such conflicts (hereinafter referred to as "the Parties to Armed Conflicts"), to assist in the establishment of a ruling apparatus by democratic means after the termination of armed conflicts or to maintain international peace and security in coping with disputes, provided that such operations be implemented by two or more participating countries at the request of the Secretary-General of the United Nations (hereinafter referred to as "the Secretary-General") and by the United Nations without any partiality to any of the Parties to Armed Conflicts, in case where agreement to cease armed conflicts and maintain the cessation has been reached among the Parties to Armed Conflicts and where consent for the undertaking of such operations has been obtained from host countries as well as the Parties to Armed Conflicts, or from host countries alone unless there have occurred armed conflicts.

(2) "International Humanitarian Relief Operations" means operations other than those implemented as United Nations Peacekeeping Operations, that are conducted in a humanitarian spirit, and upon the basis of resolutions of the General Assembly, the Security Council or the Economic and Social Council of the United Nations or at the request of international organizations listed in Appendix 1, to rescue inhabitants and other persons who actually or are likely to suffer from conflicts which are likely to endanger international peace and security (Whereas these conflicts are hereinafter referred to simply as "Conflicts", these inhabitants and persons are hereinafter jointly referred to as "Affected People".) or to make restoration out of damage caused by Conflicts, provided that such operations be implemented by the United Nations or other international organizations, or the member States to the United Nations or other countries (referred to in (2-2) and (4) below as "the United Nations and Others"), in case where consent for the undertaking of such operations has been obtained from host countries and, should the host countries be the Parties to Armed Conflicts, agreement to cease armed conflicts and maintain the cessation has been reached among the Parties to Armed Conflicts.

(2-2) "International Election Monitoring Activities" means operations other than those implemented as United Nations Peacekeeping Operations, that are conducted upon the basis of resolutions of the General Assembly or the Security Council of the United Nations or at the request of international organizations listed in Appendix 2, to ensure the fair execution of election or voting to aim at the establishment of a ruling apparatus by democratic means in areas disordered by Conflicts, provided that such operations be implemented by the United Nations and Others where consent for the undertaking of such operations has been obtained from host countries and, should the host countries be the Parties to Armed Conflicts, agreement to cease armed conflicts and maintain the cessation has been reached among the Parties to Armed Conflicts.

(3) "International Peace Cooperation Assignments" means all the following tasks implemented for United Nations Peacekeeping Operations, the tasks provided for in (j) to (q) below implemented for International Humanitarian Relief Operations and tasks provided for in (g) and (q) below implemented for International Election Monitoring Activities, wherein the incidental tasks are included respectively, provided that those tasks are conducted in Overseas Areas:

(a) monitoring the observance of cessation of armed conflicts or the implementation of relocation, withdrawal or demobilization of armed forces as agreed upon among the Parties to Armed Conflicts;
(b) stationing and patrol in buffer zones and other areas demarcated for preventing the occurrence of armed conflicts;
(c) inspection or identification of the carrying in or out of weapons and /or their parts by vehicles, other means of transportation or passers-by;
(d) collection, storage or disposal of abandoned weapons and/or their parts;
(e) assistance for the designation of cease-fire lines and other assimilated boundaries by the Parties to Armed Conflicts;
(f) assistance for the exchange of prisoners-of-war among the Parties to Armed Conflicts;
(g) supervision or management of fair execution of congressional elections, plebiscites and other elections or votings assimilated thereto;
(h) advice or guidance for and supervision of police administrative matters;
(i) advice or guidance for administrative matters not covered by (h) above;
(j) medical care including sanitary measures;
(k) search or rescue of Affected People or assistance for their repatriation;
(l) distribution of food, clothing, medical supplies and other daily necessaries to Affected People;
(m) installation of facilities or equipment to accommodate Affected People;
(n) measures for the repair or maintenance of facilities or equipment damage by Conflicts, which are necessary for daily life of Affected People;
(o) measures for the restoration of natural environment subjected to pollution and other damage by Conflicts;
(p) transportation, storage or reserve, communication, construction, or the installation, inspection or repair of machines and apparatus, not covered by (a) to (o) above.
(q) other tasks assimilated to those mentioned in (a) to (p) above, as prescribed by Cabinet Order.

(4) "Cooperation in Kind" means the alienation, free of charge or otherwise at the price lower than the current price, of goods which are necessary for the United Nations and Others engaged in the following operations:

(a) United Nations Peacekeeping Operations;

(b) International Humanitarian Relief Operations including those without the consent stipulated in (2) above if they are implemented by international organizations listed in Appendix 3. Likewise in Paragraph 1 and 3 of Article 25 following;

(c) International Election Monitoring Activities

(5) "Overseas Areas" means areas outside Japan, the high seas inclusive.

(6) "Receiving Countries" means foreign countries, the high seas not inclusive, where International Peace Cooperation Assignments are undertaken.

(7) "Administrative Agencies Concerned" means the administrative agencies referred to in paragraph 2 of Article 3 of the National Government Organization Law (Law No. 120 of 1948) and the special agencies referred to in Article 8-3 of the said Law, as designated by Cabinet Order.

The English text is an unofficial translation

INDEX

INTERNATIONAL LAW IN JAPANESE PERSPECTIVE

1. S. Oda & H. Owada: *Japanese State Practice 1971–1975* (forthcoming)
ISBN 0-7923-1405-0

2. M. Miyoshi: *Considerations of Equity in the Settlement of Territorial and Boundary Disputes*. 1993
ISBN 0-7923-2217-7

3. T. Sato: *Evolving Constitutions of International Organizations*. 1996
ISBN 90-411-0202-7

4. K. Akashi: *Cornelius van Bynkershoek: His Role in the History of International Law*. 1998
ISBN 90-411-0599-9

5. N. Ando: *Japan and International Law, Past, Present and Future. Japanese Assoc. of International Law*. 1999

6. O. Yoshida: *The International Legal Régime for the Protection of the Stratospheric Ozone Layer*. 2001
ISBN 90-411-1590-0

7. M. Igarashi: *Associated Statehood in International Law*. 2001
ISBN 90-411-1710-5

KLUWER LAW INTERNATIONAL – THE HAGUE / LONDON / NEW YORK